Studies in Diversity Linguistics

Chief Editor: Martin Haspelmath

Consulting Editors: Fernando Zúñiga, Peter Arkadiev, Ruth Singer, Pilar Valenzuela

In this series:

1. Handschuh, Corinna. A typology of marked-S languages

2. Rießler, Michael. Adjective attribution

3. Klamer, Marian (ed.). The Alor-Pantar languages: History and typology

4. Berghäll, Liisa. A grammar of Mauwake (Papua New Guinea)

A typology of marked-S languages

Corinna Handschuh

Language Science Press
Berlin

Language Science Press
Habelschwerdter Allee 45
14195 Berlin, Germany

langsci-press.org

This title can be downloaded at:
http://langsci-press.org/catalog/book/18
© 2014, Corinna Handschuh
Published under the Creative Commons Attribution 4.0 Licence (CC BY 4.0):
http://creativecommons.org/licenses/by/4.0/
ISBN: 978-3-944675-19-0

Cover and concept of design: Ulrike Harbort
Typesetting: Corinna Handschuh
Proofreading: Eitan Grossman, Daniel W. Hieber, Aaron Sonnenschein

Storage and cataloguing done by FU Berlin

Language Science Press has no responsibility for the persistence or accuracy of URLs for external or third-party Internet websites referred to in this publication, and does not guarantee that any content on such websites is, or will remain, accurate or appropriate. Information regarding prices, travel timetables and other factual information given in this work are correct at the time of first publication but Language Science Press does not guarantee the accuracy of such information thereafter.

Für Tommeck

Contents

Acknowledgments ix

List of abbreviations xi

I   Preliminaries 1

1   Introduction 3
    1.1   Marked-S coding 3
    1.2   Definition 5
    1.3   Markedness in grammar 8
    1.4   Case-labels 9
    1.5   Explaining the existence of marked-S 13
          1.5.1   Rare and geographically skewed 13
          1.5.2   Historical explanations 14
          1.5.3   Functional explanations 17
    1.6   Implications for formal approaches to case-marking 20
    1.7   Domains of alignment 24
          1.7.1   Beyond case-marking 24
          1.7.2   Head-marking 24
          1.7.3   Word order 25
          1.7.4   Behavioral properties 28
          1.7.5   The domain of investigation 29
    1.8   Outlook 30

2   Redefining alignment 31
    2.1   Introduction 31
    2.2   Split alignment 32
    2.3   Micro-alignment 33
    2.4   Contexts of investigation 37

Contents

	2.5	Incidental splits	39
		2.5.1 Contexts versus other splits	39
		2.5.2 Splits based on the semantics of the noun phrase	40
		2.5.3 Splits based on the semantics of the verb	42
		2.5.4 Splits based on morphophonological factors	43
	2.6	Usage-based factors	44
		2.6.1 Frequency	44
		2.6.2 Omission of arguments	46
		2.6.3 Optional case-marking	47
	2.7	Summary	49

II The contexts studied   51

3 Nominal predication   53
  3.1 Introduction 53
  3.2 Case-marking in nominal predication 55
  3.3 Identity predication 57
  3.4 Research questions 58
  3.5 North America 60
  3.6 Afro-Asiatic 64
  3.7 Nilo-Saharan 66
  3.8 Pacific 69
  3.9 Summary 71

4 Existential and locational predication   75
  4.1 Introduction 75
  4.2 Linguistic properties 76
  4.3 Research question 78
  4.4 Nilo-Saharan 80
  4.5 Afro-Asiatic 85
  4.6 North America 88
  4.7 Pacific 92
  4.8 Summary 96

5 Emphatic subjects   99
  5.1 Introduction 99
  5.2 Case-marking and discourse structure 100
  5.3 Zero-coded emphatic subjects 102

5.4	Overtly coded emphatic subjects	107
5.5	Research questions	110
5.6	Nilo-Saharan	113
5.7	Afro-Asiatic	116
5.8	Pacific	119
5.9	North America	126
5.10	Summary	128

6 Subjects of non-basic clauses — 131

6.1	Introduction	131
6.2	Dependent clauses	132
6.3	Valency-decreasing operations	136
6.4	Research questions	139
6.5	North America	142
6.6	Pacific	150
6.7	Nilo-Saharan	155
6.8	Afro-Asiatic	161
6.9	Summary	165

7 Non-clause-level case marking — 169

7.1	Introduction	169
7.2	Attributive possessors	170
7.3	Forms of address	172
7.4	Citation form	173
7.5	Research questions	174
7.6	Nilo-Saharan	177
7.7	Afro-Asiatic	182
7.8	Pacific	186
7.9	North America	189
7.10	Summary	194

III Analysis of the data — 197

8 Typological comparison of marked-S languages — 199

8.1	Introduction	199
8.2	Making generalizations	200
8.3	Comparison across roles	203
8.4	Comparison across languages	209

Contents

8.5	Similarity networks	213
8.6	Geographical patterns	221
8.7	Summary	225

9 Conclusion 229
9.1	Summary of the findings	229
9.2	Generalizations about the functional motivations for marked-S languages	231
9.3	Concluding remarks on the micro-alignment approach	233
9.4	Consequences for formal theories	234
9.5	Future research	238

Bibliography 241

Acknowledgments

This book started out as a PhD dissertation at Universität Leipzig by the same title, which I submitted in December 2010 and successfully defended in July 2011. The original dissertation has undergone minor revisions, but its contents have in essence remained the same.

Many people have contributed to the work in its current state, : to all of whom I would like to express my gratitude. The original research started out as part of the project 'Marked-absolutive and marked-nominative case systems in synchronic and diachronic perspective' of the *Forschergruppe* 'Grammatik und Verarbeitung verbaler Argumente' in Leipzig. Financial support for my research has been provided by the Deutsche Forschungsgemeinschaft through a grant to this project. Michael Cysouw, who was the principal investigator of the project, has patiently accompanied the development of the dissertation from the very beginning. He has always provided me with much valued feedback on all aspect of my work from methodological discussion to stylistic comments. Without his encouragement, this work would probably not have been completed. The referees for the dissertation were Martin Haspelmath and Helen de Hoop. Their comments during and after the writing process, respectively, have been much appreciated and greatly improved the final result.

The research for this book work was carried out during the heyday of the Leipzig typology community. I was lucky to have had the opportunity to conduct my research as a member of the Max Planck Institute for Evolutionary Anthropology's linguistics department. Its excellent facilities and stimulating research environment have contributed much to the completion of this work. Through the *Forschergruppe*, I also had the chance to collaborate with the larger linguistic community both at the University of Leipzig and the Max Planck Institute for Human Cognitive and Brain Science.

During this time, I presented parts of my work at various occasions in the MPI's 'work in progress' series, at the meetings and workshops of the *Forschergruppe* and at 'Typologiekolloquium' at Universität Leipzig. Through these and through the regular interaction with the members of the Leipzig linguistic community and the numerous guests over the years, my work has been greatly in-

Acknowledgments

spired. In particular, I would like to mention (in alphabetical order): Balthasar Bickel, Bernard Comrie, Tom Güldemann, Andrej Malchukov, Gereon Müller, Jochen Trommer, Søren Wichmann, and Alena Witzlack-Makarevich, with whom I also taught a course at *Leipzig Springschool on Linguistic Diversity* in 2008. The preparations for this course have been very valuable for my research. In addition, I would like to thank the following people for providing information on the languages of their expertise: Lea Brown on Nias, Gerrit Dimmendaal on Turkana, and Claudia Wegener on Savosavo. Another important factor in completing a work of this extent are your fellow sufferers, a.k.a the other PhD students. For sharing the woes of PhD life, more often a laugh and the occasional drink, I want to thank my peers at the MPI: Joseph Atoyebi, Joseph Farquharson, Diana Forker, Linda Gerlach, Thomas Goldammer, Iren Hartmann, Hagen Jung, Zaira Khalilova, Nina Kottenhagen, Christfried Naumann, Andrey Nefedov, Sven Siegmund, Eugenie Stapert, Matthias Urban, and Jan Wohlgemuth.

I would further like to thank the audiences of my presentations at the following conferences, where parts of this work were presented: *NAWUKO* 2006 at Konstanz, *ALT* 2007 at Paris, *Syntax of the World's languages* 2008 at Berlin and *Case in and across languages* 2009 at Helsinki. I also would like to thank the organizers of those conferences.

Finally, there are the people who contributed to the publication process of this very book you are holding in your hands (or more likely seeing on your screen). I am very glad for the opportunity to publish a revised and updated version of my original thesis as one of the first books of Language Science Press. I must thank Martin Haspelmath for accepting my book for the series Studies in Diversity Linguistics and thus making my work widely available. Being one of the first book being published meant witnessing many, and starting some, discussions on formatting. Martin Haspelmath and Stefan Müller were very helpful in answering my questions on all kinds of issues from alphabetization to the correct usage of hyphenation in large compounds. Together with Timm Lichte, Stefan Müller also reliably and quickly gave feedback on the more technical issues with the LaTeX-style. The tedious work of proof-reading has been done by Eitan Grossman, Daniel W. Hieber and Aaron Huey Sonnenschein. All three of them have done an incredible job in a very short time. While I was preparing the book for publication, I could rely on the great atmosphere at the linguistics department at Universität Regensburg. Special thanks go to my colleagues there, Martine Bruil, Christian Rapold and Zarina Molochieva, for their support in many ways.

Needless to say, all shortcomings, omissions and remaining fallacies of this work are my own responsibility.

List of abbreviations

'X'>'Y'	X acting on Y	CONJ	conjunction
1	1st person	COP	copula
2	2nd person	CS	construct state
3	3rd person	CVB	converb
A	most agent-like argument of transitive verb	DECL	declarative
		DEF	definite
ABS	absolutive case	DEM	demonstrative
ACC	accusative case	DEP	dependent clause
AGNM	agent nominalizer	DET	determiner
ALI	alienable possession	DETR	detransitivizer
ALLO	allocentric referent	DIR	directional
AM	associative marker	DIST	distal
ANTGEN	antigenitive case	DSBJ	different subject
ANTIP	antipassive	DSCN	discourse connective
APPL	applicative	DU	dual
ASP	aspect marker	DUBT	dubitative
ATT	attributive	DYN	dynamic
AUGV	augmentative vowel	EGO	egocentric referent
AUX	auxiliary	EMPH	emphatic
BG	background	EPEN	epenthetic segment
CA	common argument	ERG	ergative case
CAUS	causative	EXCL	exclusive
CERT	certainty marker	F	feminine
CLF	classifier	FAFF	final affix
COLL	collective	FIN	finite
COM	comitative	FOC	focus
COMPL	completive	FUT	future
COMPLX	complex marker (Gamo)	GEN	genitive case
CON	continuous tense (Maasai)	HAB	habituative
COND	conditional	HYP	hypothetical

List of abbreviations

ICML	incompletive aspect	PART	particle
IDEOPH	ideophone	PASS	passive
IMP	imperative	p.c.	personal communication
INCEP	inceptive	PFV	perfective
IND	indicative	PL	plural
INESS	inessive	PM	person marking
INF	infinitive	PN	proper noun
INS	instumental	POL	polite form
INTENS	intensifier	POSS	possessive
INTR	intransitive	PRO	pronoun
IPFV	imperfective	PRED	predicative
IRR	irrealis	PREP	preposition
LDG	Lexical Decomposition Grammar	PRF	perfect
		PRS	present tense
LIN	linker clitic (Boraana Oromo)	PRTV	partitive case
		PROG	progressive
LOC	locative case	PROPR	proprietive
M	masculine	PROSP	prospective
MDS	multidimensional scaling	PROX	proximal/proximate
MID	middle, mediopassive	PST	past tense
MODAL	modal verb	PSTCONT	past continuous
MUT	mutated form (Nias)	PSTPUNC	past punctual
N	neuter	PSTREM	remote past
N_'X'	non-'X'	PURP	purposive
NC	noun class marker	PUNC	punctual
NEG	negation, negative	PVS	preverbal selector (Arbore)
NMLZ	nominalizer	Q	question particle/marker
NOM	nominative case	REAS	reason
NP	noun phrase	RDP	reduplication
NR	nominal realis	REC	recipient
NTS	non-topical subject	REFL	reflexive
O	≡ P	REL	relative clause
OBJ	object	RES	resultative
OBL	oblique	RLS	realis
OPT	optative	S	single argument of intransitive verb
OT	Optimality Theory		
P	most patient-like argument of transitive verb	SBJ	subject
		SG	singular

SIM	simultaneous	TOP	topic
STAT	stative	TR	transitive
SSBJ	same subject	UOP	unspecific object (Wappo)
THEM	thematic suffix (Nandi)	VBLZ	verbalizer
TMP	temporal	VEN	ventive extension
TNS	tense marker	VOC	vocative

Part I

Preliminaries

1 Introduction

1.1 Marked-S coding

Syntactic typology traditionally distinguishes languages by the way they encode the single argument of an intransitive verb (S) compared to the more agent-like (A) and the more patient-like arguments (P) of a monotransitive verb (Comrie 1978; Dixon 1979, 2010a). On this basis, the two main alignment types, namely NOMINATIVE-ACCUSATIVE and ERGATIVE-ABSOLUTIVE (Figure 1.1), are distinguished. While the nominative-accusative pattern employs the same form for S and A (nominative case), the P argument receives a special form of encoding (so-called accusative case). In an ergative-absolutive system, S and P are coded alike (absolutive case) while the A argument is in a special form (ergative case).

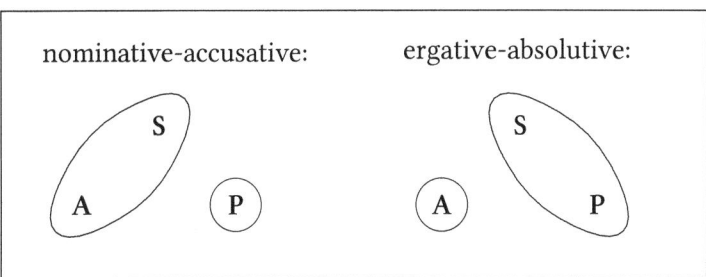

Figure 1.1: Nominative-accusative vs. ergative-absolutive alignment

In most languages, overt formal marking is employed for the P argument in nominative-accusative languages and the A argument in ergative-absolutive languages, while the relation including the S argument (i.e. S+A for the former and S+P for the latter type) is typically left zero-coded.[1] This tendency was prominently phrased in Greenberg's Universal 38:

---

[1] The label 'unmarked' is often used for the case-form lacking overt morphological marking. However, this terminology is problematic because the term 'unmarked' is used for a variety of concepts in linguistics (Haspelmath 2006). I follow Haspelmath's proposal to use the term 'zero-coded' for the formal manifestation of unmarkedness.

1 Introduction

> Where there is a case system, the only case which ever has only zero allomorphs is the one which includes among its meanings that of subject of the intransitive verb. (Greenberg 1963: 75)

However, there are clear exceptions to this generalization. I will use the term MARKED-S LANGUAGE in the following to refer to those exceptional languages. More precisely, there are two types of marked-S languages: MARKED-NOMINATIVE and MARKED-ABSOLUTIVE. Both have in common the property that the single argument of intransitive verbs is overtly-coded while one of the transitive arguments (A or P) receives zero-coding.[2] This study presents an in-depth survey of marked-S languages.

I will begin this first chapter by defining marked-S languages, which constitute a rare and somewhat unexpected type of encoding grammatical relations (Section 1.2). Following this introduction, a brief digression will be made to discuss the phenomenon known as grammatical markedness and the different usages of the term (Section 1.3). Then I will address the issue of terminology used in describing the case-forms of a nominal in a language of the marked-S type. Since a wide range of different case-terms are used in the descriptions of marked-S languages. In order to assure consistency within this work, I will employ a uniform set of case-terms. In addition, I will propose a new terminology to be employed when comparing marked-S languages with each other (Section 1.4). Following that, I will discuss the explanations and types of explanations given to justify the existence of this rare type of case-system (Section 1.5). These explanations will be grouped into two types: historical and functional explanations. The subsequent section discusses marked-S systems from the point of view of formal linguistic theories. Not only do marked-S languages constitute a typological exception, they also pose a serious problem for various formal theories of case-marking, as will be demonstrated using the example of Lexical Decomposition Grammar (Section 1.6). Alignment is most prominently associated with nominal case-marking, and this study is likewise restricted to marked-S alignment as it is found in this domain. However, the term 'alignment' is also used to refer to verbal agreement and word order, as well as with reference to behavioral properties of nominals. Marked-S coding in those other domains, or the domain-specific counterparts thereof, will briefly be discussed in Section 1.7. Finally, I will give an outline of the remainder of this study in Section 1.8.

---

[2] No examples are known to me of a language using zero-coding for both A and P but overt coding for the S argument – a pattern which would by my definition be included in the group of marked-S languages. Given the overall rarity of horizontal alignment (i.e. in which A and P are treated alike but differently from S) and the rarity of marked-S systems, it does not come as a surprise that the combination of both rarities is not (yet) found.

1.2 Definition

Marked-S languages are more traditionally known by the name MARKED-NOMINATIVE languages. I have chosen this new term in order to allow the inclusion of data from a related, yet not so widely recognized, phenomenon, namely MARKED-ABSOLUTIVE languages. The term *marked-S* also nicely summarizes the central characteristic of this type of language, namely the overt marking found on the single argument of intransitive verbs (S) combined with a zero-coded A or P argument.

The marked-nominative type is the most frequent manifestation of the marked-S coding type. As a subtype of the nominative-accusative alignment system, marked-nominative languages exhibit the basic pattern exemplified for this system in Figure 1.1. In marked-nominative systems – like in standard nominative-accusative – S is aligned with A and opposed to P. Unlike in the standard system, the P relation is left without any formal encoding of its case relation. It is in the zero-coded form, while the S+A relation (the nominative) has an overt morphological marker (cf. Figure 1.2). In contrast, the standard – 'unmarked' – nominative-accusative system uses overt marking either for both S+A (nominative) and P (accusative) or restricts it to P-marking.

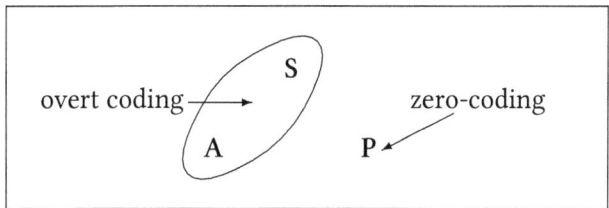

Figure 1.2: Marked-nominative coding

The two types of coding are illustrated here by some examples. The Turkish data in (1) exemplify the standard nominative-accusative system with a zero-coded Nominative[3] case and an overtly coded Accusative case-marked by the suffix *-ı*.

(1) Turkish (Altaic; Turkey; own knowledge)
    a. *Adam   gel-di*
       man.NOM come-PST
       'The man came.'

---

[3] Throughout the text, I follow the convention of capitalizing case-labels, when referring to a specific case-form in an individual language.

1 Introduction

    b. *Öğretmen adam-ı gör-dü*
       teacher   man-ACC see-PST
       'The teacher saw the man.'

The marked-nominative type is illustrated by examples from Cocopa. The S and A relation in (2a, b) is marked with the overt Nominative suffix *-c* while the P relation in (2b) is left zero-coded.

(2) Cocopa (Yuman, Hokan; Mexico; Crawford 1966: 183, 186)
    a. *apá-c   aw-yá* 'The man knows.'
       man-NOM 3-know
    b. *apá-c   kʷák   pa:-ṭím* 'The man shot the deer.'
       man-NOM deer.ACC 3>3-shoot

A parallel system to the marked-nominative type exists for ergative-absolutive languages – the marked-absolutive type. Again, the marking relations are reversed from the standard type. The standard ergative-absolutive system overtly codes the A relation (ergative) and leaves the S+P relation (absolutive) zero-coded. Conversely, in marked-absolutive languages one finds overtly coded S+P and zero-coded A. The marked-absolutive system is illustrated in Figure 1.3. Just like the marked-nominative, the marked-absolutive contradicts Greenberg's universal quoted above since it has overt marking of the S argument while zero-coding one of the transitive core relations.

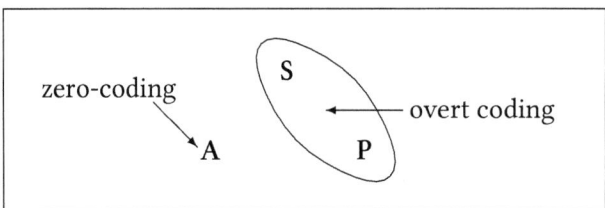

Figure 1.3: Marked-absolutive coding

To illustrate the two patterns, I provide examples for ergative-absolutive and marked-absolutive coding below. In Chechen, the S and P relation is zero coded (3a, b, c) while the A relation in (3b, c) is overtly coded by the Ergative suffix *-(a)s*. In addition to the ergative-absolutive case-marking, verbal indexing also has an ergative-absolutive basis. The verb agrees in gender with the S and P argument.

(3) Chechen (Nakh-Daghestanian; Chechen Republic; Zarina Molochieva, p.c.)

    a. *naana   baazar   j-ax-na*
       mother(F) market.ADV F-go-PRF

       'The mother went to the market.'

    b. *k'ant-as   naana   lie-j-i-na*
       boy(M)-ERG mother(F) lie-F-make-PRF

       'The boy has lied to the mother.'

    c. *naana-s   k'ant   liicna-v-i-na*
       mother(F)-ERG boy(M) wash-M-make-PRF

       'The mother has bathed the boy.'

The only known straightforward example of a marked-absolutive case-system so far is attested in Nias.[4] While the S argument in (4a) is in the overtly marked Absolutive case, the A argument is in the zero-coded Ergative form of a noun (4b). As illustrated in (4c), the P relation is also encoded in the overtly coded Absolutive form.[5]

(4) Nias (Sundic, Western Malayo Polynesian, Austronesian; Sumatra, Indonesia; Brown 2001: 343, Lea Brown, unpublished fieldwork data from 2003, Brown 2001: 346)

    a. *aukhu   **n**-idanö*
       STAT.hot ABS-water

       'The water is hot.'

    b. *i-f-o-houu   defao   **idanö**   nasi*
       3SG-CAUS-have-rust iron.ABS water.ERG sea.ABS

       'The seawater rusted the iron'

    c. *la-bunu   **m**-baßi*
       3PL.RLS-kill ABS-pig

       'They killed a pig.'

---

[4] Crysmann (2009), using a quite different definition of marked-absolutive language, argues against classifying Nias as such. In his approach, alignment is not considered to be construction specific as it is in my account and many other recent works that study alignment from a cross-linguistic perspective (cf. among others Bickel 2011). I will discuss this the notion in more detail in Section 1.7 and Chapter 2.

[5] The distinction between the Absolutive and Ergative case-form is not always as straightforward as in example (4a, c). In most cases the difference is marked by initial consonant mutation, see Section 2.5.4 for a brief discussion of the morphophonemics of nominal mutation in Nias.

1 Introduction

In addition to this definition of marked-S coding, which is purely based on the absence versus presence of overt case-marking, there is a second definition of marked-S languages. König (2006) distinguishes between Type 1 and Type 2 marked-nominative languages. Type 1 languages are classified by the criterion I have discussed above, namely the overt coding of the nominative case-form and the zero-coding of the accusative. Type 2 languages have overtly coded case-forms for both nominative and accusative. However, the accusative has a wider range of functions; it is for example the form of a noun used in citation. I will discuss this second definition of marked-S coding in Section 1.5.3.

1.3 Markedness in grammar

The term *markedness*, and more often the statement that a certain linguistic feature is *marked*, are often employed in grammatical descriptions. Markedness, in its most basic meaning, is universally associated with the presence of overt material, such as overt case morphology for example. Other aspects that are often also called *markedness* frequently correlate with formal markedness (i.e. the presence of overt material). These other factors include (often interrelated) phenomena such as restriction in use, late and/or cumbersome acquisition of a structure, specialization in meaning, or a low usage frequency of an item. Even if not correlated with formal markedness in any sense, structures that meet any of these additional criteria may be referred to as marked by many linguists. Haspelmath (2006) discusses the different meanings of the term markedness and distinguishes between twelve basic senses. These twelve senses are roughly grouped into four types that view markedness as either complexity, difficulty, abnormality or a multidimensional correlation.

The notion of markedness has a prominent position in both functionally- and formally-oriented linguistic traditions. In the functional tradition, this notion goes back to the work of Roman Jakobson and other members of the Prague School, while in the formal tradition the notion was made prominent by Noam Chomsky. In both cases the concept of markedness appears to have been inspired by phonological work. Battistella (1996) provides a detailed discussion of the understanding and evolution of the term markedness in the Jakobsoninan and Chomskyan traditions.

With respect to marked-S languages, the term *marked* is principally understood as overt coding. As mentioned at the end of the previous section, an extension of the term marked to other criteria can also be seen for marked-nominative languages, namely in the definition of Type 2 marked-nominative languages proposed by König (2006). In the following, I will attempt to make clear which one of the different definitions of markedness is presently being discussed. When referring to the form-based definition of markedness, I will use the terms OVERTLY CODED or respectively ZERO-CODED. Only when directly quoting the work of other authors, the terms 'markedness', 'marked' and unmarked' may be used for describing forms that differ in term of more versus less overt material (i.e. the form based criterion).

1.4 Case-labels

When describing the case-system of a given language, linguists often apply traditional case-terminology familiar from Latin. If a case does not resemble any case in the Latin case-system, linguistic theory today provides a huge arsenal of Latinate case-labels to be employed (cf. Haspelmath 2009). This practice of reusing terms is not uncontroversial, since the range of functions or meanings of case-forms will virtually never coincide between any two languages. Marked-S languages are a prime example of this variation of functions. Their nominative/absolutive and ergative/accusative forms show properties quite unlike the properties of case-forms that are known by the same name in standard nominative-accusative or ergative-absolutive languages. This has led many scholars working on marked-S languages to abandon the traditional labels. Yet many of the alternate labels they came up with are equally inappropriate. In this section, I will discuss the different approaches for labeling cases in marked-S languages. Furthermore, I will introduce the case-terminology to be employed in the remainder of this book.

As described in the definition of marked-S coding above (Section 1.2), the special property of the marked-S system is that it combines the standard alignment of nominative-accusative or ergative-absolutive languages with an unexpected pattern of overt/ non-overt marking of the nominal cases. The decision between choosing a label according to the function of a form or according to the overt marking relations is also the main problem when it comes to finding appropriate names for the individual cases defining this alignment system.

One possibility is to simply use the labels from the standard nominative-accusative and ergative-absolutive systems. So, the term 'nominative' is used for the S+A relation in standard nominative-accusative as well as in marked-nominative systems. Similarly, the label 'absolutive' refers to the S+P relation in standard ergative-absolutive and in marked-absolutive systems. However, the more problematic issue is how to label the zero-coded case in the marked-S systems.

1 Introduction

Not only do the terms 'accusative' and 'ergative' suggest overt marking of the case relation (Dixon 1994: 56–57), the uses of the zero-coded case-forms also go beyond those of the accusative or ergative as found in the standard versions of these alignment systems. Nonetheless the label 'accusative' is used in the description of a number of marked-nominative languages, namely Maa (Tucker & Mpaayei 1955), Murle (Arensen 1982) and K'abeena (Crass 2005: 85–86). The labels of 'nominative' and 'accusative' are also employed by König (2006, 2008) in her overview of marked-nominative languages in Africa.

Differently, Dixon (1979) proposed the term 'extended ergative' for the marked nominative case to reflect its overt marking, which is parallel to the mostly overtly marked ergative in ergative-absolutive systems. The label 'extended accusative' for the marked-absolutive would be analogous to this label, though he does not propose this term since he disputes the existence of marked-absolutive systems altogether. The 'extended ergative', however, did not make it into the terminology of grammar writers.[6] If discussed at all, it is merely mentioned as a possible alternative label, for example by Wegener (2008: 133), who irrespective of this calls the Savosavo subject-marker 'Nominative'. Dixon appears to have had a change of mind on the appropriate terminology for marked-nominative systems, as he concludes in his 1994 work that "it seems wisest to maintain the standard use of ergative to refer to marking just of A function" (Dixon 1994: 64) and proposes to stick to the term marked-nominative after all.

One strategy that avoids the terminological problem altogether is not to use any of the traditional Latinate case names at all. Most often this results in labels such as 'subject-case' and 'object-case' (or just 'subject-marker'). This approach is chosen by the grammar writers of some African languages, e.g. for Borana Oromo (Stroomer 1995: 34) or Gamo (Hompó 1990: 364). Most commonly it has been applied to languages of the North-American West-Coast – especially in the 60s and 70s of the last century. This is the case for the Yuman languages Cocopa (Crawford 1966: 104), Diegueño (Langdon 1970: 151), Mojave (Munro 1976: 18), Yavapai (Kendall 1976: 68) and Hualapai (Watahomigie et al. 2001: 38). The same is true for the non-related language Wappo (Li, Thompson & Sawyer 1977: 90). However, in their grammar of Wappo – published about thirty years later – the same authors have switched from the term 'subject-marker' to the use of *nominative* (Thompson, Park & Li 2006). The labels 'subject-case' and 'object-case' have the disadvantage that they carry theoretical connotations unrelated

---

[6] In theoretical typology, the term has done a little better. Plank (1985) uses the terms 'extended ergative/restricted absolutive' to refer to the marked-nominative system and also 'extended accusative/restricted nominative' for the marked absolutive pattern.

to marked-S case-marking. Not all nouns bearing the overt marking of subjects might be subjects in a syntactic sense, and not all syntactic subjects might have the subject case-marker in a certain language (unless one establishes overt case-marking as the only defining property of subjects in that language).

Drawing very much on the Latin grammar tradition, Mel'čuk (1997) makes an idiosyncratic proposal for labeling compared to the current practice in descriptive linguistics. For Maa, he suggests to stick to the literal translation of the term 'nominative' as 'the naming case' and therefore proposes to use it for the form used in naming a nominal (i.e. the citation form). Apart from the use as citation form, this case also encodes the P argument of a transitive verb ('Accusative' case in other descriptions of Maa). The subject-marking case he relabels as 'Oblique' in turn. This usage of the term Nominative may be well motivated from a historical and etymological perspective as Creissels (2009: 453) points out. Still, if used for the case-form encoding transitive objects, the term Nominative is bound to give rise to confusion. Beyond being extremely confusing, there is – in my opinion – a major problem with this approach, namely, that the etymological meaning is not the meaning most prominently associated with the nominative. It is rather its function as the 'subject-case' that comes to mind first, maybe along with the function as 'default' or 'elsewhere' case for some linguists.[7] Both functions are fulfilled by Mel'čuk's 'Oblique' case and not his 'Nominative'.

The terminologies traditionally employed for the marked-nominative languages of Eastern Africa are far less confusing. 'Nominative' is used in the traditional way as referring to the S+A relation. To account for the special status of the form used for the P relation, this form is not referred to as 'accusative' but as the 'absolute' case – e.g. in Turkana (Dimmendaal 1982) or Datooga (Kiessling 2007). The same terminology of 'Absolute' and 'Nominative' case was also introduced in an early description of the Yuman language Yuma (Halpern 1946: 210), although it did not catch on in the terminology of this genus, as noted above. Also Creissels (2009: 456) proposes 'absolute' as a label for nouns in extra-syntactic function such as citation forms, which tend to be zero-coded morphologically (all these function are covered by the typical East-African absolute). Some linguists also use the term 'absolutive' (rather than absolute). This is attested, for example, in the description of Harar Oromo by Owens (1985). This, however, might lead to confusion with the S+P relation in ergative-absolutive languages. Therefore absolute should be preferred as a label. Finally, König (2008: 24), in her discussion of the marked-nominative case-terminology, notes that the term 'absolute' might also lead to confusion since it is used for the zero-coded Nominative case-form in

---

[7] The notion of default case is discussed in more detail in Section 1.6.

1 Introduction

Turkish. This leads her to use the term 'accusative' also for marked-nominative languages.

Given all these different traditions and approaches to naming cases in marked-S languages, one is bound to get mixed up in the terminology when comparing data from different languages. In order to spare the reader from confusion by changing glosses from one example to the next, I decided not to stick to the case-labels chosen by the linguists working on the individual languages. Instead, I will change the glosses with the goal of achieving maximum transparency. All examples from marked-nominative languages are uniformly named and glossed as NOMINATIVE and ACCUSATIVE. I have chosen this convention for the following reasons. There seems to be a certain trend towards recognizing the overt subject-marker as parallel to the nominative case-marker in any standard nominative-accusative language. This trend is indicated by Thompson et al.'s (2006) change of terminology as well as Dixon's change of mind concerning the 'extended ergative' vs. 'marked-nominative' terminology. Moreover, this proposal involves the least amount of relabeling of case-forms and thus makes going back to the original sources less prone to requiring terminological adjustments.

'Accusative' and 'absolute' both appear to be good choices for the non-nominative case in marked-S languages. The encoding of transitive P arguments is just one of many functions the zero-coded case-form fulfills in marked-nominative languages, as I will demonstrate in the following (Chapters 3–7). The label 'accusative' is traditionally associated with a case-form with the main function of encoding P arguments. Using this label for a case-form that has a variety of additional functions may lead to mild confusion on the first encounter with examples in which the accusative argument is clearly not an object of any kind. This study aims at exploring the functions of the different case-forms in marked-S languages, and thus wants to draw attention of those functions of the object-case in marked-nominative languages that are unusual compared with standard nominative-accusative languages. In contrast, the label 'absolute' is less familiar and might be mixed up with 'absolutive' and thus lead to the wrong impression that one is dealing with an ergative-absolutive language. In the remainder of this study I will use the term 'accusative' to refer to the case-form that (among other functions) encodes transitive P arguments in marked-nominative languages. First, I do so because of the greater familiarity of the term 'accusative' over 'absolute'. Also, as noted above, the range of uses of the object case-form in marked-nominative languages is a central aspect of this study. Therefore, unexpected occurrences of accusative case, from the standpoint of the more widely known standard nominative-accusative system, are meant to be highlighted here.

For the marked-absolutive system, we are not confronted with such hard decisions about terminology, since one is not faced with any differing traditions of labeling. Brown (2001) uses the terms UNMUTATED and MUTATED form of the noun for Nias. These labels refer to the morphophonemic shape of the nouns in question. The Mutated form covers the absolutive (i.e. S+P) function, while the Unmutated form is used for A arguments among others. Since Nias is the only language with a marked-absolutive system in my study, I will adopt the language-specific terms Mutated and Unmutated form referring to the S+P relation (the absolutive) and A relation (the ergative), respectively.

The previous discussion has dealt with the issue of labeling cases in individual languages. In addition, terminology is needed to make general statements about the overtly coded and zero-coded forms in both marked-nominative and marked-absolutive languages. For this purpose I propose the following terminology, which will be employed throughout the study whenever making comparative statements. When referring to marked-S languages I use the terms S-CASE and ZERO-CASE form. The label S-case refers to the case which includes among its functions that of encoding the single argument of an intransitive verb (overtly coded in all languages under investigation by definition). This is the nominative (S+A) in marked-nominative languages and the absolutive (S+P) in Nias. The zero-case on the other hand refers to the P argument in marked-nominative languages and the A argument in marked-absolutive languages. This case-form is expressed by zero-morphology in the overwhelming majority of marked-S languages.

1.5 Explaining the existence of marked-S

1.5.1 Rare and geographically skewed

Languages of the marked-S type are a typological exception. Their occurrence is unexpected, a view expressed for example by Greenberg's (1963) Universal 38 cited above. Not surprisingly, languages of this type are extremely rare and their occurrence is geographically highly skewed. The main locus for marked-S languages is in North-Eastern Africa (König 2008: 138). Apart from the cluster in Africa, the pattern is also found in the Yuman genus of southwestern North America and a few other languages of that region, as well as in some languages of the Pacific region.

To account for the existence of this unexpected case-system, two types of explanations have been put forward, a historical one and a functional one. The

1 Introduction

historical explanation describes how the marked-S system can evolve from one of the more widespread systems. This explanation has been put forward for languages of the marked-nominative type, and considers them to be an extended variant of ergative-absolutive systems with overtly coded ergative case-marking, which has been extended to cover the S relation. Apart from ergative-absolutive systems a variety of other sources have been suggested for marked-nominative languages. What all of these historical scenarios have in common is that they propose an origin for the nominative from a category which is expected to be overtly coded from a cross-linguistic perspective. The second type of explanation draws on the number of other functions the case-forms in the marked-S system cover beyond S, A and P marking. This theory predicts that the overall distribution of the zero-coded form will be broader than the distribution of the overtly coded form if one takes into consideration other functions, such as marking of attributive possessors, marking of predicate nominals etc. Of course, these two types of explanations are more different points of view than mutually exclusive approaches.[8] Historical change in a language can certainly be explained by functional motivations in many cases. Some scholars would even argue that functional motivations are the ultimate explanation for all language change (Keller 1994; Du Bois 1987; Croft 2000).

While both types of explanations try to account for the fact that marked-S languages occur in the first place, the two approaches fall short of explaining the rarity of the phenomenon. In this section, the two lines of argumentation will be discussed in more detail starting with the historical explanation in Section 1.5.2, followed by the functional motivation in Section 1.5.3.

1.5.2 Historical explanations

A prominent advocate of the historical explanation of marked-S systems is Dixon (1979, 1994). He defines marked-nominative languages purely on the basis of the contrast between overt and zero-coding (Dixon 1994: 76ff.). Yet, he also tries to give an explanation for the existence of these typologically rare languages. Dixon argues that marked-nominative languages exist because ergative-absolutive languages constitute a somewhat unsatisfactory case-system in neglecting the 'universal concept' of subject and might eventually amend for this by extending the use of A-marking to S.

> The extension of 'marked A case' can be explained in terms of the universal syntactic-semantic identification of A and S as 'subject' (Dixon 1979: 78)

---

[8] I have to thank Eitan Grossman for reminding me of this.

1.5 Explaining the existence of marked-S

Along the same line of argumentation, Dixon denies the existence of marked-absolutive languages. Since, according to him, nominative-accusative languages are more well-formed in this respect, there is no need for overt P-marking to extend its use to mark S. There is thus no reason why marked-absolutive languages should emerge in the first place.

> There is a more slender semantic link between O and S, so that the fourth logical possibility—'marked O case' being extended to also cover S—appears not to occur.[9] (Dixon 1979: 78)

An ergative origin of the marked-nominative coding-system has also been suspected by linguists confronted with individual languages of this type. Li et al. (1977) analyze the Wappo marked-nominative system as a recent innovation. They vaguely hint that the overt subject-marker might be a trace of an earlier ergative stage "where the absolutive case was unmarked and the modern Wappo -i was the ergative case-marker that became generalized into a subject-marker" (Li et al. 1977: 98). However, they elaborate an alternative pathway for the means of encoding grammatical relations in modern Wappo, which might be in conflict with the hypothetical ergative in pre-modern Wappo. Their main argument for the innovative status of the Wappo marked-nominative is its absence from subordinate clauses and equational sentences. Both sentence types have a rigid SOV word order, while main clauses (of the non-equational type) are more flexible in the ordering of constituents. Since "subordinate clauses are known to be more conservative than main clauses in preserving" word order – citing Lehmann (1974) and Vennemann (1975) on this – they conclude that Wappo must be moving from a stage where grammatical relations were encoded by word order to a stage where this is done via case-marking (Li et al. 1977: 100). So basically they propose a change from word order to case-marking, on the one hand, and a change within the case-marking system (namely from ergative-absolutive to marked-nominative), on the other hand. Of course, it would be possible that the two events took place sequentially. First, the word order-based system changed to an ergative case-marking system with a freer word order, which then in turn became a marked-nominative system. Yet this is a highly speculative proposal, which cannot be backed up by any historical records of the language. The first records on the Wappo language date back to the early twentieth century and at this time the marked-nominative system was already established, as the first grammar by Radin (1929: 131) shows. Since doubt is cast on the classification of

---

[9] Dixon's 'O' corresponds to 'P' in the terminology used here.

1 Introduction

Wappo being closely-related to the Yukian languages by Sawyer (1980), a comparison with these languages to reconstruct earlier stages of Wappo will most likely not help in solving the riddle of the origins of the Wappo marked-S system.

The former-ergative analysis is the most widespread line of historical explanation for marked-nominative languages, yet there are a number of other explanations that have been suggested in the literature. An overview of various possible historical scenarios for the rise of overt-nominative marking is provided by König (2008: 178). She proposes for example a passive agent marker as another possible source for an overt nominative marker. She suggests that Maa could be a case of this scenario. This proposal is parallel to what has been suggested as the origin of ergative markers for many languages. Anderson (1977) lists Polynesian languages such as Tongan, Niuean and Samoan, Australian languages, such as Walpiri, as well as Indo-European languages of the Indic and Iranian subgroups, for which a passive origin of ergativity has been proposed. The parallel scenario has not been widely discussed for marked-nominative languages so far – not to mention the doubts which have been cast on this origin for ergative languages (cf. for example Hindi as discussed by Butt & King 2004).

While the theories mentioned so far all search for the origin of the marked-nominative within a prior stage of the case-system, there are other hypotheses suggesting that overt nominative-marking might have originated from a different domain of grammar altogether. The first such proposal sees the nominative marker as a reanalyzed definiteness marker, while another suggest an origin as a topic-marker. The definiteness origin is proposed for the Northern Lwoo languages Anywa, Päri, and Jur-Luwo by König (2008: 179). Note also that Reh (1996) still analyzes the form under discussion in Anywa as a definite subject and does not consider the system a fully-fledged case-system. An origin as a topic-marker is suggested for the marked-nominative of East Cushitic by Tosco (1994). He lists two reasons for this assumption. First, subject-marking only occurs with definite subjects in some of the East Cushitic languages, a feature he associates with topicality. Secondly, Tosco notes that nominative case-marking is not found with focused subjects in many of the languages under investigation.

One critical point that has been ignored by all proponents of the historical explanations of marked-S alignment is the immense rarity of this system. In other words, if there are so many routes that lead to marked-S alignment, why are there so few marked-S languages around? This point is especially problematic for the 'extended ergative' theory put forward by Dixon (1994), since this approach states a universal pressure for ergative-absolutive languages to become marked-nominative – yet standard ergative-absolutive languages are far more numerous than marked-nominative languages. Maslova (2000: 312–313) suggests two reasons why a linguistic structure might be rare on a worldwide scale. One reason is that something is rare because there are hardly any ways in which a given linguistic structure can arise – a situation that does not seem to hold for marked-S coding given all the historical scenarios discussed above. The other possible reason for cross-linguistic rarity is that even though a linguistic structure may arise through a number of pathways, there are still more pathways leading away from that structure. So once a system has come into existence, it will very quickly be lost because it changes into yet another structure.

One example for such a rise and quick demise of marked-S alignment is Old French. While the old Latin case-system was abandoned, traces of the Latin Nominative remained, which were in fact the only traces of overt nominal inflection on full NPs. Therefore nouns distinguish only two case-forms (5), the Nominative form that is encoded with the suffix -s in most cases and the zero-coded Oblique form comprising all non-subject functions (Detges 2009; Jespersen 1992 [1924]: 182).

(5) Old French (Detges 2009: 94)
 a. *li   chien-s   mort l'   ome*
     DET.SBJ dog-NOM bites DET.OBL man.OBL
     'The dog bites the man.'
 b. *le   chien   mort li   uem*
     DET.OBL dog.OBL bites DET.NOM man.NOM
     'It is the dog whom the man bites.'

In contemporary French, the Nominative endings have been eliminated, making the marked-nominative stage a transitional episode during the transfer from case-marking to positional licensing of grammatical relations. Notably, this quick episode of the marked-S coding-system in French did not come about by any of the historical sources proposed in the literature, but simply by morphophonological attrition. However, not all marked-S systems appear to be this short-lived. Since this alignment system spreads over major branches of language families, as in, e.g. Cushitic or the Yuman languages, marked-S appears to be a rather stable system in these genealogical groupings.

1.5.3 Functional explanations

The second proposal to account for the existence of marked-S systems is based on the range of functions individual case-forms have in a language. This approach reduces the impact of the formal marking of case-forms. As a consequence, a different sense of the term markedness is employed for marked-S languages by König (2006, 2008). She distinguishes between what she calls Type 1 and Type 2 marked-nominative languages. Type 1 languages overtly code the S+A relation, while using a zero-coded form for P. Type 2 languages on the other hand employ overtly coded forms for all core relations, but the form employed for P is functionally unmarked (i.e. it covers the wider range of functions). I will refer to the two types as formally (Type 1) and functionally (Type 2) marked-S languages.

The formal and functional criteria for identifying marked-S languages coincide in the majority of cases. In other words, most languages which overtly code the S-case will employ the zero-case in a wider range of functions than the S-case. And vice versa, the case which covers the widest range of functions in a language will typically receive the least amount of overt coding. However, there are some exceptions to both generalizations. As this study will show, the overtly marked S-case sometimes covers all the functions one would expect of a non-marked nominative – Maidu (Shipley 1964) is a prime example of this. And conversely, even if a non-S-case has a wider range of functions, it will not necessarily receive less overt marking than the S-case – this situation is found for example in Wolaytta (Lamberti & Sottile 1997) or Gamo (Hompó 1990).

The formal approach is the more traditional way of characterizing marked-S systems and is based on the presence or absence of overt formal marking of the different case relations. One short-coming of this approach is that it exclusively focuses on the encoding of the S, A and P arguments. Other functions the case-forms might have in the language under investigation are neglected. Those other functions are, for example, the usage to mark attributive possessors, predicate nominals or subjects of passive clauses. These other functions are taken into consideration in the second approach of defining marked-S systems – the functional one. This approach takes other functions besides S, A and P marking into account when identifying which case is the marked one and which is the default case. This definition coincides with a slightly different notion of marked-S languages in which overt marking of the S relation and zero-coding of one transitive relation is not a prerequisite. The functional definition of marked-S languages also includes languages in which all of the core verbal arguments (S, A, and P) are equally marked in terms of overt morphology, but the form used for the grammatical relation including S is used in less functions than the case-form used for the other core argument (P with nominative-accusative and A with ergative-absolutive alignment).

The functional view of marked-S alignment is advocated by König (2006). It is also the predominant take on this system by most scholars working on the marked-S languages of Eastern Africa – although it is usually not explicitly phrased. The special role attributed to the zero-coded form in these languages is for example mirrored in the label chosen for this case-form, i.e. 'absolute' or 'absolutive', which recognizes its wider use than just encoding the P relation (cf. Section 1.4).

This functional approach is put to the test within this study by examining the range of functions the different case-forms cover within marked-S languages. In her formulation of the functional approach König states quite openly that the accusative is "used with the widest range of functions" (2008: 138). However, she does not explicitly define how this widest range of functions is to be measured. It appears that she is counting the number of different functions a certain case-form has, without distinguishing how peripheral or central to the grammar a certain function is. Also, she does not clearly explain how she arrives at the list of functions she is using in her comparison. One could, for example, argue that subjects of mono- and ditransitive verbs constitute two separate functions.[10] Furthermore, certain verb classes are known to employ non-standard case-forms for their subjects in many languages, e.g. so-called experiencer-subjects. Marking the subject arguments of these verb classes could arguably be seen as separate functions. As a result, the number of function an individual case-form has will vary considerably for the same language depending on the initial set of functions one considers.

Irrespective of this, there are two possible interpretations of the claim of functional markedness of the S-case in marked-S languages, and correspondingly two hypotheses one could test. In what I call the WEAK VERSION of the functional markedness hypothesis, the widest range of functions is simply measured by comparing the range of functions of the zero-case with the range of functions of the S-case in a given language. In the STRONG VERSION of the hypothesis the range of functions of the zero-case is not only measured against the number of functions of the S-case, but also against the combined number of functions of every other case-form in the language. Of course, for languages with a two term case-system both hypotheses make the same predictions. However, as König (2008) notes, quite a number of the marked-S languages of Africa have a larger inventory of case-forms. Also the marked-S languages of North-America have somewhat more complex case-systems. In this study I will test both versions of the functional markedness hypothesis – the weak one and the strong one.

---

[10] Bickel (2011: 403) discusses a language encoding the two functions in distinct ways, namely Gyarong (Sino-Tibetan).

Like the historical explanations of marked-S coding, the functional approach does not directly address the cross-linguistic rarity of this alignment system. However, there is a promising line of argumentation for the dispreference of marked-S alignment within this approach. In what Mallinson & Blake (1981: 91–93) label the 'discriminatory theories' of case, one would expect that the S argument – which does not need to be distinguished from any other argument – will be encoded with the zero-coded case-form. Therefore the same form will be employed for any transitive argument aligning with S. Using overt morphology on the S argument – though there is no need for discriminating it from some other argument and thus no need for overt marking – is a dispreferred strategy and therefore should not be widely distributed among the world's languages. For similar reasons a number of other functions of a noun will be encoded with the zero-coded form. When using a noun in the citation form (or other isolated context), there is no need for distinguishing its argument role from some other argument.

In addition to providing the more promising explanation for the rarity of marked-S languages, the functional approach also scores better in explaining marked-absolutive languages. While for the historical approaches integration of the marked-absolutive system into the explanation is either doubtful or excluded by definition – as it is the case for the 'extended ergative' theory – no such restriction exists for the functional approach. The zero-case is the one with the widest range of functions and whether the S-case comprises an S+A or S+P relation is irrelevant.

1.6 Implications for formal approaches to case-marking

As noted in Section 1.2, the unexpectedness of the marked-S system has been expressed by Greenberg (1963), based on cross-linguistic observations. The general tendency for the nominative and absolutive to be encoded with less overt material has also been acknowledged by some formal linguists. The following quote by Chomsky (1993) expresses the same observation as Greenberg's generalization (and extends it to the domain of verbal agreement).

> The 'active' element (Agr_S in nominative-accusative languages and Agr_O in ergative-absolutive languages) typically assigns a less-marked Case to its Spec, which is higher on the extractability hierarchy, among other properties. It is natural to expect less-marked Case to be compensated (again, as a tendency) by more-marked agreement (richer overt agreement with nominative and absolutive than with accusative and ergative). (Chomsky 1993: 10)

1.6 Implications for formal approaches to case-marking

Beyond this brief statement, marked-S languages are of no further relevance for Chomsky's theory, which when it comes to case is mostly concerned with the underlying deep-structure relations. Not much room is dedicated to the actual surface case-forms which are generated in spell-out. However, there are other formally-oriented linguistic paradigms for which marked-S languages are of great relevance, since their existence poses a great challenge to the mechanisms of case-assignment underlying these theories.

Already in early work on case-systems, the nominative had a special status among the case-forms of the paradigm. This observation was often expressed by noting that, strictly speaking, only nouns in the nominative case can be viewed as nouns, while all other forms were just 'cases of a noun', i.e. they were not considered to be nouns themselves. Sweet (1876: 24) for instance held the view that all "oblique cases are really attribute-words." Likewise, in modern linguistics a strict division is often made between the nominative and all other cases. As a result of this, some scholars treat the nominative (at least if zero-coded) as an non-case altogether, as exemplified in the following quotation; similar formulations can be found in Aissen (1999, 2003) and de Hoop & Malchukov (2008: 566):

> We assume that nominative (or absolutive) case is in fact a label for 'no case': that is, we assume that the absence of special morphological marking indicates the absence of case. (de Hoop & Narasimhan 2005: 322)

Even without denying case status to it, the special status of the nominative case is undisputed by theories of case. This special status is often referred to as it being the 'default' or 'elsewhere' case. The elsewhere case is not restricted in its usage by any conditions on its occurrence, unlike, for example, German Dative subjects, which have to be licensed by certain mental state verbs. Because of its principally unrestricted usability, the nominative is the case that occurs in the widest range of functions, which is exactly the property ascribed to the zero-accusative by the functional approach to marked-nominative languages. As a consequence, some theories run into trouble when confronted with marked-S languages, since the default case nature of the nominative is hard-wired into their structure.

In some theories, the default status of the nominative is not only an underlying assumption, but is actually built into the theory via a set of features or some similar technical apparatus. The cases within the paradigm are specified with respect to those abstract features. Notably, the default case is then analyzed as the maximally underspecified case (i.e. the set of features characterizing it is the empty set). Hence there are no restrictions on the occurrence of the default case, which means it could theoretically occur in all contexts. The default case

1 Introduction

is, however, subject to the Elsewhere Principle (Kiparsky 1973). Thus if a given contexts meets the feature specification of another case-form, this more specific case-form will be picked over the default case.

As an example I will discuss Lexical Decomposition Grammar (henceforward LDG) in some detail and the difficulties arising due to the existence of marked-S languages. LDG (Wunderlich 1997; Stiebels 2002) assigns the following underspecified feature to the grammatical core cases:

- Dative: [+hr,+lr]
- Ergative: [+lr]
- Accusative: [+hr]
- Nominative/Absolutive : [ ]

Arguments are assigned case according to their theta-structure. The feature [+hr] translates to 'there is a higher role', which means in order for an argument to be assigned a case with this feature, there must be another argument that has a higher role. Conversely, the [+lr] feature requires an argument bearing a lower role necessary. The lexical entry of a verb can override the features specified in theta-structure (Wunderlich & Lakämper 2001); however, for the moment we will neglect this. The following example illustrates the case-assignment in LDG. In (6) the theta-structure and semantic form of the verb 'to see' are given. The lambda abstractors in the theta-structure generalize over the argument variables of the verb – s being the situation (or event) variable, which is not relevant for the argument structure – increasing from left to right with respect to how deeply they are embedded into the semantic form of the verb. For each argument (i.e. x and y in example (6)), there is a higher role if another argument is embedded less deeply into the semantic form. Conversely, if there is an argument that is embedded more deeply, a lower role exists.

(6) $\underbrace{\lambda x \; \lambda y \; \lambda s}_{\text{theta-structure}} \quad \underbrace{\{see(x,y)\}(s)}_{\text{semantic form}}$

The argument positions in theta-structure are fully specified with respect to their [hr] and [lr] features, thus they can be assigned both positive or negative values for the respective features. Example (7) demonstrates the mechanism of case-assignment to the arguments of a verb. In this process, a language assigns the case-forms which are at disposal in its lexical case inventory to these fully

1.6 Implications for formal approaches to case-marking

specified argument positions. Contradictions between the feature specifications of argument position and case-marker are not tolerated by the mechanism. For a position for which the language finds no better matching feature specification in its case inventory, the maximally underspecified default case will be picked. Nominative-accusative languages assign accusative case to the y arguments since its specification as [+hr] fits into this argument slot. For the x argument no case with matching features is found. Hence, the default nominative case is assigned. Conversely, ergative-absolutive languages have a matching candidate for the [+lr] feature of the x arguments – the ergative case – but no other candidate than the default case for the y argument.

(7)
	λx	λy
	-hr	+hr
	+lr	-lr
nominative-accusative	NOM	ACC
ergative-absolutive	ERG	ABS

While the LDG approach neatly derives the case-assignment in standard nominative-accusative and ergative-absolutive languages, the system is not as suitable for marked-S languages. The default case is best described, not by the case functions it covers, but by stating that it is used in all contexts in which all other cases cannot be used. For the standard systems, this property is reflected in the LDG feature specification. In marked-S languages, the role of a default case must be ascribed to the zero-case, since this is the case with the elsewhere distribution. Thus, the feature-values LDG proposes for accusative and ergative case do not do justice to zero-accusatives or zero-ergatives found in marked-S languages. Furthermore, if one adopts the LDG case feature specifications, one would have to assume a correspondence between zero-exponence (no overt morphology) and non-zero feature sets for the zero-accusative [+hr] or zero-ergative [+lr]. And conversely, one would postulate a relation between overt exponence and zero-feature specification for the marked-nominative or marked-absolutive. That leaves one with a 'NO form to meaning' relationship on the one hand and a 'form to NO meaning' relationship on the other hand. This is a most unsatisfying situation, which violates basic principles of morphological theory. In the concluding part of this work, I will come back to this issue (Section 9.4). For now, I just note that in addition to being typologically rare, marked-S languages do not seem to fit into the patterns that a number of formal theories offer for analyzing case-assignment.

1 Introduction

1.7 Domains of alignment

1.7.1 Beyond case-marking

The discussion of marked-S languages so far has exclusively focused on nominal case-marking. The labels *nominative-accusative* and *ergative-absolutive* are commonly employed to classify the system of case-marking on the noun phrase (i.e. dependent-marking). However, the terms are also applied more generally for any morphosyntactic device treating S like A or P, and thus including verbal indexing (i.e. head-marking). In some instances, the terminology has even been expanded to word order (Buth 1981; Andersen 1988). In addition, behavioral properties have been used to characterize the alignment system(s) of a languages (Bickel 2011), thereby extending the term alignment beyond coding-properties.

I will discuss these other domains of alignment – head-marking (Section 1.7.2), word order (Section 1.7.3) and behavioral properties (Section 1.7.4) – and clarify for all of these domains what the marked-S equivalent would look like. All of these domains have some limitation with respect to the possibility of investigating the marked-S system in them. For nominal case-marking, some restrictions exist as well. In the final section (Section 1.7.5), I will state these limitations and thus define the exact domain of this study on marked-S languages, namely, nominal case-marking of full noun phrases.

1.7.2 Head-marking

For indexing the S+A (or S+P) arguments, overt morphological marking is the norm cross-linguistically (if a language chooses to employ head-marking devices at all); cf. the Chomsky (1993) quote at the beginning of Section 1.6. So for the indexing-system of a language, it would be unusual to lack overt coding of the S+A (or S+P) relation, and instead only indexing the P (or respectively A) argument. Thus, a system that overtly marks S arguments via verbal indexing is actually the expected, and most common system (for languages that encode their arguments on the verb at all). A system that would be comparable to marked-S case-marking in terms of its unexpectedness accordingly would lack overt marking of S arguments on the verb, while indexing some other arguments. The head-marking counterpart of marked-S would thus be more appropriately called 'unmarked-S'.

Just like the marked-S dependent-marking, its equivalent in head-marking appears to be rare typologically. Miestamo (2009) lists Khoekhoe as the only language with verbal indexing for objects but not subjects, while there are three languages with a marked-S case-system in his 50 languages world-wide sample.

1.7 Domains of alignment

Drawing on the larger sample of the *World Atlas of Language Structures* (WALS), when combining the data from the two chapters devoted to verbal person marking (Siewierska 2005a,c), there are 18 languages that have nominative-accusative alignment in their verbal person marking while indexing only their P argument. These languages stand against 192 languages marking either only the A or both A and P arguments. In addition there are 3 languages with ergative-absolutive alignment cross-refencing only their A argument, which are compeeting with 14 language marking either only P or both A and P arguments.[11]

However, except for the fact that marked-S case-marking and unmarked-S indexing are both rare, there is no structural or logical reason to compare the two structures. Including both phenomena into this study would even lead to methodological restrictions. In Chapter 2, I will outline an approach to comparing marked-S languages by means of a number of functions such as attributive possessor or subject of positive and negative existential constructions; a number of these functions cannot be studied in indexing-systems. This is the case for those structures which are below clause level or extra-syntactic, namely, attributive possessors and the form of a noun used in citation or address. Furthermore, in some of the more complex constructions the comparison of case- and agreement-marking languages is also problematic. In nominal predications, for example, not all languages employ a construction that exhibits verbal agreement. On the one hand, there are languages in which no overt verbal element at all is employed in this context. Zero-copulas are in fact most common in nominal predications and only occur in other types of non-verbal predications when also found there (Stassen 1997: 62–65). Also, overt copulas are most likely to be absent in third person contexts (Stassen 1997: 65), which comprise clauses with full noun phrases – the domain of this investigation. On the other hand, if a language makes use of a copula in nominal predications, this copula might not behave like other verbs in terms of agreement and other properties. Pustet (2003) notes the tendency of copulas not to behave like verbs in terms of morphosyntax.

1.7.3 Word order

When extending the notion of marked-S to word order, first of all, a few considerations have to be made on how alignment systems can be translated into the ordering of constituents. While word order is seen as an alternate means

---

[11] The languages with the unmarked-S agreement system are ‖Ani, Anejom, Batak, Ijo, Indonesian, Kera, Khoekhoe, Kisi, Mupun, Nakanai, Noon, Palikur, Panyjima, Selknam, Sema, Tiguk, Warao, and Yapese, for the nominative-accusative alignment, and Atayal, Chamorro and Nadëb, with ergative-absolutive alignment. The total number of languages shared between the two WALS maps is 378.

/ *1 Introduction*

to distinguish arguments on a par with case-marking and verbal indexing, the notion of nominative-accusative or ergative-absolutive word order is not commonly found in grammars. A reason for this might be that word order is thought to be on the nominative-accusative basis almost without exceptions.[12] However, there are a few examples of languages for which an ergative word order has been proposed. This is the case in Päri (Andersen 1988) – though only in main clauses – and Luwo (Buth 1981), which have a SV+PVA word order.[13]

One complication in associating the different types of alignment with specific word orders is the inherently relational nature of this property. The ordering of a specific argument can only be identified in relation to some other element. At least three factors could be taken into account here. First, there is the ordering of an argument with respect to another argument. This measure can obviously only be applied in clauses with more than one argument. So this factor in itself is not helpful for identifying nominative-accusative or ergative-absolutive alignment in a language, since the S argument of intransitive clauses is not parallel to the A or P argument in preceding or following the other argument. Secondly, one can take into account the ordering of an argument with respect to the verb. Two sub-criteria can be called upon here, strict ordering (i.e. precedes/follows the verb) and direct adjacency to the verb. And finally one can classify the ordering of an argument with respect to clausal boundaries, i.e. whether it occurs at initial position (or final or any other salient position one might be interested in investigating) of the clause.

In verb-medial languages, there is an overlap between these two last factors. The argument that precedes the verb will also typically be in clause-initial position and be directly adjacent to the verb (unless there are good reasons to assume an intervening clause structure position). For these types of languages, positioning with respect to the verb and with respect to clausal boundaries will identify the same type of alignment system: nominative-accusative for the ordering of SV+AVP or VS+PVA and ergative-absolutive for languages with SV+PVA or VS+AVP word order. If both transitive arguments are positioned on the same side of the verb, the two criteria identify different alignment systems. Taking the adjacency and positioning to the verb as the unit of measure, SV+APV languages are ergative-absolutive, but with respect to the clause initial position, they are nominative-accusative. Also there is the theoretical possibility – though not

---

[12] Cf. the debate on syntactic ergativity (Anderson 1976, 1977; Dixon 1994) and whether such a phenomenon exists at all – though this debate is not restricted to word order.

[13] In order to make the alignment systems that are to be identified through word order more clear, I will consistently use the S, A, and P labels for the arguments, rather than employing the traditional word order abbreviations such as SOV or SVO.

attested and supposedly highly unlikely to be found – of a language where both transitive arguments are found on the same side of the verb, but intransitive S occurs on the other side. Here in the ordering with respect to the verb, S does not align with either A or P, but in terms of verb-adjacency it behaves like whichever transitive argument is adjacent to the verb.

In conclusion, the definition of nominative-accusative or ergative-absolutive word order is somewhat problematic for verb-initial and verb-final languages. Only if a language is verb medial can a distinction based on word order be made between a nominative-accusative (SV+AVP/VS+PVA) and an ergative-absolutive basis to the word order (SV+PVA/VS+AVP).

Furthermore, the notion of marked versus unmarked ordering must be clarified for identifying the marked-S equivalent in word order. As noted earlier, when defining alignment systems, the ordering of the A and P argument with respect to each other is not of much use. However, previous research on the ordering of subject and object has revealed that subjects tend to precede objects in word order. This might be a good starting point to identify the marked types of word order. Like marked-S case-marking, languages with objects preceding subjects are rare on a worldwide basis. This finding suggests that the straightforward equivalent of a marked-nominative language would be a language in which the object precedes the subject in the canonical word order.

The tendency of ordering A before P was already stated by Greenberg as the first universal of his seminal paper on word order:

> In declarative sentences with nominal subject and object, the dominant order is almost always one in which the subject precedes the object. (Greenberg 1963: 61)

This observation is, however, biased toward languages with nominative-accusative word order. Though this is the cross-linguistic norm, there are some remarkable languages not conforming to the S+A vs. P word order, as discussed above. Therefore, in ergative-absolutive languages the 'marked' status of the object-precedes-subject ordering might be questionable, since the term 'subject' is not applicable for the A argument in a language exhibiting a syntactic S+P pivot by grouping those two arguments together in terms of word order.

Greenberg's observation on the ordering of A and P was confirmed by large scale studies. For example, Dryer (2005b) finds 1017 languages in his sample in which the subject precedes the object, while only 39 have the subject following the object (172 languages are listed as having no dominant order of S, O and V). With this figure, one has to take into account that – as discussed above –

1 Introduction

not all of these languages will allow for a clear classification of having either nominative-accusative or ergative-absolutive alignment in terms of word order. Only verb-medial languages allow for an unambiguous classification. Out of the 39 languages with O-S order in Dryer's sample, there are nine verb-medial ones (two of which – Päri and Mangarayi – will be discussed in this study due to the marked-S properties in their case-marking systems).[14]

As with verbal indexing, there are no good reasons to enlarge the scope of this study of marked-S languages to this domain. The two phenomena are different in nature, and as with head-marking, some of the contexts of interest for nominal case-marking have no equivalent. In addition, the definition of alignment systems based on the ordering of constituents should be put on firmer theoretical ground, before attempting to do a unified study of any alignment system through all domains. As a consequence, word order as a means of classifying languages as marked-S will not be used within this study. However, there will be some discussion of the word order of marked-S languages in Chapter 5, which deals with information structure.

1.7.4 Behavioral properties

Traditionally, the overt coding of case and verbal agreement have featured prominently in studies of alignment systems. Additionally, behavioral properties such as relativization, equi-NP deletion, conjunction reduction or control/raising are also possible factors in establishing the alignment systems of a language (Bickel 2011).

Studies of behavioral properties have shown that the typical subject arguments often allow for behavior that cannot be found with other arguments. So one definition of behavioral marked-S would be a language in which subjects (or S+P pivots in ergative-absolutive languages) are more restricted in their behavior than non-subjects. For the domain of relativization, for example, it has been shown that subjects are the most widely relativizable elements across languages. Further, languages that allow for other types of relativization must also allow subjects to be relativized (Keenan & Comrie 1977). All proposed counterexamples to this so-called 'Accessibility Hierarchy' have not touched upon the special status of subjects, but rather made amendments to the non-subject part of the hierarchy. So, there do not seem to be any cases of 'marked-S relativization'.

---

[14] The remaining seven languages with marked-S word order are: Asuriní, Cubeo, Hixkarayana, Selknam, Tiriyo, and Ungarinji. These languages could be considered marked-S word order languages, unless they are revealed to be instances of ergative word order like Päri.

It may well be that there are other interesting behavioral properties of marked-S languages, but their investigation requires an extensive description of these topics in a grammar. Hardly any of the materials available on marked-S languages provide such an in-depth discussion of these issues.

1.7.5 The domain of investigation

For the reasons listed above, I concentrate on marked-S as a phenomenon in the domain of nominal case. I adopt the broad definition of case as given by Bickel & Nichols (2009), which includes all instances of morphological case-marking (affixes, stem change, tone, clitics) and also adpositional marking rather than only case-marking via inflectional affixes. Furthermore, it is case-marking of full noun phrases (NPs) rather than pronominals which is the focus of this survey. The reasons for this restriction are the following:

First of all, formal zero vs. overt coding is usually easier to identify for full NPs. The pronominal system of a language often consists of two or more sets of pronouns for the individual cases which are not historically related to each other (or such a relation might be blurred through language change). In these cases, the identification of the zero-coded vs. the overtly coded form of a pronoun either in terms of non-affixed vs. affixed form, or underived vs. derived form, cannot be performed easily and uncontroversially.

Secondly, not all languages make ready use of pronominal arguments. A large number of languages (so-called 'pro-drop' languages) will not overtly realize pronominal arguments in many instances. Moreover, if the pronoun is expressed in one of these languages, then the pronominal element will bear some special discourse status, such as expressing a contrast (either against the expectations of the listener, or to highlight a change in participants). Such contrastive contexts are an important part of this study. However, they have to be compared to contexts with a neutral information structure, in which often no overt pronouns occur at all. Therefore, overt pronominals as the element most prone not to be neutral with respect to their information structure are not the ideal domain for this investigation.

Finally, the pronominal and the nominal systems of a language sometimes behave differently in terms of their alignment. Split alignments along the so-called Silverstein Hierarchy, which have long been noted for ergative-absolutive languages (Silverstein 1976; Dixon 1994) are also found in marked-S languages (Handschuh 2008, 2014). A discussion of all alignment splits found with marked-S languages – including those on the Silverstein Hierarchy – is presented in Section 2.5.

1 Introduction

Instead of lumping together the categories of pronominal and nominal case-marking, full NPs have been selected for this study. Unavoidably, some of the examples presented do contain pronouns, but this is only done when the description of the language makes it clear the behavior of pronouns and full NPs is identical for the feature under investigation. Wherever possible, examples are chosen where the relevant item is a full noun phrase.

1.8 Outlook

In the remainder of this study, an in-depth investigation of marked-S coding-systems will be provided as found in the case-marking system of full noun phrases. The next chapter will present the methodology of this investigation. This methodology is based on the notion of MICRO-ALIGNMENT. That is the notion that the alignment system of a language can be established in a large number of contexts, and that in fact the alignments regularly differ between these contexts within one and the same language. This phenomenon is often referred to as *split alignment*. Part two (Chapter 3–7) comprises the discussion of the contexts selected for this investigation (these will be introduced in the next chapter) and demonstrates the strategies employed by marked-S languages to encode these contexts. Based on these data, I will investigate how uniform or diverse the marked-S languages are. Special emphasis will be put on systematic patterns arising in term of genealogically or areally defined groups of languages (Chapter 8). Finally, I will conclude this survey in discussing the validity of the findings, the overall applicability of the methodology, the implications for theoretical linguistics, and propose further lines of investigation (Chapter 9).

2 Redefining alignment

2.1 Introduction

The functional approach to marked-S coding (König 2006, 2008) claims that the zero-case will have a wider distribution than the S-case in every language. However, measuring the distribution of case-forms in such a way as to be comparable across languages is not a trivial enterprise. A number of factors have to be taken into account. In this chapter, I discuss these different factors and develop a methodology for measuring these distributions.

Traditionally, typological work on alignment systems has always considered languages in a more finely-grained manner than simply to state that language X has, for example, nominative-accusative alignment. Rather than classifying languages as a whole as belonging to type A or B, a large part of the typological literature has been focused on the investigation of the alignment in specific domains of the grammar. Central to this take on alignment are languages with a so-called split alignment-system – i.e. languages employing different alignments in different parts of their grammar. This study follows the spirit of such approaches, which are discussed in more detail in Section 2.2.

The methodology of this study is outlined in the subsequent sections. Several meta-linguistic contexts are defined for which the case-realization in the individual marked-S languages is investigated (Section 2.3). These contexts constitute possible split-up points for alignment, such that a language will use one case-form to encode an S-like argument in one context but a different case-form in the next context. The contexts that turned out to be most interesting are discussed in depth in separate chapters. These contexts are introduced in Section 2.4. Further, there are various types of splits found only in a small number of languages in my sample – in most cases only in a single language. These idiosyncratic splits will be presented in Section 2.5.

Finally, I will look at the usage-based factors that influence the distribution of zero-case and S-case (Section 2.6). These factors have not been dealt with in previous studies on marked-S alignment. However, without taking the actual overall usage of the case-form into account – as measured, for example, through textual frequencies – any claim about the distribution of S-case and zero-case can only be of preliminary nature. The lack of well-designed corpora for marked-S languages prevents me from doing a quantitative analysis of usage-based factors. Therefore, I will discuss the influence of such factors only from a qualitative point of view.

2.2 Split alignment

The standard method for identifying alignment systems is to compare the morphosyntactic treatment of the S argument of intransitive verbs with the A and P arguments of transitive verbs. In the previous chapter, it has been discussed how on this basis the basic types of nominative-accusative and ergative-absolutive alignment are distinguished (Section 1.1). However, it has long been noted that the classification of a languages as a whole as being ergative-absolutive or nominative-accusative is problematic.

> [...] it is rather misleading to speak of ergative languages, as opposed to nominative-accusative languages, since we have seen that it is possible for one phenomenon in a language to be controlled on an ergative-absolutive basis while another phenomenon in the same language is controlled on a nominative-accusative basis. Thus one should ask rather to what extent a language is ergative-absolutive or nominative-accusative, or, more specifically, which constructions in a particular language operate on the one basis and which on the other. (Comrie 1978: 350–351)

The prototypical kind of languages not having a uniform alignment throughout are languages exhibiting so-called 'split ergativity'. As the terminology suggests, this phenomenon has most prominently been studied for languages of a basically ergative type (cf. Silverstein 1976; Dixon 1994). As a more general term, I will use the term SPLIT ALIGNMENT SYSTEM for all cases in which two different alignment systems are employed in two domains of a grammar. Differences in coding will also be subsumed in this analysis of splits, since, strictly speaking, marked-nominative and marked-absolutive systems are coding variants of the basic nominative-accusative and ergative-absolutive alignment types.

Several observations have been made about split ergative languages. First, splits in the alignment system seem to occur in a limited set of grammatical domains (Dixon 1994). Most frequent are splits along the line of some kind of a nominal prominence hierarchy and splits based on temporal or aspectual information of the clause. Second , the ergative pattern is in most cases found on the same side of those splits, namely in the more salient part of the nominal hierarchy (Silverstein 1976) and in the past tense/perfective aspect (Malchukov 2014). The view that one side of a hierarchy is uniformly associated with the same type of alignment system across languages has recently been challenged (Bickel 2008a). Third, it has been observed that hardly any overlap is found between those two splits, i.e. when a language has a split along the nominal hierarchy, it will not have a tense/aspect split, and vice versa (Trask 1979).

Examples of the NP split ergative system can be found in many Australian languages. In Dyirbal (Dixon 1972) Accusative case (which is overtly coded) is distinguished from (zero-coded) Nominative for first and second person pronouns. All other nominals (i.e. third person pronouns, proper names and common nouns) show a distinction between (overtly coded) Ergative forms and (zero-coded) Absolutives. Splits based on tense, aspect, or modality of the clause are attested in the Indo-Aryan languages and in Georgian (see Malchukov (2014) for a discussion of splits of this type). In Section 2.5, I will discuss the extent to which the split systems in marked-S languages behave in the same way as classical split-ergative languages.

2.3 Micro-alignment

The goal of this study is to provide an in-depth view of the marked-S system that goes beyond the encoding of the primitive S, A, and P. Instead, I will survey a variety of grammatical domains with respect to which case-forms are employed. Ultimately, this study aims to test the claim that in marked-S languages the zero-coded form of a noun has a wider range of functions than the overtly coded S-case (König 2006). So, instead of determining alignment by considering three different possible occurrences of case-marking (the well-known S/A/P trinity of alignment), I will look at fourteen possible different contexts in which case-marking can occur. The focus is on areas of grammar that are coded by the S-case in typical languages of the standard nominative-accusative or ergative-absolutive kind. The contexts define the possible split-up points for alignment. The larger the number of contexts one considers, the more room there is for cross-linguistic variation. Compared with broad classifications of languages as nominative-accusative or ergative-absolutive, this approach studies alignment on a microscopic level. Hence, I call this take on alignment MICRO-ALIGNMENT. Various current typological approaches are attending to ever finer-grained distinctions between languages. For example, Bickel (2007) proposes a multivariate approach to language typology that aims at more precisely quantifying how different individual languages are. This approach is employed for the domain of grammatical relations by Witzlack-Makarevich (2011). A fine-grained classification of the linguistic structures under investigation is vital for such quantitative work.

When doing language typology, one has to consider the important issue how the data from different languages can be compared at all. The need for a TERTIUM COMPARATIONIS has been highlighted in many works. Seiler (2000: 28–19) criticizes the practice of choosing an individual language as the unit of measure to compare other languages against. Furthermore, he agrees with earlier scholars, such as Heger (1990/91), that the *tertium comparationis* should also not be taken from beyond the domain of language activity. Wierzbicka (1995: 185) argues that meaning is the only possible source a *tertium comparationis* can be derived from since linguistic form and structure differ among individual languages. Croft (2003: 13–14) discusses the common practice in typological research of choosing a semantic definition of the domain to be investigated (at least for typological research that is concerned with morphosyntactic structures). He notes that the traditional notion of semantics is too narrow to subsume all relevant aspects and thus includes pragmatic structures into the domain from which means of comparison can be drawn. A similar stance is taken by Haspelmath (2010), who notes that comparison across languages should not be done on the basis of grammatical categories, since these are of language-specific nature. He suggests that one should rather resort to 'comparative concepts', which are not language-specific but specifically defined as a cross-linguistic means of comparison.

The methodology underlying this study is visualized in Figure 2.1. The distinction between language-specific categories and comparative concepts is captured on the horizontal axis – the left side being dedicated to language-specific categories, while metalinguistic comparative concepts are to be found on the right side of the figure. The term *surface* on top of the left-hand side of the figure is not to be understood in opposition to any deep structure level. Case-forms or constructions that one wants to postulate for a given language must be identifiable on the surface level. However, whether they are directly mapped from the language-independent *conceptual level* or from a language-specific deep structure representation (which in turn receives its information from the conceptual level) is not relevant here. For this approach I assume at least these two levels, the conceptual level, which is employed to make comparisons across languages possible, and the surface level, which reflects the observable data from a language. An additional language-specific level that comprises an underlying representation could be integrated if need be.

2.3 Micro-alignment

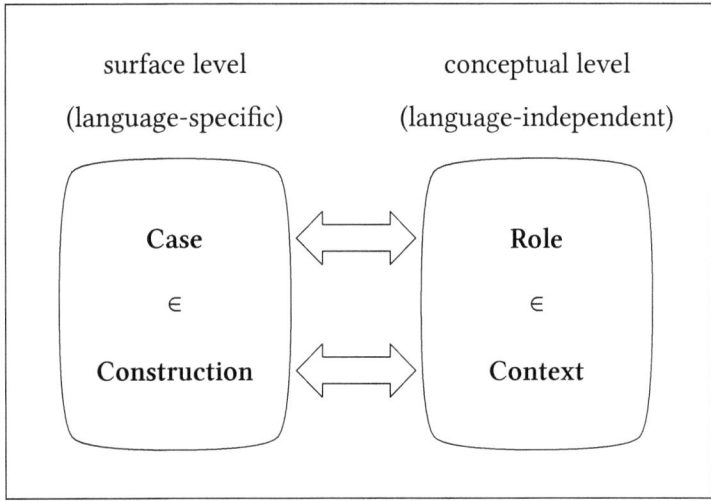

Figure 2.1: Cross-linguistic comparison of case-forms based on the contexts of use

Another aspect depicted in the figure is the level of granularity of the elements considered; granularity increases from top to bottom. The left side of the graph consists of two elements: CASE and CONSTRUCTION. Case refers to a specific case in a given language, e.g. the German Dative, the Latin Ablative or the Finnish Partitive. A construction in the sense used here is a linguistic entity roughly corresponding to a clause. The notion of construction is defined more narrowly than in Construction Grammar (Goldberg 2006: 18) where constructions go "all the way down" and up. While in Construction Grammar individual case-forms are considered to be constructions as well, in my definition, constructions are larger entities. A typical construction in my view is a predication and thus takes at least one argument. Note, however, that not all contexts I discuss in this work easily fall under this definition, namely, the extra-syntactic forms of citation and address. A use of the notion construction similar to mine can be found in descriptive grammars, where labels such as 'copula construction', 'existential construction' or 'locational construction' are used for language-specific ways of expressing a certain meaning. For example, the most commonly used existential construction in English is the 'there is an X' construction. Nominals marked in a given case-form constitute a part of a construction, i.e. cases are elements of constructions.

On the right side of Figure 2.1 the topmost concept are ROLES, which are elements of the larger meta-linguistic CONTEXTS. The notion of role is quite familiar from works such as Fillmore's 1968 'case roles' or the 'semantic/thematic/θ-' roles of other schools of linguistics. No consensual term has yet been established for what I have labeled context here. Labels such as 'meaning', 'function' or 'sense' could be employed as well. This level of representation is meant to represent some larger chunk of meaning that can have varying levels of abstractness. Semantic forms along the lines of Dowty (1991) are a way to envisage this level of representation, as in: $\exists e[kissing(e)\ \&\ Agent-of(John,e)\ \&\ Patient-of(Mary,e)]$. However, these can be paired with additional contextual information like the discourse properties of a given role within the specific contextual occurrence (like: "mono-transitive verb whose A is a contrastive topic").

The double-headed arrows connecting the language-independent conceptual level with the language-specific surface level represent the relation between the two sides in a given language. The correspondences between the two sides can be manifold (one-to-one, many-to-one, one-to-many or many-to-many). A given context might be expressed by only a single construction in a language, but for another context (or in another language) there can be multiple constructions encoding the same meaning. Conversely, a language may use a construction to encode a whole array of contexts or it might have a construction that is exclusively used for encoding a specific context.[1]

In Figure 2.2 the mapping between a number of contexts to individual constructions in English and German is illustrated. English has a specific construction for contexts A, B, and F while C, D, and E are all encoded by the same construction. German on the other hand uses one construction for contexts B, C, and D, while individual constructions are employed for A, E and F. For E even two different constructions are used.

English and German already differ notably with respect to the mapping of contexts and constructions. The difference between the languages is also apparent when considering the case-forms employed in the constructions. English uses Accusative case for the only role in context A and B as well as for the patient role in context F. All other roles are in the Nominative case. In German, the Accusative is used for the only role in context A and in one of the constructions to express context E. In the other construction expressing E, this role is encoded by Dative case. The patient role in context F is encoded in the Accusative again, and every other role in the contexts listed is in the Nominative.

---

[1] During the final stage of production, Eitan Grossman pointed out to me that a very similar idea is presented in Frajzyngier & Shay (2003). I was not aware of this work previously and the production schedule does not permit me to review this work here in any detail.

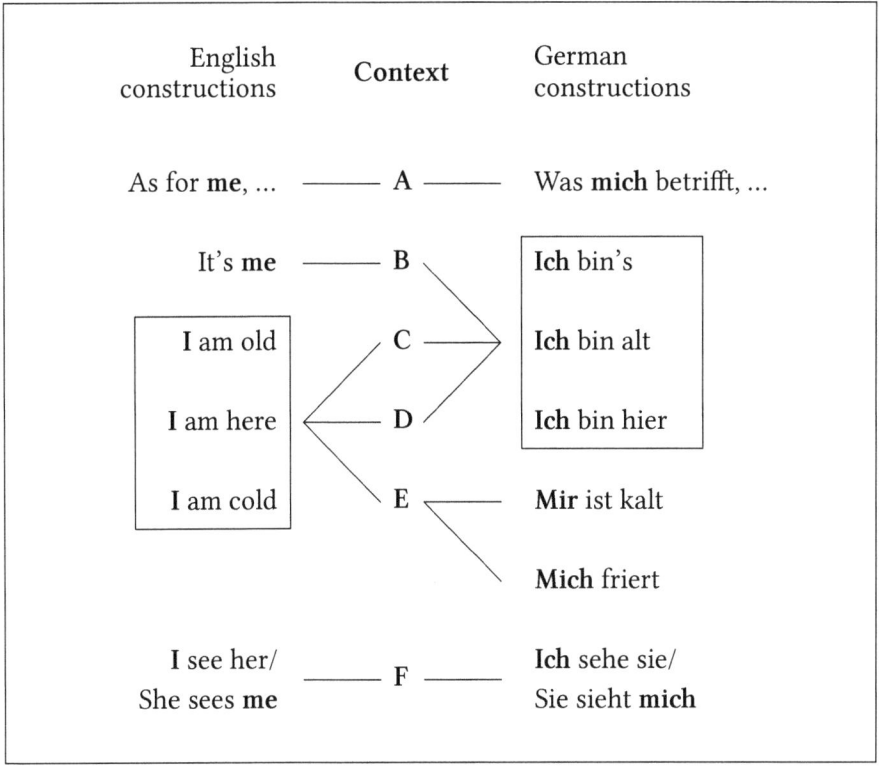

Figure 2.2: Mapping between contexts and constructions in English and German

2.4 Contexts of investigation

For this study, I have selected a number of contexts which contain roles typically encoded by the unmarked nominative/absolutive case in non-marked-S languages. Of course there is variation in the encoding of different roles between the languages of the standard nominative-accusative as well. However, in a small test sample of non-marked-S languages all the roles studied here have indeed been encoded with the nominative case in the majority of the languages. [2] For each context one or more constructions will be discussed that are used to express the context in each language. Special attention is given to the case-marking employed in these constructions. The full discussion of all data will be presented in

---

[2] The test sample has not been of any representative size, however, the languages have been chosen in order to represent different genera. The following languages have been included: German, Finnish, Turkish, Japanese, Maori and Kanuri.

2 Redefining alignment

the following five chapters. Here I will introduce the contexts which have been selected for this survey. A more detailed discussion is provided in the chapters dedicated to a certain context.

For each language data on the encoding of prototypical transitive and intransitive clauses have been collected (i.e. the traditional marking of S, A and P). In addition, the following contexts have been investigated:

- subject of nominal predication
- predicate nominal
- subject of positive existential predication
- subject of negative existential predication
- subject of locational predication
- emphatic subject[3]
- subject of dependent clauses (more precisely: relative, adverbial and complement clauses)
- subject of valency-decreasing operations
- attributive possessor
- noun in citation form
- noun used for addressing someone

The term *subject* used here is short hand for the argument that would be encoded with a nominative case in an ordinary nominative-accusative language. For each context a more specific definition is provided in the chapter it is treated in. Subjects of nominal predication and nominal predicates are discussed in Chapter 3. Chapter 4 deals with subjects of positive and negative existential and locational predications. Subjects marked as having a specific role in the discourse (referred to as EMPHATIC SUBJECTS) are dealt with in Chapter 5. Subjects of valency-decreasing (passives, antipassives) and subordinate clauses are subsumed under non-basic clause-types, discussed in Chapter 6. And finally a number of contexts

---

[3] The term *emphatic*, which is used in the same way in many grammars, refers to an argument that receives a certain amount of highlighting in the given context. Typical examples of this are focused arguments and contrastive topics.

that are below clause level (attributive possessors) or extra-syntactic altogether (citation, address) are investigated in Chapter 7.

Unfortunately, the information on the encoding of all contexts is not available for every language of the sample. I have included data as far as it is available, with the result that some languages will only be discussed for a small number of contexts. Those languages described in less detail are not very useful for the typological and statistical analysis. However, since the data are still informative for the more descriptive discussion, I have nonetheless included them. An in-depth statistical analysis will be presented in Chapter 8 for a smaller sample of languages for which I have sufficient data.

2.5 Incidental splits

2.5.1 Contexts versus other splits

The contexts listed in the previous section are set up in order to investigate different types of alignment (and also different coding systems) that may exist in a language. As noted already, not all splits encountered in marked-S languages – let alone the world's languages – are mirrored in this set of contexts I have picked for more detailed investigation. This section discusses the residual splits that will not be taken into account in the chapters to follow.

While it would in principle be possible to define the contexts listed in Section 2.4 above in such a way that all splits are covered by them, this would radically increase the number of contexts surveyed. Therefore I decided to take only those splits into account that regularly show up in the marked-S languages of my sample. It is of course a matter of debate how to assess whether something shows up regularly. I have made this decision on a somewhat impressionistic basis rather than taking any hard arithmetic criterion, because of the limited amount of information that could be gathered from grammars for some contexts. Otherwise, a number of splits would have had to be discarded even though they show up quite frequently in the small number of languages. Another factor leading to the inclusion of a context is the applicability of a domain across the sample (e.g. excluding splits between genders, which are not applicable for languages without a grammatical category of gender).

In the following three subsections, I will discuss all the types of split marking found in marked-S languages that are glossed over in the remainder of this study. These are splits based on the semantics of the case-marked noun phrase (Section 2.5.2), the semantics of the verb (Section 2.5.3), and splits conditioned by morphophonological properties of the noun or noun phrase (Section 2.5.4).

2.5.2 Splits based on the semantics of the noun phrase

The classical examples of split ergative languages discussed by Silverstein (1976) are splits between pronoun and full NPs or within the different persons of the pronominal system. This type of split is also found in languages of the marked-S type, for example in Oirata. This language marks first and second person pronouns functioning as S or A arguments of the verb by the Nominative suffix *-te* (1). Third person referents (whether expressed by demonstratives – proper 3rd person pronouns do not exist – or full NPs) receive no case-marking in either S, A or P function (2). Thus there is a split marked-S system with marked-S coding (i.e. a subtype of nominative-accusative alignment) for first and second person and neutral alignment for all elements lower on the referential hierarchy.

(1) Oirata (Timor-Alor-Pantar; Maluku, Timor; Donohue & Brown 1999: 66)

a. *in-te*   *ee*   *asi*
1PL.EXCL-NOM 2SG.POL see
'We saw you.'

b. *ee-te*   *in*   *asi-ho*
2SG.POL-NOM 1PL.EXCL see-NEG
'You didn't see us.'

c. *an-te*   *ete na'a ippa*
1SG-NOM tree OBL fall
'I fell out of the tree.'

(2) Oirata (Donohue & Brown 1999: 67)

a. ***maaro*** *mede-n kopete-he*
person eat-REL black-NEG
'The person who is eating isn't black.'

b. ***ihar*** *ani*   *asi-le*   *mara*
dog 1SG.ACC see-SSBJ go
'The dog$_i$ saw me$_j$ and ∅$_i$ left.'

Other marked-S splits on the nominal hierarchy can be found in K'abeena of the Cushitic language family (Crass 2005) and the Nilotic language Datooga (Kiessling 2007). A more detailed discussion of marked-S splits along the nominal hierarchy and their implications for the theoretical analysis of split marking in general can be found in Handschuh (2008, 2014).

Another domain of nominal semantics that has been noted to affect the alignment system is in the gender system of a language (or of nominal inflection

2.5 Incidental splits

classes in general). The Neuter nouns of several Indo-European language (like German and Russian) are known for notoriously conflating their Nominative and Accusative case-forms. Looking at these systems from a split alignment perspective one could describe them as having nominative-accusative alignment for some nouns (e.g. those with masculine gender) and neutral alignment for another class of nouns (neuter nouns). Gender-based splits in marked-S languages which look similar to the Indo-European situation can be found in some Cushitic languages (Sasse 1984). This is for example the case in Qafar (Hayward 1998) where only masculine nouns have marked forms for S+A function versus zero-coded P function. All other genders do not distinguish these two cases.

Another – more complex – instance of gender-based splits is exhibited by the Australian language Mangarayi (Merlan 1989). In each of the three genders (Masculine, Feminine and Neuter), a different alignment or coding system is employed. While Feminine nouns use a standard type of nominative-accusative system (3), Masculine nouns are of the marked-nominative type (4) and Neuter nouns are ergative-absolutive (5). [4]

(3) Mangarayi (Australian; Northern-Territory; Merlan 1989: 59, 61, 64)

    a. **ɲaḷa-gadugu** ∅-*ya-ɟ*
       NOM.F-woman 3SG-go-PSTPUNC
       'The woman went.'

    b. *buy? ɲan-wu-na*   **ɲaḷa-bugbug**   **ɲaḷa-X?**
       show 3SG>2SG-AUX-PSTPUNC NOM.F-old_woman NOM.F-X
       'Did old woman X (name deleted) show you?'

    c. **ɲan-guḍugu** *buy? wuḷa-wu-na*   *ɲani*
       ACC.F-woman show 3PL>3SG-AUX-PSTPUNC language(N)
       'They taught the woman language.'

(4) Mangarayi (Merlan 1989: 59, 61, 63)

    a. **ɲa-malam** ∅-*gala+wu-yi-ni*   *ŋa-landi-yan*
       NOM.M-man 3SG-hang-MID-PSTCONT LOC.N-tree-LOC
       'The man was hanging in the tree.'

---

[4] Of particular historical interest is the fact that the Ergative marker of Neuter nouns is the same form as the Nominative found with Masculine nouns. There seems to be a clear diachronic relation between these two alignment systems. However, the exact historical scenario (either the Ergative extended its domain to Masculine nouns, or the Nominative ceased to be used for S arguments that were Neuters) has not been established so far. Also, the tendency for Neuter nouns in some contexts to receive overt case-marking even as S arguments can be either analysed as an innovation or as a remainder of an older system.

b. ***ɲa-muyg*** *ŋan-daḻag*
   NOM.M-dog 3SG>1SG-bite.PSTPUNC
   'The dog bit me.'

c. ***malam*** *ŋa-ḓaṛa+wu-b*
   man(M) 1SG>3SG-find-PSTPUNC
   'I found the man.'

(5) Mangarayi (Merlan 1989: 59, 61)
   a. *wumbawa **ḻandi** ɟir ∅-ɟaygi-ni   wuburgba*
      one   tree(N) stand 3SG-AUX-PSTCONT halfway
      ŋa-budal-an
      LOC.N-billabong-LOC
      'One tree is standing in the middle of the billabong.'
   b. ***ɲa-gunbur*** *ŋan-gawa-ɟ   ɟib-ŋanju*
      ERG.N-dust 3SG>1SG-bury-PSTPUNC eye(N)-mine
      'Dust buried (i.e. blew into) my eye.'

2.5.3 Splits based on the semantics of the verb

Another domain in which languages might have multiple alignments in different categories of their grammar is verbal semantics. Splits in the domain of intransitive subjects which are based on the semantics of the verb are often viewed as a form of split ergativity (Dixon 1994: 70–83). This phenomenon is also known under the name of stative-active, split-S/fluid-S or semantic alignment. More generally, it has been recognized that most languages have different alignment patterns that are found with specific classes of verbs or even individual verbs – be they intransitive, monotransitive or ditransitive. In her survey of the worldwide distribution of stative-active languages, Nichols (2008), for example, uses a quantitative approach to identifying alignment systems. Only if a certain proportion of verbs in a language uses the same alignment pattern does she refer to this language as being of that alignment type.

In Nias, an Austronesian language of Indonesia, some types of verbs show specific alignment patterns. Mental state verbs take both of their arguments – the one in experiencer role as well as the one in stimulus role – in the Mutated (i.e. absolutive) form of a noun (6a). Change of state verbs exhibit another special case frame: the participant undergoing the change is in the Mutated form while the target of change is in the Unmutated (i.e. zero-coded) form of a noun (6b). Since most other marked-S languages do not exhibit any differences in alignment

2.5 Incidental splits

between different semantic classes of verbs, this domain – although a very interesting one – will not be treated further in this study. For Nias, verbs of the types exemplified in (7) are used for the further typological comparison.

(6) Nias (Sundic, Western Malayo Polynesian, Austronesian; Sumatra, Indonesia; Brown 2001: 345,591)

a. *a-ta'u* **mba'e** *n-ono matua*
STAT-fear monkey.MUT MUT-child male
'The monkey is afraid of the boy.'

b. *tobali n-idanö es*
become MUT-water ice
'The water changed into ice.'

(7) Nias (Brown 2001: 343, 208)

a. *aukhu n-idanö*
STAT.hot MUT-water
'The water is hot.'

b. *asese la-tandraigö va-nanö* **goßi** *Balanda ba Danö*
often 3PL.RLS-try NMLZ.MUT-plant tuber.MUT Dutch LOC land.MUT
Niha
person.MUT
'The Dutch have often tried to plant potatoes in Nias.'

Another factor which falls under the heading of verbal semantics involves splits based on the tense/mood/aspect properties of the clause. Though these splits are commonly observed for ergative-absolutive languages, no straightforward example of a TAM-based split has been found for marked-S languages. Urban (1985) proposes an analysis of Shokleng (Gê) that suggests marked-nominative coding for stative aspect and ergative-absolutive alignment for dynamic aspect, but his data are rather controversial. In particular, the question whether the elements discussed by him should be considered case-marking at all – or rather as some kind of resumptive pronouns – remains to be answered conclusively.

2.5.4 Splits based on morphophonological factors

A final factor that can lead to the absence of case-marking in a predictable context is morphophonology – though this is usually not viewed as a form of split case-marking. If the segment(s) that a case-marker consists of are deleted in a certain phonological environment, any host (noun or other case-marked element) meeting these requirements will be lacking this case-marking even in a context where it usually would be assigned this case by the construction it is used in. This situation holds in Cocopa where according to Crawford (1966: 104) the subject-marker -c "is not usually attached to a noun ending in more than one consonant or in /ṭ/." Also in Nias the process of nominal mutation is not visible on all nouns. Nominal mutation is straightforward with vowel initial nouns and those beginning in a voiceless obstruent. Other segments do not (or do not always) undergo this process (Brown 2001: 69). Considering that voiceless consonants become voiced through the process of nominal mutation, the most likely explanation for such a 'split' is a morphophonological one, namely that those segments cannot receive any more voicing and thus do not undergo any visible transformation between the Unmutated and Mutated form. I will ignore such 'apparent' splits in the remainder of this study.

2.6 Usage-based factors

2.6.1 Frequency

After investigating the ways in which the grammar of a language can influence the overall use of the different case-forms, I will now turn to language usage. In studies of marked-S languages, the main focus has been on grammar-based factors, and the present study is no exception. However, usage-based factors can strongly influence the distribution of the case-forms in actual language data.

For the present study, 'usage-based factors' basically is equated to 'textual frequency of the individual case-forms'. This factor is strongly influenced by the possibility of a language to omit overt arguments (and the use the language makes of this possibility) and the optionality or non-optionality of the overt case-markers. These two aspects of usage frequency will be discussed in more detail in Section 2.6.2 and Section 2.6.3 respectively. First, however, I will address the topic of textual frequencies and how it is relevant for the present study from a more general point of view.

Zipf (1935: 38) prominently noted "that the length of a word tends to bear an inverse relationship to its relative frequency." While this observation refers to a language's vocabulary in its totality, it can also be applied to the paradigmatic structure of individual words, such as the different case-forms of a noun. An observation which more specifically addresses the relation between frequency and the length of morphological forms (of the same word) was made by Fenk-Oczlon (2001) – among numerous other frequency effects she postulates:

> So we may say that relatively independent of its degree of markedness, that which is more frequent because of its natural salience and/or cultural importance: [...] is encoded in shorter morphological form (Fenk-Oczlon 2001: 435)

Translated into the domain of case-marking this means that a case-form which does not employ overt morphological marking should be more frequent than case-forms which bear overt coding. For marked-S languages this can be broken down to the formula: zero-case is more frequent than S-case. This prediction in principle goes in the same direction as the functional approach to marked-S, though it proposes a completely different direction for research. While a case-form might be used in a wider number of functions throughout the grammar (because it covers a larger set of roles and/or appears in a larger number of constructions), this does not have to be reflected in any kind of usage frequency effect. A case-form that appears in a large number of marginal constructions might still be significantly less frequent than a case-form that is employed in the most widely used construction. So the survey of the grammar of a language and the contexts where case-forms are used does not necessarily give any insights into usage frequencies.

In order to get informative results on the usage frequencies of individual case-forms one would need extensive corpora with data from a wide variety of different genres (narratives, spoken discourse etc.). Statistically meaningful comparison across languages can only be achieved when the types of data used in the analysis are comparable across languages. Otherwise the results cannot be interpreted. If, for example, one compares languages A and B and the data for language A comprise naturalistic examples from spoken discourse but language B is only represented through elicited narratives, one runs into severe problems. In this constellation any differences arising between languages A and B could either be due to a differences between the languages studied or due to the different types of data. For a discussion on how representativeness in corpora can be achieved see Biber (1990, 1993) and McEnery et al. (2006: 13–21).

Unfortunately the situation is such that for most of the languages from my sample data of the nature described above are not accessible or do not exist at all. Setting up corpora for twenty or so languages – for most of which quite an amount of data would have to be gathered in the first place – is certainly beyond the scope of this work. Therefore, as regrettable as it is, a frequency-based study of marked-S systems is precluded from this study.

As just pointed out, it is absolutely necessary to have extensive, reliable and balanced data from actual language use in order to make any strong claims about the distribution of certain forms in a language. However, this does not mean that the usage data of a language are completely detached from its grammar. The grammar of a language can specify a number of parameters which will strongly influence language usage. The parameters in question here are the ones which determine what can and cannot be left out (and under which circumstances) in a language. With regard to marked-S languages, and more specifically with regard to the range of usage of the zero- and S-case-forms, this boils down to two factors, which are discussed in the following sections. First, can core arguments be omitted? And second, is the use of the overt markers of core arguments optional in the language? If a language allows for any of these possibilities, the question arises, how frequently speakers make use of these possibilities, and what are the factors that influence the choice between omission and occurrence of the marker.

2.6.2 Omission of arguments

The tendency to leave out arguments that are required by a verb's semantic profile has long been noted for a number of languages of otherwise completely different typological profiles. Gilligan (1987: 131–132) finds that in his genealogically balanced sample of 100 languages around 80 % allow the omission of topical subjects. In addition, at least one third of the languages allow for non-topical subjects to be omitted as well. This phenomenon is often referred to as 'pro-drop', a term that is prevalently used for the phenomenon of subject omission – especially by linguists of a more formal persuasion – but has been extended to the domain of object omission by at least some scholars (e.g. Rizzi 1986).

Many languages allow for the omission of overt NPs if they can be understood from the context, and indeed speakers of such languages make wide use of this. Since subjects are typically highly topical, and subject NPs are especially prone to lacking overt realization. This suggests that the actual textual frequency of overt subjects (and thus S-case-marked NPs) will be lower than the frequency of overt objects. For the reasons listed above, a corpus analysis supporting the fact that subject NPs are omitted significantly more often than object NPs in marked-S languages will have to wait until representative corpora for the languages studied will be available. At the current stage, I can only give an impressionistic evaluation of the preferences in dropping overt arguments in speech for the languages of my sample.

2.6 Usage-based factors

Most of the languages under investigation here allow for the possibility of omitting arguments in actual speech. This is especially obvious where collected texts are available. In cases in which the author of a grammar used mainly naturalistic data for illustration instead of elicited examples, this has even led to the situation that hardly any examples could be found of a given construction to illustrate the nominal case-marker for the purpose of this study. Transitive subjects expressed by overt nominals were the hardest to find throughout all languages surveyed. This again hints at a lower frequency of S-case-marked forms, at least in the languages of the marked-nominative type. For Nias, overt transitive subjects were particularly hard to find. This should lead to a lower figure for the zero-coded Unmutated (Ergative) in textual counts, resulting in a situation in which the overtly coded Mutated form of the noun (the absolutive) could actually be the most frequent case-form in a corpus.

2.6.3 Optional case-marking

A final factor influencing the frequency of each case-form is the optionality of case-marking. In some situations, an overt marker is employed only occasionally to mark the subject relation, while in other instances the marker is absent from an NP in the very same role. This is the case for quite a number of marked-S languages. These will briefly be discussed in this section. The reasons usually listed for this behavior are often related to need to distinguish between different participants and their relevant roles in a given situation. However, these explanations are rather tentative, for the most part.

In the description of the Australian language Malakmalak, it is noted that there is an optional Nominative suffix. Birk (1976: 112) describes the distribution of the marker with the following words "[it] can be suffixed to transitive or intransitive subject, but not to transitive object." The case-suffix is only employed when it cannot be distinguished otherwise, if an argument is the subject or object of the verb (i.e. if they are of the same person and gender, otherwise verbal indexing gives clues for identification). The need for disambiguating between participants does not appear to arise very frequently in Malakmalak since the examples in the grammar hardly provide any instances of the Nominative case-form. Two of the few examples is given in (8).

(8) Malakmalak (Australian; Northern Territory; Birk 1976: 113)
    a. *alalk **yikpi-waŋ**   yin^{y}a tař yimin^{y}nö*
       child little.SG.M-NOM man bite 3SG.M.SBJ.PUNC.3SG.M.OBJ
       'The little boy bites/bit the man.'

b. *yinʸa alalk **yikpi-waŋ** tař yiminʸnö*
   man child little.SG.M-NOM bite 3SG.M.SBJ.PUNC.3SG.M.OBJ
   'The little boy bites/bit the man.'

This phenomenon is often discussed under the title 'optional ergativity', even though a language might permit this optional ergative marker to occur on intransitive subjects as well. The phenomenon appears to be particularly widespread in Australia and the non-Austronesian languages of Oceania (commonly referred to as Papuan). The absence or presence of the overt marker is often linked to the discourse structure of a given utterance (for a discussion of optional ergativity see McGregor & Verstraete (2010) and the other papers in the special issue of *Lingua* dedicated to this very topic). A more detailed discussion of the interaction of these kinds of information will be provided in Chapter 5.

A similar situation seems to hold in some Yuman languages of North-West America, though the Nominative marker seems to be used more often in these languages. Munro (1976: 19) notes that in Mojave "[o]ccasionally, when the context is clear, the subject case-marker may be omitted, particularly in fast speech, and with intransitive verbs." In the closely-related language Jamul Tiipay, the Nominative marker *-ch* is optional with most noun phrases. According to Miller (2001: 160), it "appears obligatorily on lexical demonstratives and on the interrogative/indefinite word *me'a* 'where?, somewhere'" and is almost exceptionless "on noun phrases marked with the demonstrative clitic *-pu*", but in other context the case-marker is optional. Also, some African languages allow for the omission of S-case-marking, as for example has been noted for the Cushitic language Boraana Oromo (Stroomer 1995: 93).

The discussions of the mechanisms triggering the presence of the case-marker are very sparse, if present at all, especially in the languages of Australia and Oceania. This makes it very difficult to include their data into this present study. Usually, the discussion is restricted to the presentation of a few odd examples. In the rest of the grammatical description, the phenomenon is not treated in any more detail, so that for a given construction it is usually not clear whether it would allow for the presence of the respective case-marker on either of its arguments. Any judgments, whether a given role in encoded by the zero-case only, or if marking with the S-case is also possible, would have to be based on negative evidence. Eyeballing texts from the languages in which the S-case-marker is optional hints that they only rarely make use of the overt-S marker, so that for textual frequency one has to expect a clear dominance of the zero-case.

2.7 Summary

In this chapter, the methodological basis of this study of marked-S systems was presented. This methodology draws heavily upon the notion of split alignment systems, which has been a central aspect in the research on morphosyntactic alignment in past decades. In my approach, the idea of different alignments existing in different domains of a grammar is taken one step further. The alignment systems of marked-S languages are investigated at a micro-level by surveying a set of very specific contexts. By looking at all these contexts, the claim that the zero-case in marked-S languages has the widest distribution is to be tested.

In the final section, I have discussed another factor influencing the distribution of case-forms in a language, namely textual frequency. I have argued that a corpus analysis would provide the ultimate measure for which case-form has the widest distribution in a given language. For marked-S languages dealt with here, no such corpora exist at present.[5] However, coming up with actual figures on the usage of the two case-forms for at least a subset of the languages from my sample is a very desirable enterprise for future studies.

---

[5] One exception to this is Savosavo, on which a large amount of corpus work has been done in recent years, e.g. Haig et al. (2011). However, this work was only published after the completion of the original research for this book.

Part II

The contexts studied

3 Nominal predication

3.1 Introduction

In nominal predications, a predication over a noun (henceforward called the SUBJECT OF THE NOMINAL PREDICATION) is expressed by means of another nominal element (henceforward called the PREDICATE NOMINAL) rather than by a verb. Since this construction consists of two nominals, which can both potentially be case-marked, both functions – the subject of the nominal predication and the predicate nominal – are of interest for this study.

The Wappo example in (1) demonstrates the general pattern of nominal predications. The subject of the nominal predication is the noun phrase *ce k'ew* 'that man', while the second noun phrase *i ek'a* 'my son' is the predicate nominal. Note that, unlike in other transitive or intransitive clauses in Wappo, the subject does not receive Nominative case-marking, and neither does the predicate nominal receive any overt marking.

(1) Wappo (Wappo-Yukian; California; Thompson et al. 2006: 12)
    ce   k'ew ce?e? i   ek'a
    DEM man COP   1SG son
    'That man is my son.'

Many languages employ additional grammatical means in nominal predications such as copulas. This is, for instance, the case in the Wappo example above. However, no matter whether a language employs a copula in this context or not, the predicate nominal functions as the predicator and not the copula. Hengeveld (1992: 28–29) demonstrates that for all non-verbal predications (of which nominal predications are a subgroup), selectional restrictions on the arguments of a predicate are due to the meaning of the predicate and independent of any copula element.

Stassen (1997: 62–100) makes a number of observations about the distribution of zero and overt copulas in the languages of the world, or in his terms 'zero strategies' and 'full strategies'. The usage of zero-copulas in nominal predications has by far the widest distribution among the types of non-verbal intransitive

3 Nominal predication

predication and in fact is a prerequisite for the zero strategy to be used with other non-verbal predication types. Furthermore, Stassen (1997: 65) notes that the zero strategy is most commonly found with third persons – a subset of which are full noun phrases, on which this study centers. For some languages of my sample the question whether there is a copula in nominal predications or not is crucial since nominal case-marking is different in the two constructions. I will address this issue in greater detail in Section 3.4, in which the research questions on nominal predications for this study are outlined. However, the absence or presence of a copula in a given language or context is not the only noteworthy property. Copulas have quite different properties cross-linguistically, ranging from more verb-like (taking regular verbal inflections etc.) to less verb-like (mere particles, which do not behave like other verbs of the relevant languages). However, these differences will not be taken into consideration in this study (for a detailed study of the category copula across languages, see Pustet 2003).

In the discussion of nominal predications a distinction is often made between 'identity' and 'class-membership' predications (Stassen 1997: 100). Since in almost all languages of my sample, the formal encoding does not differ in the two types of nominal predication, both types will be discussed in parallel in this chapter. The distinction between these two types of nominal predication will be explicitly discussed in Section 3.3. In that section, the data from Tennet (Nilotic) – the only example I am aware of of a marked-S language with different constructions for encoding identity and class-membership – will be presented in greater detail.

As I noted before, both the subject and the predicate nominal are of interest for this study due to their nominal nature and the resulting potential for case-marking. For the predicate nominal, however, there might be some uncertainty with regard to the part of speech it functions as in this construction. It is possible for the predicate nominal to have verb-like encoding – Stassen (1997) calls such cases 'verbal takeover' of class-membership predicates. If the predicate nominal shows morphological marking used exclusively on verbs in that language otherwise, I will consider it to function as a verb rather than a noun in this construction. Thus the absence of case-marking on a lexical noun clearly showing exclusively verbal marking in nominal predications will not be considered an instance of zero-coding but as 'not applicable'. In contrast, zero-coded predicate nominals in a language that does not require any inflection on the verb could just as well be treated as verbs as as nouns. In cases in which there is no evidence for or against a nominal status of predicate 'nominals' I will consider predicate nominals as belonging to the nominal rather than the verbal category.

In the following section (3.2), I will review the (rather sparse) literature on case-marking in nominal predications. Afterwards, the distinction between the two semantic types of nominal predication – class-membership and identity predication – is discussed (Section 3.3). In Section 3.4, I will identify four patterns of case-marking found with nominal predication, as well as outline further research questions of the present study. The subsequent sections demonstrate the presence/absence of these four patterns in the marked-S languages of North America (Section 3.5), the Afro-Asiatic (Section 3.6), and Nilo-Saharan (Section 3.7) phyla and the languages of the Pacific region (Section 3.8). Finally, a summary of the data discussed in Sections 3.5–3.8 will be given in Section 3.9.

3.2 Case-marking in nominal predication

Case-marking is not a prominent topic in the literature on nominal predication. Payne (1997: 111), for example, in his chapter on predicate nominals, discusses various strategies of encoding with respect to the presence/absence or type of the copula, but does not mention case-marking at all. The literature that discusses case-marking in nominal predications is largely concerned with the case of the predicate nominal. On the subject of nominal predications, most authors seem to assume that the same mechanisms apply as to subjects elsewhere. One exception to this general tendency is Dixon (2010b: 162, 165–168), who treats subjects of nominal predication – his 'copula subjects' (CS) and 'verbless clause subjects' (VCS) – as a distinct category (more accurately two distinct categories) from transitive and intransitive subjects. He notes that in individual languages CS and VCS can have different syntactic properties than the other types of subjects, among these properties being case-marking. The data in (2) exemplify a language which uses different case-marking for subjects in nominal predication than in basic (in)transitive clauses.

(2) Mesa Grande Diegueño (Yuman; California; Gorbet 1976: 15)
ixpa-pu a:sa:-c yis
eagle-DEM bird-NOM is_indeed
'The eagle is a bird'

Comrie (1997) proposes two possible accounts for case-assignment to nominal predicates (under which he also subsumes predicative adjectives): case-assignment through government by the verb and case-assignment through agreement with the subject of the nominal predication. He argues that both possibilities are attested in the languages of the world. Hence, the mechanism of case-assignment

3 Nominal predication

to the predicate nominal – either through government or agreement – is a typological variable that languages vary with respect to. For languages in which the subject and predicate nominal do not match in case-marking only the government hypothesis is plausible. If, however, both nominals have the same case, both analyses could potentially account for the observed behavior. To test which analysis is correct, one needs detailed data on nominal predications in that language. Also, the language must allow subjects to have a non-uniform case-marking in the first place, otherwise there would not be any observable difference between the two hypotheses. Most marked-S languages of my sample use different case-forms for the subject and predicate nominal, hence the agreement hypothesis would not work for them. Of the remaining languages, there are not enough data on nominal predications to decide which account works best to explain the case-assignment to predicate nominals.

A more formal approach dealing with case-assignment to predicate nominals is provided by Yip et al. (1987: 243–246). In their approach, case is represented on a tier separate from phrase structure; case-assignment to individual NPs happens through association of the two tiers (unless case is lexically assigned through the verb). Yip et al. give two possible accounts for languages in which the predicate case agrees with the subject-case (their example language being Icelandic). In one account, the case assigned to the subject spreads to the nominal predicate; Yip et al. compare this process to the phonological principle of 'Geminate Integrity', and state that this is implemented in the lexicon through a joint linking of the two nominals. In the second account, the nominal predicate receives its case from copying the case of the subject, with which it is co-indexed. In this approach the predicate nominal is assigned a special case – called 'predicative' by Yip et al. (1987) – through the lexical entry of the verb 'to be' (i.e. the copula). This predicative case has the property of copying the case of the co-indexed argument. Since Yip et al. (1987) only model the data from Icelandic, in which the subject and predicate of nominal predications agree in case, no implementation is proposed for languages that use different cases for the two roles. The second approach appears to be more promising for implementing such languages, since one would simply have to change the lexical case-assignment to the nominal predicate from 'predicative' to the respective case found on predicate nominals in a language.

Finally, Fillmore (1968: 84) – in his seminal paper on the semantic roles in language (referred to as 'case roles' by him) – makes some reference to nominal predications. He states that "they represent a distinct type from those involving any of the case relations discussed above, though more than one case relation may be provided in these sentences." He ponders introducing the terms 'essive' and 'translative' for the type of case relations introduced in sentences of this type. Still, he views the requirement of number agreement between subject and predicate nominal as an issue that lacks implementation in an approach that simply introduces a new case-label for the nominal predicate.

3.3 Identity predication

So far, I have discussed nominal predication defined as a clause containing two nominal elements, one serving as the subject and the other as the predicate of the construction. The distinction between identity predication and class-membership predication has been glossed over.[1] The two types of nominal predication differ with respect to the semantic type of their predicate nominals. If the predicate nominal uniquely identifies an individual, then the predication is of the identity type. This type of nominal predication is illustrated in (3). Otherwise the predication is one of class-membership. In that case, the predicate nominal identifies a certain class of which the subject is a member as in (4).

(3)   a.   *That man is her husband.*
       b.   *The morning star is the evening star.*

(4)   a.   *She is a teacher.*
       b.   *Whales are mammals.*

From a semantic perspective, this distinction is crucial, as Doron (1988) argues. For English (and to some extent also for French), she suggests that this semantic distinction also has syntactic relevance, putting forward a number of tests to distinguish between the two types of predicate nominal constructions. Adger & Ramchand (2003) claim that there is no structural distinction between the two types of clauses. They support their claim with data from Scottish Gaelic and argue that the two types of clauses are identical in their syntactic representation.

Stassen (1997) distinguishes between identity and class-membership, yet he claims that the strategy of encoding identity is very frequently extended to class-membership. His 'principle of identity pressure' states that whenever predicate nominals are encoded by a strategy different from all other types of intransitive

---

[1] The terminology of 'class-membership' vs. 'identity' is taken from Stassen (1997). Other terms used for the same distinction are 'predicational' vs. 'equative copula clauses' (Adger & Ramchand 2003) or 'predicational' and 'referring predicate nominals' (Doron 1988).

3 Nominal predication

predication, the strategy will be taken over from the encoding of identity predication (Stassen 1997: 111). The overlap of the encoding strategies of identity and class-membership predication is also revealed in my sample of marked-S languages. Only in one language of my sample, Tennet, the two types of predication are encoded by different constructions.

In Tennet, the subject is in the Accusative form rather than the Nominative for sentences interpreted as identity predications. This is irrespective of whether the clause contains an overt copula (5a) or not (5b).[2] In class-membership predications the subject is in the Nominative, as is illustrated in (5c).

(5) Tennet (Surmic, Nilo-Saharan; Sudan; Randal 1998: 234, 233)

  a. ***anẹ̣t*** *cí k-ẹẹ́nį́ dẹmẹ́z-zọ́h-t*
     1SG.ACC AM 1-be   teach-AGNM-SG
     'I'm the teacher.'

  b. ***anẹt*** *mọ́t-tọ́h-t*
     1SG.ACC be.angry-AGNM-SG
     'I am the brave man.'

  c. *k-ẹẹ́nį́* ***anná*** *dẹmẹ́z-zọ́h-t*
     1-be   1SG.NOM teach-AGNM-SG
     'I am a teacher.'

3.4 Research questions

The following examples (6–9) demonstrate the variability of case-marking with subjects and predicates of nominal predication in marked-S languages. Maidu (6) marks both nominals with the overt Nominative case-suffix -*m*. In Savosavo (7) only the subject of a nominal predication is marked with the Nominative case (=*na*) while the predicate nominal is zero-coded. Conversely, Mesa Grande Diegueño marks the predicate nominal with the Nominative case-suffix -*c* while the subject remains zero-coded. Example (2) from above is repeated as (8). Finally, in Wappo (9) both the subject and predicate nominal are zero-coded, as was already seen in (1) that is repeated here.

---

[2] In some marked-S languages of my sample, case-marking depends on whether or not a clause has an overt copula (see Section 3.4).

(6) Maidu (Maiduan, Penutian; California; Shipley 1964: 30)
*mym kylókbe-**m***   *ma-káde mín-kotò-**m***
this old_woman-NOM be-Q   2-grandmother-NOM
'Is that old woman your grandmother?'

(7) Savosavo (Solomons East Papuan; Solomon Islands; Wegener 2008: 128)
zu lo   *gola kiba sisi=**na***   *te*   *lo*   *ulunga*
and DET.SG.M green   orn_flower=NOM EMPH DET.SG.M pillow
lo-va   *taghata*
3SG.M-GEN.M on_top
'and the green flower (is) on top of the pillow' (lit.: 'and the green flower (is) the pillow its top')

(8) Mesa Grande Diegueño (Yuman, Hokan; California; Gorbet 1976: 15)
ixpa-pu   *a:sa:-**c***   *yis*
eagle-DEM bird-NOM is_indeed
'The eagle is a bird'

(9) Wappo (Wappo-Yukian; California; Thompson et al. 2006: 12)
ce   *k'ew ce?e? i*   *ek'a*
DEM man COP 1.SG son
'That man is my son.'

These are all four logical possibilities of case-marking that can be derived from a set of two case-forms – S-case and zero-case – and two roles – subject and nominal predicate.³ However, these four patterns are quite unevenly distributed within the languages of my sample, as will become apparent in Sections 3.5–3.8, in which the nominal predications in the marked-S languages of my sample will be presented in greater depth.

After introducing the four patterns of case-marking found in nominal predications, I will now turn to the other element often present in the constructions encoding this context: the copula. With respect to the occurrence of copula elements in nominal predications, the languages of my sample also exhibit a number of distinct patterns. Some languages do not have a copula element, while others must have a copula present in this context, yet again other languages exhibit

---

³ If one includes the possibility of additional case-forms, the number of possible patterns is multiplied. The vast majority of languages of my sample does, however, restrict the case-forms used in this context to the S- and zero-case. Arbore, the only exception, will be discussed in Section 3.6.

variation between presence and absence of the copula in nominal predications. For the last type of language – those languages in which a copula can be either present or absent – finer distinction can be made. First, some languages seem to have free variation between the two constructions while other languages behave in a more systematic fashion. The systematic languages employ copula elements in certain contexts, usually in clauses that are negated or non-present tense. The copula in these contexts serves as a means to mark tense or negation, a pattern well known from many languages of the world, not just marked-S languages (Payne 1997: 119). Another distinction addresses the case-marking of the nominals in the relevant construction(s). In some of the languages that exhibit variation between presence and absence of the copula (either free or systematic), this distinction correlates with a difference in case-marking. While the overt S-case is found in the constructions with having an overt copula, this case-marking is absent in the construction lacking the copula. For the languages in which some of the described variation is found, this will be addressed in more detail in the following sections discussing the data. The data are subdivided by macro-area and genealogical affiliation. The latter classification is only applied to the African languages since for the other areas the number of languages is rather small and most genealogical units have only one member in the sample. Furthermore, the data are organized by the four patterns of case-marking for nominal predications introduced above, repeated here for convenience:

- overt marking of both nominals
- overt marking of only the predicate nominal
- overt marking of only the subject of nominal predication
- no overt marking on either nominals

3.5 North America

The North American languages of my sample are all located near the Pacific Coast in an area reaching from Northern California to Mexico and stretching inland as far as Arizona. Among these languages, the remarkable pattern exemplified in (8) above is found, in which the nominal predicate is marked with Nominative case and the subject is zero-coded. This pattern appears exclusively in the Yuman genus. It is predominant in the Yuman languages, but does not appear to be attested in any other language worldwide. However, as we will see below, some Yuman languages employ some of the other patterns under certain conditions.

As in Diegueño (cf. 8), in Mojave the Nominative suffix -č is attached to the predicate nominal and – unlike in other clauses – not to the subject, which in turn remains zero-coded (cf. 10).

(10) Mojave (Yuman; California; Munro 1976: 49)
 ʔinʸep ʔ-ičuy-nʸ kʷaθəʔide:-č ido-pč
 1SG.POSS 1-husband-DEM doctor-NOM be-TNS
 'My husband is a doctor.'

Comparable structures can be found in most other Yuman languages. This is illustrated by the examples from Maricopa (11), Yavapai (12) and Walapai (13)[4] below.

(11) Maricopa (Yuman; Arizona; Gordon 1986: 38)
 a. *mmdii-ny-a chyer-sh duu-m*
 owl-DEM-AUGV bird-NOM be-RLS
 'Owls are birds/ The owl is a bird.'
 b. *'iipaa-ny-a kwsede-sh (duu-m)*
 man-DEM-AUGV doctor-NOM be-RLS
 'The man is a doctor.'

(12) Yavapai (Yuman; Arizona; Kendall 1976: 66)
 can ʔ-ñ-pa: ʔichwa:-v-c yu-m
 John 1-POSS-enemy-DEM-NOM be-FAFF
 'John is my enemy.'

(13) Walapai (Yuman; Arizona; Redden 1966: 160; Watahomigie et al. 2001: 480)
 a. *ɲá apà-v-č yú*
 1SG.ACC human-REFL-NOM be
 'I am a human being.'
 b. *nya boś-v-č yu*
 1SG.ACC cat-REFL-NOM be
 'I am a cat.'

In the closely-related language Havasupai, this pattern is also found for encoding nominal predications. As is demonstrated in (14a), in this construction the

---

[4] Since the two Walapai examples come from different sources, the orthographies and levels of phonetic detail represented differ between the examples.

3 Nominal predication

noun phrase referring to the predicate nominal is marked with the Nominative suffix -c, while the subject remains zero-coded. However, this is not the only possibility for encoding nominal predications in that language. In (14b), another possible construction is illustrated. If a sentence expressing nominal predication does not contain an overt copula, a zero-coded predicate nominal – as well as a zero-coded subject – is found according to Kozlowski (1972). However, there is no general correlation in the Yuman language family of zero-coding of predicate nominals with copula-less sentences. Other Yuman languages do mark the predicate nominal with overt Nominative case, even in sentences that lack a copula.

(14) Havasupai (Yuman; Arizona; Kozlowski 1972: 35, 33)

    a. *jan ña-ñuwa ha-c yu*
       John 1-friend DEM-NOM be
       'John is my friend.'

    b. *jan ña-ñuwa-ha*
       John 1-friend-DEM
       'John is my friend.'

While in Havasupai the example in (14b) exemplifies an alternative construction, in Jamul Tiipay it is the only possibility for expressing nominal predications. As can be seen in (15a), both the subject of nominal predications and the predicate nominal are zero-coded. However, there is another construction in the language consisting of two nominals in which the subject is in the Nominative case (15b). Miller (2001: 184–185) explicitly distinguishes this construction from nominal predication. She calls it the 'copula construction', since, unlike the regular nominal predication in Jamul Tiipay, it contains the verb 'to be'. In this copula construction, the subject is in the Nominative case and the other noun is zero-coded. At least in some cases, there seems to be a difference in meaning between the copula construction, as in (15b), and the regular nominal predication, as in (15a). While the (a) example clearly makes a statement about class-membership, the (b) example does not.

(15) Jamul Tiipay (Yuman; California; Miller 2001: 181, 185)

    a. *nyech'ak-pu metiipay*
       woman-DEM indian
       'That woman is an Indian.'

    b. *nyech'ak-pe-**ch** metiipay we-yu*
       woman-DEM-NOM indian 3-be
       'That woman is playing Indian/pretending to be an Indian.'

3.5 North America

Another North American language with zero-coded subject and predicate in nominal predications is Wappo, as was already noted in the previous section. This pattern has already been illustrated in example (9) above with two full noun phrases. (16) exemplifies an instance of class-membership predication with a pronominal subject.

(16) Wappo (Thompson et al. 2006: 43)
 i ceʔeʔ yomtoʔ
 1SG.ACC COP doctor
 'I am a doctor.'

Only one of the North American marked-S languages marks both the subject of nominal predication and the predicate nominal with the overt Nominative case-marker. This language is Maidu. Although this pattern is the one that is most familiar from nominative-accusative languages of the standard type, for marked-S languages it seems to be an exceptional pattern. As demonstrated in (17), both subject and predicate nominal are marked with the Nominative suffix *-m* in Maidu nominal predications. In general, Maidu employs the overtly coded Nominative more than one would expect from a standard nominative-accusative language, that is, in a wide variety of contexts. It thus behaves counter to the expectation of König (2008) that in a marked-nominative language the zero-coded accusative will have a wider range of functions than the overtly coded nominative.

(17) Maidu (Maiduan; California; Shipley 1964: 30)
 my-m kyle-m ka-k'an nik-po-m
 DEM-NOM woman-NOM be-3 1SG.POSS-daughter-NOM
 'That woman is my daughter.'

In the Yuman languages, a reinterpretation of the nominal predication construction appears to be ongoing. In some instances, the subject of a nominal predication receives Nominative case-marking as well, as Gordon (1986: 39–40) demonstrates for Maricopa. According to Munro (1977: 469–471), this tendency can be observed in other Yuman languages as well.

(18) Maricopa (Yuman; Arizona; Gordon 1986: 40)
 '-ny-kwr'ak-sh pakyer-sh duu-m
 1-POSS-old_man-NOM cowboy-NOM be-RLS
 'My husband is a cowboy.'

3 Nominal predication

The data provided in this section are summarized in Table 3.1. The table provides an overview of the case-marking in nominal predications in the marked-S languages of North America. Maidu is exceptional – not only for this region – in marking both nominals with overt Nominative case. Wappo, on the other hand, has both nominals zero-coded, a pattern that is also found as one possible pattern in the Yuman languages Havasupai and Tiipay, where it is the most common pattern. The other Yuman languages have the remarkable pattern of using nominative case on the predicate nominal and zero-coding the subject in this context. This pattern is also found for Havasupai in clauses with an overt copula).

language	subject	predicate nominal
Diegueño (Mesa Grande)	ACC	NOM
Havasupai	ACC	NOM/ACC
Jamul Tiipay	ACC/NOM	ACC
Maricopa	ACC	NOM
Mojave	ACC	NOM
Walapai	ACC	NOM
Yavapai	ACC	NOM
Maidu	NOM	NOM
Wappo	ACC	ACC

Table 3.1: Marking of nominal predication in the marked-S languages of North America

3.6 Afro-Asiatic

The predominant pattern in the Afro-Asiatic marked-S languages is to have overt nominative case-marking on the subject of the nominal predication and zero-coding on the predicate nominal. This pattern can be found in numerous languages of the Eastern Cushitic and Omotic genera. Yet in some cases the predicate nominal does receive overt case-marking, which does not necessarily have to be the nominative case.

In Boraana Oromo, the Nominative suffix *-ii* marks the subject of the nominal predication in (19), while the predicate nominal – *obboleesa kiya* – remains zero-coded. In the closely-related Harar variety of Oromo, a parallel structure is used, as shown in (20).

(19) Oromo (Boraana) (Eastern Cushitic; Kenya; Stroomer 1995: 34)
*mamic-**ii** kuninii obboleesa kiya*
man-NOM DEM.NOM brother 1SG.POSS
'This man is my brother.'

(20) Oromo (Harar) (Eastern Cushitic; Ethiopia; Owens 1985: 100)
 a. *mak'áa-**n** axaaxúu xiyyá álii*
    name-NOM grandfather my Ali
    'My grandfather's name is Ali.'
 b. ***innii** angafa xiyyáa-mihi*
    he.NOM elder_brother my-NEG
    'He is not my elder brother.'

This typical Afro-Asiatic pattern of marking nominal predication with the subject in Nominative case and the predicate nominal in the accusative is also found in Gamo (21), K'abeena (22), and Zayse (23)[5]

(21) Gamo (Omotic; Ethiopia; Hompó 1990: 370)
***Č'aboi** lo?o asi d-∅-∅-enna*
Chabo.NOM good man.ACC2 be-PM-TNS-NEG
'Chabo is not a good man.'

(22) K'abeena (Eastern Cushitic; Ethiopia; Crass 2005: 264)
*ku **manc^u** moggaancoh^a*
DIST.M man.NOM thief.ACC.COP.M
'This man is a thief.'

(23) Zayse (Omotic; Ethiopia; Hayward 1990: 280)
*ʔe-**ʔaśi** wóotaś'-ú-tte*
DET.M-man.NOM farmer-EPEN-COP
'The man is a farmer.'

Wolaytta has a construction parallel to the Afro-Asiatic languages discussed so far (24a). However, it is also possible to mark the predicate nominal with

---

[5] It might appear a bit puzzling at first glance that the 'zero-coded' predicate nominal has extra material following the noun stem. Hayward (1990: 280–281) gives the following description of the copular element popping up in this construction: "[t]he copula attaches to a phrase (NP or PP) which is focused". He also demonstrates the use of the copula in cleft-like constructions with focused subjects, objects, temporal nouns, and prepositional phrases.

3 Nominal predication

Nominative case, as there is no difference in meaning between examples (24b) and (24c). According to Lamberti & Sottile (1997), this alternation is especially common with feminine nouns.

(24) Wolaytta (Omotic; Ethiopia; Lamberti & Sottile 1997: 225)
   a. *he bitann-ey laagge*
      that man-NOM friend.ACC
      'That man is a friend.'
   b. *ha-nna gelawi-ya*
      this-F girl-NOM
      'This is a girl.'
   c. *ha-nna gelawi-y^u*
      this-F girl-ACC
      'This is a girl.'

Finally, Arbore has a dedicated case-form for encoding predicate nominals, the so-called 'Predicative' case (25). The subject of nominal predications, as in the other Afro-Asiatic languages, is in the Nominative case.

(25) Arbore (Eastern Cushitic; Ethiopia; Hayward 1984: 136)
   mó   bal ʔiyya-ħ-aw-a
   man.NOM was father-M-1SG.POSS-PRED
   'The man was my father.'

All data from the Afro-Asiatic marked-nominative languages are summarized in Table 3.2 on the facing page. Uniformly the subject of nominal predications is marked with the Nominative case in the Afro-Asiatic marked-S languages. The predicate nominal exhibits some minor variation with respect to the overt encoding. While most languages use the zero-coded Accusative form to encode this function, Wolaytta exhibits an alternative variant of encoding it with the Nominative case (at least for some nouns) and Arbore has a special dedicated case-form for this role.

3.7 Nilo-Saharan

Like Afro-Asiatic, the Nilo-Saharan languages prefer nominative case-marking on the subject and zero-coding of the predicate nominal. Similar to the situation described above for Yuman Havasupai (14), there is also an interaction be-

language	subject	predicate nominal
Arbore	NOM	PRED
Gamo	NOM	ACC
K'abeena	NOM	ACC
Oromo (Boraana)	NOM	ACC
Oromo (Harar)	NOM	ACC
Wolaytta	NOM	ACC/NOM
Zayse	NOM	ACC

Table 3.2: Marking of nominal predication in the Afro-Asiatic marked-S languages

tween presence/absence of a copula in the nominal predication and the presence/absence of overt case-marking in one Nilo-Saharan language, namely Turkana.

The most widespread pattern of marking nominal predications in Nilo-Saharan is to mark the subject of the construction with nominative case, while the predicate nominal remains in the zero-coded accusative form. This pattern is found in the Surmic languages Murle (26) and Tennet (27). A parallel structure is also found in the Nilotic languages, such as Maa (28)[6] or Nandi (29), and to some extent in Turkana (30).

(26) Murle (Surmic; Sudan; Arensen 1982: 110)
 boŋboŋec-i kibaali
 pelican-NOM bird.PL
 'The pelican is a bird'

(27) Tennet (Surmic; Sudan; Randal 1998: 233)
 *k-ęę́ní **anná** dęméz-zóh-t*
 1-be 1SG.NOM teach-AGNM-SG
 'I am a teacher.'

(28) Maa (Nilotic; Kenya; Tucker & Tompo ole Mpaayei 1955: 175)
 á-rá Sirónkà
 1SG-be Sironka.ACC
 'I am Sironka.'

---

[6] Maa case is marked through a variation in the tonal pattern of the noun. The tone pattern of the Accusative case is assigned lexically, while the tonal shape of the Nominative is derived from the lexical tone in a regular pattern.

3 Nominal predication

(29) Nandi (Nilotic; Kenya; Creider & Creider 1989: 121)
ná:nti-i:n-tèt **kípe:t**
Nandi-SG-THEM Kibet.NOM
'Kibet is a Nandi.'

(30) Turkana (Nilotic; Kenya; Dimmendaal 1982: 75, 76)
a. mèèrɛ` a-yɔ̀ŋ ɛ-kapılanı̬
   not   NC-1SG.NOM NC-witch.ACC
   'I am not a witch.'
b. è-à-raı` ŋesı̀ ɛ-kapıla-nı̬
   3-PST-be he.NOM NC-witch.ACC
   'He was a witch.'

Apart from the predominant pattern just described, there is also another pattern in Nilo-Saharan. In this minor pattern, both the subject of nominal predications and the predicate nominal are in the zero-coded accusative form. This pattern occurs in Turkana when the clause lacks an overt copula – this is the case in all positive, non-tense-marked clauses (31). In the related language Datooga, both nouns, the subject and predicate nominal, are also in the zero-coded Accusative case, even if an overt copula appears in the construction (32). The Tennet equational predication already discussed in Section 3.3 is of the same type.

(31) Turkana (Dimmendaal 1982: 75)
a-yɔŋ` ɛ-kapılanı̬
NC-1SG.ACC NC-witch.ACC
'I am a witch.'

(32) Datooga (Nilotic; Tanzania; Kiessling 2007: 172)
a. sàawà màanàŋóodìgà gîl
   3PL.ACC wealthy_people.ACC DEM
   'They are wealthy people.'
b. nìɲ   à[a] mùránéedà gîl
   3SG.ABS COP hero.ACC   DEM
   'He was a hero.'

The data presented above are summarized in Table 3.3 on the next page. As can be seen, all Nilo-Saharan marked-S languages mark the predicate nominal in the zero-coded accusative case. The subject of nominal predications is treated like

language	subject	predicate nominal
Datooga	ACC	ACC
Maa	NOM	ACC
Murle	NOM	ACC
Nandi	NOM	ACC
Tennet (*class-membership*)	NOM	ACC
Tennet (*identity*)	ACC	ACC
Turkana	NOM/ACC	ACC

Table 3.3: Marking of nominal predication in the Nilo-Saharan marked-S languages

other S/A arguments in most languages. Only the Nilotic languages Datooga and Turkana deviate from this pattern. While in Datooga subjects of nominal predications are always zero-coded, Turkana has a split between nominal predications that have an overt copular element and those that lack an overt copula. In the construction with the overt copula, the subject is in the Nominative case, while the Accusative case is used for subjects in the construction without an overt copula. Tennet, the only language of the sample with a distinct construction for identity predication, uses a construction with both nouns in the zero-coded case-form for encoding identity.

3.8 Pacific

The marked-S languages of the Pacific (Savosavo, Ajië and Nias) pattern similarly to the African languages in marking the subject of nominal predications with the standard subject-case and leaving the predicate nominal zero-coded.

This pattern is illustrated by the Savosavo examples in (33a, b). However, Wegener (2008: 212) notes that the Nominative case-marking on the subject noun is often dropped in this type of clause, as is exemplified in (33c).

(33) Savosavo (Solomons East Papuan; Solomon Islands; Wegener 2008: 210, 222, 214)

a. *Ururu=gha   lava   ko-va   zuba=na*
   be.fragrant=PL PROPR.SG.M 3SG.F-GEN.M child=NOM
   '[Talking about eggs of a megapode] Her child (i.e. egg) has a nice smell (when cooked).',
   lit. 'Fragrance having (is) her child.'

b. *ghoma lo mapa=e ai lo biti=na*
   NEG DET.SG.M person=EMPH this DET.SG.M volcano=NOM
   '(It was) not a conscious being, this volcano.'

c. *anyi ghajia Solomone sua mapa*
   1SG self Solomo_Islands ATT.SG.M person
   'I was the only Solomon Islander.'
   lit. 'I myself (was) a Solomon Island person.'

The marked-absolutive language Nias has a parallel pattern of zero-coding the predicate nominal, while the subject of the nominal predication receives overt marking (34).[7]

(34) Nias (Sundic, Western Malayo-Polynesian, Austronesian; Sumatra, Indonesia; Brown 2001: 443)
*a-me'e-la **ganunu-a** ha'a*
IPFV-give-NR IPFV.MUT.burn-NMLZ PROX
'This pan was a gift.'

Apart from the noted tendency of Savosavo to leave the subject zero-coded, there is another type of nominal predicate clause without Nominative case-marking on the subject (35). In Nias, a similar structure exists with subject of nominal predications in the Unmutated case (36). For both languages, the respective context involves a high discourse prominence of the subject of the nominal predication. This behavior is, however, not restricted to nominal predications as such. There is a general tendency of marked-S languages to use the zero-coded form of a noun if the noun is emphasized (see Chapter 5).

(35) Savosavo (Wegener 2008: 221)
Ko nini=koi Polupolu
3SG.F.GEN name=EMPH DET.SG.F Polupolu
'Her name (was) Polupolu.'

(36) Nias (Brown 2001: 444)
a-nunu-a ha'a, a-me'e-la
IPFV-burn-NMLZ PROX IPFV-give-NMLZ
'This pan, (it was) a gift.'

---

[7] Recall that the so-called nominal mutation in Nias is used for S and P arguments, while A arguments are in the basic non-mutated form (Brown 2001).

language	subject	predicate nominal
Ajië	-	ACC
Nias	ABS	ERG
Savosavo	NOM/ACC	ACC

Table 3.4: Marking of nominal predication in the marked-S languages of the Pacific

Nominal predications are not discussed as a construction in the descriptions of Ajië. I found only two examples of it in the data (37, 37b), both of which do not have the subject expressed as an independent nominal. The third singular form in example (37) is the pre-verbal subject-marker rather than the independent form of a third person pronoun *ce*. In (37b), one also finds the subject agreement marker for the first person rather than the independent form *gɛ-ɲa*. The only generalization for Ajië thus must be that predicate nominals are zero-coded (at least as one of the options of the language), while the marking of the subject remains unknown so far.

(37) Ajië (Oceanic, Eastern Malayo-Polynesian; Austronesian; New Caledonia; Lichtenberk 1978: 99, 103 after de la Fontinelle 1976: 264, 210, 211)

    a. *na dɔ pani-ɲa*
       3SG INTENS mother-1SG
       'She is my true mother.'

    b. *(ki) gɔi ɔrɔkaʔu*
       HYP 1SG chief
       'I wish I were chief'

The data from the marked-S languages of the Pacific region are summarized in Table 3.4. All three language of that region have zero-coded predicate nominals. The subject of nominal predications can be coded in the S-case, which is also used also for subjects of intransitive clauses in Savosavo and Nias (and possibly also in Ajië). However, at least in Savosavo zero-coded subjects are often found.

3.9 Summary

Table 3.5 summarizes all data given on the marking of nominal predications in marked-S languages in the above sections. For each language, the case-form used

3 Nominal predication

for subjects of nominal predications (shortened to 'subject' in the table) as well as the predicate nominal are listed. In addition, I list the information on whether or not an overt copular element is used in the construction. If a language has alternative constructions for the encoding of nominal predication, e.g. one with an overt copula and one without, each construction has its own line in the table. Supposedly free variation of case-marking on either of the arguments that cannot be pinned down to any clear conditions, such as: NOM in copula clauses, ACC in copula-less clauses, is represented with a slash in the respective cell.

Most genealogical units of languages behave rather uniformly with respect to case-marking in nominal predications. For some of the languages with a deviating pattern, this is conditioned by other structural properties of the construction such as presence or absence of a copula (Turkana and Havasupai), or a difference in the case inventory (Arbore's Predicative case). Some languages behave differently from genealogically related languages without there being a base for this in any apparent structural conditions (Daatoga and Jamul Tiipay). Also, there is in general no correlation between whether a copula is obligatory, optional, or never present in a language and the case-marking found in nominal predications – though for individual languages, such as Turkana and Havasupai, this may be different.

language	subject	pred. nominal	zero copula
Ajië	-	ACC	possible
Arbore	NOM	PRED	possible
Datooga	ACC	ACC	possible
Diegueño (Mesa Grande)	ACC	NOM	possible
Gamo	NOM	ACC	possible
Havasupai (*construction 1*)	ACC	NOM	no
Havasupai (*construction 2*)	ACC	ACC	always
Jamul Tiipay (*construction 1*)	ACC	ACC	always
Jamul Tiipay (*construction 2*)	NOM	ACC	never
K'abeena	NOM	ACC	no
Maa	NOM	ACC	no
Maidu	NOM	NOM	no
Maricopa	ACC	NOM	no?
Mojave	ACC	NOM	possible
Murle	NOM	ACC	yes/always
Nandi	NOM	ACC	always
Nias	ABS	ERG	always
Oromo (Boraana)	NOM	ACC	possible
Oromo (Harar)	NOM	ACC	possible
Savosavo	NOM/ACC	ACC	always
Tennet (*class-membership*)	NOM	ACC	no
Tennet (*identity*)	ACC	ACC	yes
Turkana (*construction 1*)	NOM	ACC	no
Turkana (*construction 2*)	ACC	ACC	always
Walapai	ACC	NOM	no
Wappo	ACC	ACC	only future
Wolaytta	NOM	ACC/NOM	restricted
Yavapai	ACC	NOM	no
Zayse	NOM	ACC	no

Table 3.5: Overview of the marking of nominal predication

4 Existential and locational predication

4.1 Introduction

In this chapter, two types of predications are discussed: existential and locational predications. The two types are exemplified by the English sentences in (1a) and (1b) respectively.

(1) a. *There is a tree (in the garden).*
    b. *The tree is in the garden.*

While in the existential construction (1a) a statement about the existence of an entity is made, existence is presupposed in the locational construction (1b) and said entity is categorized with respect to its location in space. In many languages the formal properties of the constructions, such as definiteness/indefiniteness of the arguments, correlate with these pragmatic implications of the two structures.

From a descriptive as well as a formal semantic point of view, existential and locational sentences have been treated as similar to one another, if not identical in their underlying semantic structure. Sometimes, other contexts such as predicative possession and nominal predication are also put into the same category (Payne 1997: 111–113). Nominal predication in marked-S languages has already been discussed in Chapter 3. I have chosen to treat that topic separately since in some languages in my sample nominal predication has a number of special properties that are not shared with existential or locational predications. In contrast, the context of predicative possession did not reveal any special properties in my study. The languages of my sample employ two strategies for expressing this context: either there is a transitive verb 'have' or predicative possession uses the same construction as existentials (while adding the possessor either as an adpositional phrase or an attributive possessor). These are also the two main types that Stassen (2009) distinguishes in his typology of predicative possession. He further introduces three subtypes of the locational possessive construction – the 'locational possessive', 'with-possessive' and 'topic-possessive' – the details of which are not relevant here. Another approach to the classification of types of

4 Existential and locational predication

predicative possession are the eight types of possessive 'event schemata' distinguished by Heine (1997: 47). Five of these eight schemata use a formula including a predicate 'exist' or 'be located', while a sixth uses a predicate 'be with' which can be considered a locational concept. This approach also indicates a strong relation between the encoding of location and existence, on the one hand, and possession, on the other. For those languages of my sample that have an existential/locational/possessive construction, the data from possessive contexts are included in this chapter. Otherwise, this context is not treated in this study.

For a small number of languages in my sample, a different case-form is used for the subject of negative and positive existential predications. From a cross-linguistic perspective, this behavior is not unheard of, though also not very common (Matti Miestamo, p.c.). For instance, in Russian and Finnish, subject case-marking is different for positive and negative clauses in a number of contexts. While positive copula clauses mark their subjects with Nominative case, in the negative counterparts, Finnish employs Partitive case while Russian uses the Genitive (Dixon 2010b: 167).

The overwhelming majority of languages in my sample use the same construction to express locational and existential predication. This is, however, not a peculiar fact about languages of the marked-S type, but has been noted for the majority of the world's languages. Historical as well as philosophical explanations have been given in order to account for this relation. In addition, when the two predications are not encoded by the same construction, the structural differences appear to be triggered by the same types of factors across languages. A brief overview of the literature treating these topics is given in Section 4.2. Afterwards, I will present the different patterns found in existential and locational constructions for the languages of my sample and formulate the research questions for the present study (Section 4.3). In the subsequent sections, I will present data from Nilo-Saharan (Section 4.4), Afro-Asiatic (Section 4.5), North-American languages (Section 4.6), and languages from the Pacific area (Sectin 4.7). Finally, I summarize the languages in my sample in Section 4.8.

4.2 Linguistic properties

Lyons (1967, 1968) argues that existential constructions are historically derived from locational constructions in most of the languages of the world, unless the two kinds of constructions are completely identical to each other. Indeed, the locational nature is still very obvious in the existentials of many languages since they require some locational phrase – be it as vague as 'here' or 'there' – to be present in this construction (cf. the English existential construction 'there is a X'). As a motivation for this historical connection, Lyons (1968: 499) argues for an ontological relation between existence and location since existence implies existence at a specific (though possibly unspecified) location. And, conversely, absence of a entity from all locations implies non-existence.

While Lyons' discussion is concerned with the semantic and ontological relation of the two types of constructions, other scholars have concentrated on the syntactic relation between the two. Among these scholars is Freeze (1992), who argues that the underlying syntactic structure of existentials and locationals is identical. Any differences in the surface realization of the two structures in a given language are triggered by other factors such as definiteness of the S argument.

One structural correlate of these factors is an alternation of word order in the two types of constructions. These word order effects are the main focus of the study by Clark (1978) on existential, locational and possessive constructions. She(, argues that the ordering correlates with the properties of the subject in terms of definiteness and specificity. This is shown, for example, by the English data (cf. example (1a) and (1b) above), in which the indefinite subject of existentials is not in the canonical subject position but instead a dummy location is inserted in this position.[1] The (usually) definite subject of locationals on the other hand preferably occurs in the canonical subject position (i.e. sentence initially). Clark's findings suggest that this is not only the case in English, but that the correlation between word order and predication type is a cross-linguistic tendency, since the overwhelming majority of her sample of 30 languages (with some bias toward European languages) showed this tendency. The correlation between word order and existential vs. locational sentences was particularly high for languages without a morphosyntactic means to distinguish definites and indefinites.

Though Clark's findings are intriguing, her collapsing of the categories existential and locational with the notion of indefinite versus definite subject may be somewhat problematic. To distinguish between existentials and locationals, the criterion whether the subject of a clause in definite or indefinite is a good approximation, but counterexamples do occur. The following made-up tabloid headline would probably be interpreted as a statement about existence rather

---

[1] The example such as (i.a) and (i.b) are possible in English, but very unusual. Example (i.a) gets better when the locational phrase is added.

(i)   a.   *A tree is (in the garden).*
       b.   *A tree exists.*

than location by most speakers of English, yet the subject is marked with the definite article (2).

(2) The Yeti exists.

So the question has to be answered whether Clark's correlation really is between word order and existential versus locational predications, or rather between word order and definiteness, which in most cases coincides with the distinction between existentials and locationals.

In studies of existential and locational predication, not much is said about the case-marking of subjects in these constructions. Or, to put it in other terms, the question is whether the S-like argument in existentials and locationals behaves like other S elements. Given the topic of this study, this is my main interest with regard to these contexts. Payne (1997: 123) notes that there "[u]sually is no or reduced evidence of grammatical relations in existential constructions." If this is true, one would not expect S of existential predications to be encoded like more typical intransitive subjects in marked-S languages.

4.3 Research question

In the subsequent sections, I will present data on locational and existential predications in the languages of the marked-S type. The special focus is on the case-forms employed for the S-like arguments in these clauses. More specifically, I selected three contexts: locational predications, as well as positive and negative existential predications. In each of these contexts, the marking of the respective subject is investigated. Thus, data for the following three roles were collected for each language of the sample:

- subject of positive existential predication
- subject of negative existential predication
- subject of locational predication

The distinction between negative and positive predications is only made for existentials here. If a language uses the same construction for existential and locational contexts, any differences between negative and positive existentials will also be found with negative locationals. However, there are languages in which the difference between positive and negative contexts is only found with existentials to the exclusion of locationals, while no language makes such a distinction exclusively in the locational context.

4.3 Research question

Most marked-S languages use the same constructions for existential and locational predications. Usually, these constructions encode their subjects like subjects of regular intransitive clauses. A distinction between the encoding of subjects of positive and negative contexts is only found in few of the languages. Not all languages appear to have dedicated constructions for locationals and/or existentials. The contexts (or subset of these contexts) are often expressed through the use of a generic intransitive verb expressing some kind of local orientation, such as 'sit', 'stand' or 'lie'. In these cases, the locational and existential predications can be regarded as instances of regular intransitive clauses. Thus subjects are expected to be in the S-case.[2]

First, I will give an example of this majority pattern. The S element in (3a) and (3b) is marked with the Nominative case-suffix -č in Mojave, just as any intransitive S argument is. Note that Mojave does not have a single existential or locational verb, using instead a number of stative verbs in both existential and locational predications.

(3) Mojave (Yuman; Arizona; Munro 1976: 33, 212)

    a. *hukθar-č*   *ʔaviː-θ-lʸ*   *idiː-k*
       coyote-NOM mountain-DEM-LOC lie-TNS

       'There are coyotes in those hills.'

    b. *piːpa*   *nʸamaθaːm kʷəloyaw kʷ-tapoy-h-nʸ-č*   *ʔavaː-lʸ*   *iva-m*
       person tomorrow chicken   REL-kill-IRR-DEM-NOM house-LOC sit-TNS

       'The man who's going to kill the chicken tomorrow is in the house.'

Nias also uses the same type of construction to encode locational and existential meanings. However, different constructions are used for positive and negative contexts. While the construction used for positive contexts (4a) employs the S element in the Mutated form of a noun (i.e. the same as for regular intransitive S), in negative contexts the S-like element is in the Unmutated form (4b).

(4) Nias (Sundic; Sumatra, Indonesia; Brown 2001: 344, 358)

    a. *ga* *so* **göcoa**
       here exist cockroach.MUT

       'There's a cockroach here.'

---

[2] Recall that the label S-CASE is a shorthand for: the nominative case if a language has nominative-accusative alignment and the absolutive case if a language has ergative-absolutive alignment.

4 Existential and locational predication

    b. *löna*   **baßi** ba mbanu   *ha'a*
       NEG.exist pig LOC village.MUT PROX
       'There are no pigs in this village.'

Finally, there is one language in my sample in which different constructions are used for existentials and locationals (at least by some speakers). While in Tennet existentials the subject can be zero-coded (5a), with locationals the Nominative case is always used (5b).

(5) Tennet (Surmic; Sudan; Randal 1998: 236, 236)

    a. *ányák* **mám** *cééz-a*
       have   water house-OBL
       'There is water in the house.'

    b. *ạ̈ve*   **loụ̈dọ́**   keét-á   vụ́rt-ạ̈
       be_located Loudo.NOM tree-OBL under-OBL
       'Loudo is under the tree.'

The following sections provide a detailed study of the contexts of positive and negative existential predication and locational predication in marked-S languages. The data are divided by genealogical and areal grouping into the Nilo-Saharan (4.4) and Afro-Asiatic languages (4.5), and the languages of North America (4.6) and the Pacific area (4.7). In many cases, it has been difficult to obtain information on the contexts studied here for individual languages. This is probably due to the fact that clauses of the existential and locational type are often encoded like regular intransitive clauses and thus are not explicitly discussed in many grammars. Hence, in the following sections there are no data on one or the other context for a number of languages.

4.4 Nilo-Saharan

For most marked-S languages of the Nilo-Saharan stock, the S arguments of existential and locational predications are encoded alike, since the same constructions are used in both contexts. However, some languages show interesting patterns, especially in having alternative constructions in the different subdomains.

In Murle, the prototypical situation is attested, in which parallel constructions are used for existential (6a) and locational predication (6b). And indeed this construction is also parallel to other intransitive verbs (6c). Nandi (7) and Datooga (8) behave similarly.

(6) Murle (Surmic; Sudan; Arensen 1982: 49, 50)
    a. *abil   guumun-**i** kɛɛt taddina*
       stands owl-NOM tree up
       'There is an owl up in the tree.'
    b. *ɛɛl   tor-ɛt-**a**   ceeza*
       stand gun-PL-NOM in_house
       'The guns are in the house.'
    c. *akɔ agul-**i**   ci appi liila*
       goes crocodile-NOM REL big into_river
       'The big crocodile goes into the river.'

(7) Nandi (Nilotic; Kenya; Creider & Creider 1989: 123)
    a. *mì:t-éy **ngetún**-ta*
       COP-IPFV lion.NOM-THEM
       'There is a lion.'
    b. *mì:t-éy **kípro:no**   kitâ:li*
       COP-IPFV Kiprono.NOM Kitale
       'Kiprono is in Kitale.'

(8) Datooga (Nilotic; Tanzania; Kiessling 2007: 184, 171)
    a. *mà-ndá   **dúu**-sù   jáa   gá-wá gwá-róoɲí*
       3.NEG-be_there cattle.NOM-PROX.PL NOM.FUT.REL 3-go   3-meet
       'There are none of these cattle that he may go to meet.'
    b. *gwándà   **gádéemgá** jèedá dûhwa̞*
       3-be_there women.NOM among cattle.ACC
       'The women were among the cattle.'

As noted before, the same is true for the majority of languages in my sample. However, there are some languages which have an alternative construction for one of these two types of predication that differs from the encoding of the other type. Also, in some languages at least some types of existential and/or locational predications do not encode their subject in the same way as prototypical intransitive clauses encode their subjects (S). In the following, I will focus on these languages.

The first Nilo-Saharan language which exhibits some variation with respect to the encoding of the S argument in existential and locational predications is Turkana. At least two different constructions are used in Turkana for encoding

4 Existential and locational predication

existential and locational contexts. First, existentials can be encoded like nominal predicates. As seen in the previous chapter (3.7), this construction usually does not have a verb, unless it is negated or in non-present tense. In those verbless clauses, the S argument is in the Accusative case (9a). If a verb is present – whether to encode negation or past tense, or because construction with a lexicalized verb is used, as in the next example – Nominative case is used for the S argument (9b).[3]

(9) Turkana (Nilotic; Kenya; Dimmendaal 1982: 74, 75)

   a. *ŋɪ-dɛ`  omwɔn`*
      NC-children.ACC four

      'There are four children.'

   b. *è-màa-sè ŋɪ-dɛ̀ omwɔn`*
      3-drink-PL children.NOM four

      'There are four children.'

The second construction I will discuss here is interpreted as either existential, locational or possessive. Other than the nominal predication construction, in which an overt copula only occurs when it is needed to host negation or tense marking, the copula is usually used in all cases. As is to be expected in constructions which have an overt verb, the Nominative case is used for the S argument (10). In the possessive interpretation of this construction, the possessee is always interpreted as being indefinite (11a). If one wants to formulate a possessive sentence with a definite possessee, the non-verbal construction used in nominal predications has to be employed (11b) according to Dimmendaal (1982: 82).

(10) Turkana (Dimmendaal 1982: 82)

   a. *è-yàka-sì ŋa-àtùk*
      3-be-PL NC-COWS.NOM

      'There are cows (or the cows are there).'

   b. *è-yè-i` a-pèsɛ a-pèy*
      3-be-ASP NC-girl.NOM NC-one.NOM

      'There is one girl (or one girl is there).'

---

[3] The example in (9b) is an idiomatic expression, in which the verb 'drink' is deprived of its lexical meaning. The high potential of verbs of eating and drinking to undergo metaphorical extensions is discussed in Newman (2009).

(11) Turkana (Dimmendaal 1982: 82)

a. è-yàka-sì a-yɔŋ` ŋa-àtùk
 3-be-PL NC-me NC-cows.NOM
 'I have cows.'

b. **ŋa-atuk`ŋugu`** ŋa-kaŋ`
 cows.ACC these.ACC NC-mine
 'These cows are mine'

Maa is another language that shows some variation on the constructions used for existential and locational contexts. According to Payne (2007), there are two types of existentials in Maa, those constructed with the verb *tii* 'be at' and those constructed with the verb *ata* 'have'. The first construction, i.e. the one with *tii*, encodes both existential and locational contexts. In this construction, the S argument is always marked with the Nominative case (12a, b). Existentials constructed with the verb *ata* on the other hand have zero-coded S arguments and do not have a locational meaning (12c).

(12) Maa (Nilotic; Kenya; Payne 2007: ex. 19a, ex. 17, ex. 20a)

a. N-é-tíí apá, **ɔl-mʊrraní óbo**
 CON-3-be.at long_ago M.SG-warrior.NOM one.NOM
 'Long ago, there was a warrior.'

b. e-tíí ɛnk-áyíóní ol-kɛjǒ
 3-be_at F.SG-boy.NOM M.SG-leg.ACC
 'The boy is at the river.' (lit. 'The boy is at the big leg.')

c. n-é-yioló-u áàjò k-é-áta-ɪ ɛnk-áí ná-râ
 CON-3-know-INCEP that.PL DSCN-3-exist-PASS F.SG-God.ACC REL.F-be
 papâ
 father.ACC
 'They knew that there is God who is the father.'

In the above example of the *ata*-existential, the verb is in the passive. Since passive verbs always take their subjects in the zero-coded Accusative form in Maa, this is not surprising.[4] However, there are some non-passive *ata*-existentials which nevertheless take zero-coded subjects. Examples of the type demonstrated in (13) make up a quarter of the instances of *ata*-existentials in Payne's corpus.

---

[4] The following examples, from Payne (2007: ex.16, ex.15), demonstrate the Maa Passive and the corresponding active clause:

4 Existential and locational predication

(13) Maa (Payne 2007)

    a. ...*amʊ̂ m-ɛ-átà **ɔl-tʊŋání** ó-ítieu*
        because NEG-3-exist M.SG-person.ACC M.SG.REL.ACC-dare
        '...because there is no one who can face him.'

    b. *M-ɛ-étà **ɔl-mʊ́rrání** lé-m-é-nyɔ́rr*
        NEG-3-exist M.SG-warrior.ACC REL.M-NEG-3-like
        te=n-e-i-pus-íék-ì ɛnk-áíná
        OBL=CON-3-VBLZ-blue-INS-PASS F.SG-arm.ACC
        'There isn't a warrior who doesn't want to (have his) hand be made blue.'

In the previous section, data from Tennet have already been introduced. Randal (1998: 236) notes that in Tennet not all speakers use parallel constructions for existential and locational predications. Some speakers use the standard locational construction for existentials as well. In this construction, the S argument is in the Nominative case (14a, b). Other speakers use a different construction for existential contexts, which has a zero-coded S argument (15a). For negative existential and locational predications the subject is always zero-coded (15b). The basic variation between the two groups of speakers is thus whether the positive existential context is covered by the same construction as the negative existential context or as the positive locational context.

(14) Tennet (Surmic; Sudan; Randal 1998: 223)

    a. *ą́ve **lo̧ų́do̧** keét-á vų́rt-ą̂*
        be_located Loudo.NOM tree-OBL under-OBL
        'Loudo is under the tree.'

    b. *ávte **bu̧rú-nâ** lebel-á*
        stay.PL eggs-NOM platform-OBL
        '(The) eggs are on the platform.'

(i) a. *ɛ-te-ɛn-ák-ì **ɔl-apúrrònì***
      3-PRF-tie-PRF-PASS M.SG-thief.ACC
      'The thief was arrested.'

  b. *ɛ-ɪbʊ́ŋ-á ɪ-s'ɪkarɪní **ɔl-apúrrònì***
      3-catch-PRF PL-police.NOM M.SG-thief.ACC
      'The policemen have arrested the thief.'

(15) Tennet (Randal 1998: 236)

a. *ányák* **mám** *céẹ́z-a*
   have water house-OBL
   'There is water in the house.'

b. *iḷḷóí* **mám** *céẹ́z-a*
   absent water house-OBL
   'There's no water in the house.'

The Nilo-Saharan data are summarized in Table 4.1. The data from Maa and Tennet are split up between two lines for each of the two languages. For Maa, the first line represents the construction with *tii* 'be at', while the second line represents the construction with *ata* 'have'. In Tennet, the two lines represent the inter-speaker variation regarding which construction to use for positive existentials. The table shows that all languages use nominative case for locational subjects. Most languages also make use of the nominative for existential subjects, but in this context more variation is found. A distinction in encoding between negative and positive existenials in only found in Turkana and with some Tennet speakers. While in Turkana negative existentials receive Nominative case-marking, in Tennet this context is zero-coded.

language	S exist. (+)	S exist.(-)	S loc. pred.
Datooga	NOM	NOM	NOM
Maa (*be at*)	NOM	-	NOM
Maa (*have*)	ACC	ACC	n.a.
Murle	NOM	-	NOM
Nandi	NOM	-	NOM
Tennet (*variety 1*)	ACC	ACC	NOM
Tennet (*variety 2*)	NOM	ACC	NOM
Turkana	ACC/NOM	NOM	NOM

Table 4.1: Overview of the marking of existential and locational predication in the Nilo-Saharan languages

4.5 Afro-Asiatic

For the Afro-Asiatic marked-S languages, very little information on existential and locational predications is given in the relevant grammars. Most of the data

4 Existential and locational predication

given in the following were gathered by extensively studying all examples provided throughout the grammars and trying to identify the ones with locational or existential meanings. The data that could be gathered on the relevant contexts did not reveal any remarkable patterns. Whether a grammar provided data on existentials, locationals or both types, the subject element always was marked with the S-case. A minor exception to this pattern was attested in Harar Oromo and will be discussed below. Also, no variation between negative and positive contexts could be identified in any Afro-Asiatic language, but then again, hardly any negative examples were found at all.

The only Afro-Asiatic language in which alternations in case-marking on the S argument of existential and locationals can be observed is the Harar dialect of Oromo. The subject of locational phrases is normally in Nominative case, especially when definite (16b). In some situations, the emphatic subject form is used (16c) and thus no Nominative case-marking occurs on the subject. The construction with the emphatic subject-marker appears to be limited to the existential reading, but this might just be a tendency parallel to the correlation between indefiniteness and existential reading observed by Clark (1978) and not an absolute selectional restriction. For negative contexts, no examples were found.

(16) Oromo (Harar) (Eastern Cushitic; Ethiopia; Owens 1985: 101, 109)

    a. *c'uf-tíi xéesá jir-an*
       all-NOM in exist-PL
       'All are inside.'

    b. *kitaab-**nii** miizá rrá jira*
       book-NOM table on exist
       'The book is on the table.'

    c. *miizá rrá kitaabáa-túu jira*
       table on book-EMPH.SBJ exist
       'There is a book on the table.'

In K'abeena (17), locationals as well as existentials mark the S argument in Nominative case. Also, there does not seem to be any alternation between positive and negative sentences – unless the non-accessible negative existentials reveal an alternative pattern. However, since the same verb is used for existential and locational predications, even though *yoo* is sometimes glossed as 'to exist' and sometimes as 'to be located' by Crass (2005), negative existentials very likely employ the same pattern as negative locationals.

(17) K'abeena (Eastern Cushitic; Ethiopia; Crass 2005: 98, 115, 98)
    a. *wiim^u 'abogodáa'nut^i yoo-s^i*
       many friends.NOM.PL exist.3-3SG.M.OBJ
       'He has got many friends,' lit.:'Many friends are to him.'
       original translation: 'Er hat viele Freunde'
       lit.: 'Viele Freunde existieren [bei] ihm.')
    b. **máncu-s^e** *bokku yoo*
       man.NOM-DEF.M house.ACC be_located.3
       'The man is in the house.'
       original translation: 'Der Mann ist im Haus.'
    c. *wolk'itt'een^i tees^u* **wuu** *yoo-ba*
       Wolkite.LOC now water.NOM exist.3-NEG
       'In Wolkite there is no water right now.'
       original translation: 'In Wolkite gibt es jetzt kein Wasser.'

In Arbore, only examples of the existential predication could be identified. The subject of this construction in the Nominative case as demonstrated in (18).[5]

(18) Arbore (Eastern Cushitic; Ethiopia; Hayward 1984: 132)
    ʔiNgir-é ʔa-y gírta
    louse-NOM PVS-3SG exist.3SG.F
    'There is a louse.'

For Boraana Oromo (19), Gamo (20), and Wolaytta (21), only locational examples could be extracted from the grammatical descriptions. The Nominative case is always used to encode the S argument.

(19) Oromo (Boraana) (Eastern Cushitic; Kenya; Owens 1982: 54)
    nàm-i jànn-i dìbi-in sùn arm jìr
    man-NOM brave-NOM other-NOM DEM here be
    'That other brave man is here.'

(20) Gamo (Omotic; Ethiopia; Hompó 1990: 384)
    iza naʔi-t-ii goššanča-z-aa-ko-n d-ettes
    his child-PL-NOM peasant-DEF-ACC-COM-LOC be-COMPLX
    'His children are around the peasant.'

---

[5] The Nominative form *ʔiNgiré* is distinct from the zero-coded form of the noun *ʔingir*.

4 Existential and locational predication

(21) Wolaytta (Omotic; Ethiopia; Lamberti & Sottile 1997: 587, ex: 332)
 eet-i banta horaatta keettaa-n^i de?osoona
 3PL-NOM 3PL.POSS new house-PL-LOC be.3PL
 'They are in their new houses.'

For Zayse, finally, it was not completely clear whether the only relevant sentence that could be found should be classified as an existential, as the English translation suggests, or rather as a locational. Regardless of this question, the construction demonstrated uses the Nominative case for the S argument (22).

(22) Zayse (Omotic; Ethiopia; Hayward 1990: 261)
 ʔas̀-í kará yesatte
 man-NOM indoors exist-COP
 'There is a man in the house.'

The data are summarized in Table 4.2. There are a lot of missing data for the Afro-Asiatic languages on the contexts of existential and locational predications. Therefore, any tendencies described here have to be viewed as a preliminary result. The languages of this family encode existential as well as locational subjects in the nominative case. No differences between the encoding of subjects in positive and negative existential predications could be found in the Afro-Asiatic marked-S languages.

language	S exist. (+)	S exist.(-)	S loc. pred.
Arbore	NOM	-	-
Gamo	-	-	NOM
K'abeena	NOM	NOM	NOM
Oromo (Boraana)	-	-	NOM
Oromo (Harar)	emphatic subjet	-	NOM
Wolaytta	-	-	NOM
Zayse	NOM	-	NOM

Table 4.2: Overview on the marking of existential and locational predication in the Afro-Asiatic languages

4.6 North America

The marked-S languages of North America tend to have no dedicated constructions for encoding existential and locational predications. They usually employ stative verbs in these contexts. However, at least for the Yuman languages, the option not to use the S-case on subjects in existential contexts seems to exist, or even to be preferred or obligatory for some languages. This is generally the case if the S-case is an optional marker (cf. also Section 2.6). This tendency is in accordance with the claim by Payne (1997: 123) that existentials mark grammatical relations only to a limited degree.

Mojave has been shown in Section 4.3 to use the same type of construction for locational (23a) and existential predications (23b). In this construction, a number of stative verbs can occur, and the S argument is usually encoded with the Nominative case. Hence, these contexts can best be analyzed as being regular intransitive clauses. Negative existentials also exhibit this intransitive pattern with Nominative marking on the S argument (23c).

(23) Mojave (Yuman; Arizona; Munro 1976: 21, 212, 70)
  a. *pi:pa-č k^wəča:nava:-l^y uwa:-k*
     person-NOM Yuma-LOC   be_in-TNS
     'There is someone in Yuma ...'
  b. *pi:pa n^yamaθa:m k^wəloyaw k^w-tapoy-h-n^y-č   ?ava:-l^y iva-m*
     person tomorrow chicken   REL-kill-IRR-DEM-NOM house-LOC sit-TNS

     'The man who's going to kill the chicken tomorrow is in the house.'
  c. *hatčoq havasu:-č kava:r-ta:han-e*
     dog   blue-NOM not-very-AUGV
     'There are no blue dogs'

Out of the dozens of existential examples that I found for Mojave, the S argument is always in the Nominative case, with one exception. Example (24) suggests that the Nominative case-marker can be missing on this argument. Since Munro (1976) notes the optionality of the Nominative case-marker, this is no surprise.

(24) Mojave (Munro 1976: 70)
   n^ya-v-k   ?aha: kava:r-k
   this-DEM-LOC water not-TNS
   'There's no water here'

In Jamul Tiipay S arguments of presentational clauses are always zero-coded (25a), whereas in locational contexts Nominative marking does occur (25b). In the closely-related language Diegueño[6], S arguments of existential clauses are

---
[6] Until recently, Jamul Tiipay was treated as a dialect of Diegueño.

4 Existential and locational predication

apparently also zero-coded (26a). Whether they also allow for encoding of the S argument in the Nominative like locational clauses (26b) is not clear, since unfortunately none of the materials on the language give information on this question.

(25) Jamul Tiipay (Yuman; Mexico; Miller 2001: 231; Miller 1990: 148)

    a. ***toor** tewa-ch   u-wiiw*
       bull be_located-SSBJ 3-see
       'There was a bull there, and he saw (the boy).'

    b. *nyaa-**ch** peyii ta'-wa-ch-pu   puu-ch ny-u'yaaw*
       1-NOM here 1-be_located-NR-DEM 3>1-see ???
       'She knows that I was there.'

(26) Diegueño (Mesa Grande) (Yuman; California; Gorbet 1976: 27, Langdon 1970: 176)

    a. *'i:kʷic 'xin nʸwa:yp t+wa: i:tay+pu+i*
       man one live   PROG+be_sitting forest+DEM+LOC
       'There was a man who lived in the forest.'

    b. *ʔikʷic pu=**c**   nʸuk pa*
       man that_one=NOM already he_got_here
       'That man is already here.'

For Yavapai, all examples listed in the grammar are of an existential nature if one takes the English translation into account. Whether a locational reading is also possible cannot conclusively told from the information in the grammar. All S arguments are in the Nominative case. And finally, in Havasupai, only one example was found, which is existential according to the translation provided. In this example the S argument is in the Nominative case (28).

(27) Yavapai (Yuman; Arizona; Kendall 1976: 28, 98)

    a. *hʷat-**c**   viya-k wi-o-m*
       blood-NOM here-LOC have-APPL-FAFF
       'There is blood here.'

    b. *cmyul ñ-wa:-**c**-**c**   via ʔ-wa:-v-m   pay-a yo:*
       ant POSS-house-PL-NOM here 1-house-DEM-around all-TNS exist
       'There are ant hills all around my house.'

c. *cnapuk-**c*** *miyyul-l yu-m*
red_ant-NOM sugar-LOC be-FAFF

'There is an ant in the sugar.'

(28) Havasupai (Yuman; Arizona; Kozlowski 1972: 61)
*pa-c-**v*** *hlah-l θa-l yu-k-yu*
man-DEM-NOM moon-LOC there-in be-IND-AUX

'There is a man in the moon.'

The Wappo data provide a mirror image of the Yavapai situation. The translations suggest an existential reading of the following examples. Possibly, examples such as (29c) can also be interpreted as locationals, depending on the previous discourse, but the grammar does not provide any information on this topic. One reason for this might be the lack of textual data due to the fact that, as Thompson et al. (2006) note in the introduction to their grammar, their informant (and last speaker of the language) did not enjoy working on narratives. Be that as it may, all the examples have Nominative S arguments, and no difference is made between positive (29a) and negative clauses (29b).

(29) Wappo (Wappo-Yukian; California; Thompson et al. 2006: 105)
a. *pol'-**i*** *ŏi:-khiʔ*
dirt-NOM exist-STAT

'There's a bucket of dirt.'

b. *heta hut'-**i*** *la-khiʔ*
here coyote-NOM missing-STAT

'There aren't any coyotes here.'

c. *c'ic'a-t-**i*** *hol-wil'uh leʔa-hkiʔ*
bird-PL-NOM tree-on many-STAT

'There are lots of birds on the tree.'

In Maidu the S argument of existential (30) and locational clauses (31) is marked with Nominative case.

(30) Maidu (Maiduan; California; Dixon 1912: 10)
"*ʋnuñ' ko'doi-di kan sede-**m**' uma'pem,*" *atsoi'a*
this word-LOC and blood-NOM shall_exist say.PST.3SG

' "There shall be blood in the world", he said'

(31) Maidu (Shipley 1964: 58)
ʔadóm my-kʾí pándak-**am** kykým ma-ʔám mymý-k kapóta-m
then DEM-GEN rifle-NOM PSTREM be-PT_PST.3 he-GEN coat-NOM
kʾanájdi
under
'His rifle was there under his coat.'

A summary of the data is provided in Table 4.3. In Jamul Tiipay and Diegueño, existential subjects are in the zero-coded accusative. Both languages mark locational subjects with the Nominative. All other marked-S languages of this area appear to use the nominative case in locational as well as existential contexts. Although for many of the examples, the grammars give an existential translation, the same sentences can probably also be translated as locationals in a given contexts since they employ regular intransitive verbs such as 'sit/stand/lie', and in many cases a locational phrase is added. For none of the languages of this area was any variation found in the subject-marking of positive and negative existentials.

language	S exist. (+)	S exist.(-)	S loc. pred.
Diegueño (Mesa Grande)	ACC	-	NOM
Havasupai	NOM	-	NOM
Jamul Tiipay	ACC	-	NOM
Mojave	NOM	NOM	NOM
Yavapai	NOM	-	NOM
Maidu	NOM	-	NOM
Wappo	NOM	NOM	NOM

Table 4.3: Overview of the marking of existential and locational predication in the languages of North America

4.7 Pacific

The languages of the Pacific region, though there are only three of them with informative data in my sample, exhibit the most interesting patterns with regard to existential and locational predications. All languages have at least two different constructions to encode this domain of grammar. The semantic distinctions that individual constructions encode vary to quite an extent between the languages. Differences between negative and positive contexts are wide-spread in this very limited selection of Austronesian and non-Austronesian languages of this region.

The distinction between positive and negative existentials in Nias has already been demonstrated in Section 4.3. Now I will discuss the data in more detail. In Nias, existential and locational predications use parallel constructions (possessive constructions use the same pattern as well). For both types of predication, there is one construction that is used for positive sentences (existence, location) and another one for negative ones (non-existence, absence). Positive existential/locational constructions are built with the verb *ga* which takes the Mutated form of the noun it predicates over (32). Negative existential/locational constructions contain the verb *löna*[7], which takes a noun in Unmutated form (33).

(32) Nias (Sundic; Sumatra, Indonesia; Brown 2001: 344, 570)

    a. *ga so **göcoa***
       here exist cockroach.MUT
       'There's a cockroach here.'

    b. *so **nono**-nia do-**mbua***
       exist child.MUT-3SG.POSS two-CLF.MUT
       'She has two children.'

(33) Nias (Brown 2001: 358, 575)

    a. *löna **baßi** ba mbanu ha'a*
       exist.NEG pig LOC village.MUT PROX
       'There are no pigs in this village.'

    b. *löna ono-nia.*
       exist.NEG child-3SG.POSS
       'She doesn't have any children.'

Ajië is an Austronesian language from New Caledonia. It has two positive existential constructions, one positive locational construction, and one construction used for both negative existentials and locationals. First there is the 'unmarked' existential verb *wii/wi* (34a,34b). With this verb, the Nominative marker is optionally used (Lichtenberk 1978: 109).

---

[7] *Löna* is also the form of the standard verbal negator in Nias. When used as verbal negator, the case-marking is the same as it would be with the non-negated verb (Brown 2001: 471–475).

4 *Existential and locational predication*

(34) Ajië (Oceanic; New Caledonia; Lichtenberk 1978: 102)

    a. *na wii **rha mʌʔu** ka kani ə*
       3SG exist one yam REL grow good
       'There is a yam that grows good.'

    b. *wi tɔ-wɛ **na** pũ-ẽ?*
       exist be_where NOM trunk-3SG
       'Where is its trunk?'

Apart from this construction, there is the human existential verb *ta/tʌ*. The Nominative is always used to mark the subject with this verb (35a). In addition, there is a locational verb *tɔ* 'be at a place'. Most examples given of this verb do not have an overt subject nominal. Those that do have one mark it with the Nominative preposition *na* (35b). For the negative contexts, the same construction is used for existentials and locationals. For both non-human and human S arguments in negative existential/locational predications, it is not possible to be marked with the Nominative preposition, thus they are always zero-coded. Those sentences are constructed with the negative existential *yɛri* (36).

(35) Ajië (Lichtenberk 1978: 110)

    a. *na ta mã **na** bweʔ ye kaunuaɛ*
       3SG exist PSTREM NOM woman from K.
       'Long ago there was a woman from Kaunuae.'

    b. *gɛ yɛ ta tɔ-a **na** gɛi*
       2SG PROSP be be_there NOM you
       'You are going to stay over there.'

(36) Ajië (Lichtenberk 1978: 110)

    a. *na yɛri **kamoʔ** rro-i*
       3SG NEG.exist man in_there
       'There was no-one there.'

    b. *na yɛri **mwane***
       3SG NEG.exist money
       'There is no money.'

Savosavo – the only non-Austronesian languages of the Pacific discussed in this chapter – has a large number of locational constructions. Only one of these constructions can have an existential interpretation. In this type of locational construction (a subtype of what Wegener (2008) calls 'predicate-subject locational') the predicate is marked by the focus emphatic =e, and the following S argument may (37a) or may not (37b) be marked with the Nominative clitic. Other than for positive existentials, which do not seem to have a dedicated construction, negative existentials are formed with the verb *baighoza* 'not exist'. The S argument is marked with the Nominative in this construction (37c).

(37) Savosavo (Solomons East Papuan; Solomon Islands; Wegener 2008: 209, 122)

    a. *apoi   ata=e   te   lo   keva=**na***
       because here=EMPH EMPH DET.SG.M path=NOM
       'Because here (is) the road.'

    b. *lo   lo   buringa=la=e   edo kola=ga*
       3SG.M 3SG.M.GEN back=LOC.M=EMPH two tree=PL
       'At his back (are) two trees./ There are two trees at his back.'

    c. *lo   mama mau lo-va   nanaghiza=**na** te*
       DET.SG.M mother father 3SG.M-GEN.M teaching=NOM EMPH
      baighoza-i
      NEG.exist-FIN
      'The teaching of the parents does not exist (any more)'

Locational contexts can be expressed with a number of different constructions in Savosavo. In addition to the 'predicate-subject locational with an emphatic predicate' (38a) already discussed above, there is also the 'predicate-subject locational with a particle subject enclitic' (38b) as well as the 'subject-predicate locational' construction (38c). The S argument of all these locational constructions is in the Nominative case. However, as noted above, zero-coding is possible for the 'predicate-subject locational' with an emphatic predicate.

(38) Savosavo (Wegener 2008: 92, 208, 209)

    a. *Apoi   ata=e   te   lo   keva=**na***
       because here=EMPH EMPH DET.SG.M path=NOM
       'Because here (is) the road.'

    b. *ny-omata te=**lo***
       1SG-at   PART=3.SG.M.NOM
       'With me (is) it.' lit.: 'At me (is) it.'

c. *lo-va   sokasoka=**na** lo-va   kata   papale=la*
   3SG.M-GEN.M brush=NOM 3SG.M-GEN.M bushwards side=LOC.M
   'His brush is at his bushwards side.'

The data from the marked-S languages of the Pacific area are summarized in Table 4.4. Subjects of locational sentences are predominantly coded by the overt S-case (Nominative in Savosavo and Ajië, Absolutive in Nias), but in one of the Savosavo locational constructions they can also be zero-coded.[8] All languages of this region have – at least optionally – variation between negative and positive existential contexts. While this variation is always found in Nias, Ajië and Savosavo have two coding options for postive existentials – overt nominative case or zero-coding – but only one in negative contexts. Ajië negative existentials are always zero-coded, Savosavo on the other hand codes negative existentials with Nominative case.

language	S exist. (+)	S exist.(-)	S loc. pred.
Ajië	NOM/ACC	ACC	NOM
Nias	ABS	ERG	ABS
Savosavo	NOM/ACC	NOM	NOM/(ACC)

Table 4.4: Overview of the marking of existential and locational predication in the marked-S languages of the Pacific

4.8 Summary

The encoding of subjects in positive and negative existential predications as well as locational predications is summarized in Table 4.5. In locational predications, all languages allow for the marking of subjects with the overt S-case. In most languages, this is the only pattern available for this role. Languages that show variation in the encoding of existentials (either between positive or negative contexts, or simply have multiple coding options) may also exhibit the same variation in locationals (e.g. Nias and Savosavo). With existentials in a number of languages encoding the subject in the zero-case is at least one of the options. This is, for example, the case for North American Jamul Tiipay and Diegueño, Nilo-Saharan

---

[8] Remember that for the locationals only the positive context is included here, since no language has a variation between negative and positive locationals but not with existentials. Thus the Nias negative locational construction is not represented in the table.

4.8 Summary

Tennet and Turkana and all three Pacific languages. Variation in subject-marking between positive and negative existentials can be found in a small number of languages (for example Nias and Turkana). However, there is no clear directionality in the distribution of overt versus zero-coding between positive and negative contexts. Ajië, Nias, and Tennet use the zero-coded form in the negative contexts, while the positive contexts have overtly coded case-forms (at least as an option). In Turkana and Savosavo, overt marking is used in the negative context, while positive existentials can have zero-coded subjects. Since zero-coding of subjects is more commonly found with existentials than with locationals, the data to some extent support the claim that existentials exhibit a limited degree of grammatical relation marking (Payne 1997: 123).

language	S exist. (+)	S exist.(-)	S loc. pred.
Ajië	NOM/ACC	ACC	NOM
Arbore	NOM	-	-
Datooga	NOM	NOM	NOM
Diegueno	ACC	-	NOM
Gamo	-	-	NOM
Havasupai	NOM	-	NOM
Jamul Tiipay	ACC	-	NOM
K'abeena	NOM	NOM	NOM
Maa	NOM/ACC	ACC	NOM
Maidu	NOM	-	NOM
Mojave	NOM	NOM	NOM
Murle	NOM	-	NOM
Nandi	NOM	-	NOM
Nias	ABS	ERG	ABS
Oromo (Boraana)	-	-	NOM
Oromo (Harar)	emphatic subjet	-	NOM
Savosavo	NOM/ACC	NOM	NOM/ACC
Tennet	NOM/ACC	ACC	NOM
Turkana	NOM/ACC	NOM?	NOM
Wappo	NOM	NOM	NOM
Wolaytta	-	-	NOM
Yavapai	NOM	-	NOM
Zayse	NOM	-	NOM

Table 4.5: Overview of the marking of existential and locational predication

5 Emphatic subjects

5.1 Introduction

For the languages of East Africa, it has been repeatedly observed that discourse function plays a crucial role for case-marking of subjects. König (2008: 240–271) concludes that overt nominative markers in many of these languages are absent in pre-verbal position. More generally, she notes a tendency of all languages of North-Eastern Africa not to employ overt case-marking in this position. This tendency is referred to as the 'no case before the verb' rule by König. The Nilotic languages, for example, are predominantly verb-initial, thus the canonical position for all arguments is post-verbal. Whenever a subject argument is fronted – usually for discourse structure reasons – it will occur in the zero-coded form.

(1) Turkana (Nilotic; Kenya; Dimmendaal 1982: 390, 177)
    a. tɔ̀kɔ̀na ` nèg ` a:a,   ŋèsi `   e-los-ì   nà-wuyę̀
       now   here TOP he.ACC 3-go-ASP DIR-home
       'Now, HE goes home.'
    b. tɔ-rʊk-ɔ́-ʊ   ŋesì   k-ìpʊd-ɔ̀d   a-màna
       3-meet-EPEN-VEN he.NOM 3-trample-RES field.ACC
       'He found the field in a trampled state.'

Most grammars are vague on the exact function that this fronting of arguments fulfills. What seems to be common to all languages is that special emphasis is put on the fronted argument, hence, I refer to the context to be studied in this chapter as EMPHATIC SUBJECTS.[1]

In this chapter, I will investigate the marking of discourse-prominent subjects in marked-S languages. First, I give a very brief overview of the different patterns of interaction between the marking of discourse structure and case-marking, as well as a general overview (Section 5.2). Following this brief introduction, I will

---

[1] Remember that I use the term subject as a shorthand for the S argument of intransitive verbs plus whichever transitive argument is encoded in a parallel fashion in terms of the overt case-marking.

discuss the accounts offered for the absence of case-marking in emphatic contexts (Section 5.3). Next, I will discuss overt case-marking exclusively found on emphatic subjects, another pattern of interaction of the domains of case-marking and discourse structure, which can be analyzed as a very special instance of marked-S coding, though the languages in question are not typically included in the study of marked-nominative languages (Section 5.4). Afterwards, I will summarize the different patterns and point out the research questions that are of interest for this study (Section 5.5). The subsequent sections provide detailed information on how the individual languages of the Nilo-Saharan (Section 5.6) and Afro-Asiatic stocks (Section 5.7), as well as the Pacific (Section 5.8) and North American areas (Section 5.9) behave with respect to the interaction of case-marking and discourse structure. Finally, a summary of these data will be provided in Section 5.10.

5.2 Case-marking and discourse structure

Zero-coded emphatic subjects are not an exclusive feature of African marked-S languages. A similar structure can be found in some languages of the Pacific region. Also in the Pacific region, another opposite type of discourse-structure sensitive marked-S system exists: languages in which overt marking of the S argument is exclusively found in emphatic contexts. The discussion of this kind of marked-S system is commonly subsumed under the phenomenon of optional ergativity (McGregor & Verstraete 2010), even if the optional ergative marker is found on intransitive S. Further, case-marking does not distinguish between emphatic and non-emphatic contexts in a number of marked-S languages. These languages are mostly found in North America but some African languages are of this type as well.

The main focus of this chapter will be on the two patterns that distinguish between emphatic and non-emphatic subject arguments in terms of case-marking. For both systems, different explanations have been proposed on how the respective system arose. The two systems and proposed explanations are discussed in the subsequent sections (5.3 and 5.4). First, I will introduce the basic concepts of information structure in this section.

The term 'information structure' has been coined by Halliday (1967), but the study of this domain of grammar can be traced back to the classical works of Aristotle. Nowadays, information structure is often treated within the larger field of discourse analysis. It is concerned with the introduction and tracking of referents within a larger discourse and the formal means used for this purpose.

The whole domain of information structure is a field in which little consensus on the basic concepts or the meaning of specific terms appear to exist (Payne 1997: 261–276). In contrast, information structure is a field that is only rarely treated by linguists working on little described languages. Possibly as a result of this, typological work on discourse structures is still rarely carried out (Myhill 2001). The following discussion is meant to introduce the basic concepts of the study of information structure as well as to define the terminology used in this chapter.

The two concepts 'topic' and 'focus' are the most widely used types of discourse relations in the literature. The terms 'theme' and 'rheme' are often used instead for these concepts. Lambrecht (1996) for example dedicates a complete chapter of his book to each of the two concepts. TOPICS are generally understood to be the things that one is talking about, or formulated less vaguely, they have a high level of mental activation with the discourse participants and are repeatedly expressed as arguments within the discourse. As a result, topical elements are often expressed through very little overt material once they have been established. Pronominals are typical discourse representations of topics. If a language has the option to not overtly express an argument, topical elements are the prototypical candidates for this process (see also the discussion on the omission of arguments in Section 2.6.2). FOCUSED ELEMENTS, in contrast, are unexpected in the given context. They do not have to be mentioned in the previous discourse and typically have a low level of mental activation. Focused elements tend to be realized with more overt material (e.g. as full noun phrase rather than as pronoun). In more philosophical treatments, topics are often equated with the subject of a clause while focus is linked to the predicate. The following English examples are typical topic (2a) and focus (2b) structures.

(2)   a. *Speaking of **John**, he was involved in a car crash.*
      b. *It was **John** (not Susan) who was involved in a car crash.*

The broad notions of topic and focus are often subdivided into subcategories, which might have quite different properties with respect to their linguistic expression. A special kind of topic is the so-called 'contrastive topic' (Lambrecht 1996: 291–296). This type of construction is used in cases where more than one possible discourse topic has been established and after referring to one of them, reference to another of these topical elements is made. This switch of topic is usually marked overtly, but usually no more overt material is used than is necessary to establish the reference. In languages that have gender-specific pronouns, for example, the switch between a male and a female topical participant is transparent through the use of the respective pronoun. In addition, topics are some-

5 *Emphatic subjects*

times classified with respect to their position in the clause. One cross-linguistic generalization that is often repeated is that "old information precedes new information" (Ward & Birner 2001: 119). However, this is just a tendency. Apart from the observation that topics (i.e. old information) can also be left out from overt realization since they are already known, a number of languages have a special topic construction, the so-called 'afterthought topic'. In this construction the topical element, which has not been prominently realized in a proposition, is added after the proposition has been made as a sort of addition to the clause into which it is not syntactically integrated.

Focus constructions are often distinguished by the grammatical status of the element in focus (Lambrecht 1996: 226–235). The first type of focus construction is 'predicate focus'. In this situation a topic (most likely a person) is established within the discourse and some additional information on this participant is given. 'Argument focus' constructions, in contrast, are used if what happened is already known but there is some uncertainty or misunderstanding about the involved participant(s), as exemplified by (2b) above. Furthermore, an entire sentence can consist of new information, in which case one speaks of 'sentence focus'. A different terminology for sentences like this is 'thetic', which is contrasted with 'categorial' sentences (Sasse 1987). In addition, the term 'contrastive focus' is also used for constructions in which the focused element is opposed to another element of the same syntactic category. All of the focus constructions introduced above can be used contrastively. This type of focus corrects an assumption that the listener had about an event (concerning the predicate, argument(s) or entire proposition respectively).

5.3 Zero-coded emphatic subjects

As noted above, the absence of nominative case-marking in pre-verbal position is one of the signature features of the African marked-nominative languages. However, this pattern is not found exclusively in this region of the world. A similar pattern is also found in some languages of the Pacific region.

The following are some examples of languages in which the emphatic S is not marked for case in the same way as the non-emphatic S. The (a) example is always the one with the emphatic subject while in the (b) example no emphasis is put on the subject. In the Nilotic languages Nandi (3) and Turkana (4) emphatic subjects are in the zero-coded accusative case and occur in pre-verbal position. In non-emphatic contexts, on the other hand, subjects are in the nominative case-form, which has a different tonal pattern and is derived from the accusative form of a noun. The Western Malayo-Polynesian language Nias behaves in a similar fashion. When S or P arguments occur in the non-canonical pre-verbal position, they are in the Unmutated form (5a) while in post-verbal position they would be in the Mutated form (5b). The fronting of an argument is a communicative means employed to express the importance in discourse of the respective argument.

(3) Nandi (Nilotic; Kenya; Creider & Creider 1989: 124, 125)

    a. ***kipe:t***   kó   kê:r-éy   la:kwé:t
       Kibet.ACC PART see-IPFV child.ACC
       'KIBET is looking at the child.'

    b. kè:r-éy ***kípe:t***   la:kwé:t
       see-IPFV Kibet.NOM child.ACC
       'Kibet is looking at the child.'

(4) Turkana (Nilotic; Kenya; Dimmendaal 1982: 82)

    a. ***ŋa-atuk`***    ***ŋa-arey`***   màke`e-yakà-sɪ a-yɔŋ`
       N_N.PL-COW.ACC N_N.PL-two.ACC self   3-be-PL   1SG.ACC
       'Two cows is all I have.'

    b. a-yɔŋ` e-yakà-sɪ ***ŋa-àtùk***    ***ŋa-àrèy***    màke`
       1SG.ACC 3-be-PL   N_N.PL-COW.NOM N_N.PL-two.NOM self
       'I only have two cows.'

(5) Nias (Sundic; Indonesia; Brown 2001: 262)

    a. ***si'o*** hö'ö ma+i-taru-'ö   ba danö
       stick DIST PRF=3SG.RLS-plant-TR LOC ground.MUT
       'That stick he planted in the ground.'

    b. i-taru-'ö   ***zi'o***   hö'ö ba danö
       PRF-3SG.RLS.plant-TR stick.MUT DIST LOC ground.MUT
       'He planted that stick in the ground.'

There are two types of explanation for this alternation in case-marking with emphatic subjects. The first explanation argues that the emphatic S argument is in a structural position in which it cannot be assigned the regular S-case. The second approach is only suitable for those languages that mark the emphatic S argument by some other device, e.g. a focus-marker. For the languages of this type the occurrence of the S-case-marker might simply be blocked by the presence of another marker on the S argument and not by its structural position.

5 Emphatic subjects

The first explanation – i.e. the one claiming that emphatic subjects are outside of the domain in which they can be assigned S-case – comes in a more specific and a more general version. The more specific variant analyzes the whole structure as a biclausal cleft-construction while the second analysis more generally states that the emphatic argument is outside the domain of case-assignment.[2] I will first turn to the more specific version of the structural explanation, which I will refer to as the CLEFT ANALYSIS. It states that sentences with an emphatic subject have a structure similar the the one exemplified by the English cleft-construction in (6).

(6) *It is John who lost his wallet.*

The whole structure of the clause with an emphatic subject argument is interpreted as actually consisting of two clauses. The first clause, i.e. the cleft, only consists of the logical subject of the entire structure. However, it is not realized as a grammatical subject but as a predicate nominal. The second clause is a headless subject relative clause modifying the predicate nominal. This analysis predicts that since the logical subject does actually function as a predicate nominal, the emphatic S will have the same marking as a predicate nominal in the respective language. As has been shown in Chapter 3, many marked-S languages indeed employ the zero-coded form for predicate nominals. This analysis of emphatic subjects as biclausal structures is put forward by König (2008) for African marked-S languages. Also Payne (1997: 278–281) discusses cleft-constructions as a source for focus-constructions in general.

This line of argumentation can either be interpreted as a synchronic analysis or merely as the historical source of the modern construction. In either way, this analysis is only plausible if a language meets the following typological requirements (or met them at the point in time, when the emphatic S construction developed):

1. The formal marking of predicate nominals and emphatic subjects must be the same.

2. The language must allow for nominal predications to lack an overt copula (or an additional marker, that functions as a copula must be present in the construction).

---

[2] The more general analysis of the emphatic argument being outside the domain of case-assignment also captures the more specific cleft-analysis.

5.3 Zero-coded emphatic subjects

3. The language must either allow for relative clauses to be formed without an overt relative marker, or such a marker that introduces relative clauses must be present in the constructions.

These requirements are easy to check as a synchronic claim. However, as a diachronic claim this check is not always possible. In addition, there will be languages that meet only some of these criteria, that one would nevertheless want to analyze in a parallel fashion.

For some languages this analysis appears to be quite promising, since they meet all requirements. With regard to Tennet, Randal (1998: 261) strongly argues in favor of an analysis of emphatic statements like (7a) as structures consisting of a predicate nominal plus a headless relative clause. The so-called 'associative marker' (AM) linking the predicate nominal to the relative clause is also used with other nominal modifiers such as adjectives. Randal also states that the same utterance can be made in the longer variant in (7b), making the nominal predication more transparent. However, this approach does not explain why in the fuller version of the nominal predication both arguments are in the Accusative case. From the description of nominal predication in Tennet, one would expect the subject argument of the nominal predication (i.e. 'Lokuli') to be in the Nominative case.

(7) Tennet (Surmic; Sudan; Randal 1998: 261)

a. ***lokúli*** *cí á-rúh lohâm*
Lokuli AM IPFV-beat Loham
'It is Lokuli who is beating Loham.'

b. ***lokúli*** *néné cí á-rúh lohâm*
Lokuli the_one AM IPFV-beat Loham
'Lokuli is the one who is beating Loham'

A good argument for the status of the initial noun as a predicate nominal is provided by Arbore. In Arbore there is a special case-form used only for predicate nominals – the so-called 'Predicative' case – which is also found on emphatic subjects (8a), while non-emphatic subjects receive standard Nominative case (8b). Also there is a reduced amount of morphological marking found on the verb in the emphatic context. For instance, the so-called 'pre-verbal selector' (PVS) is missing, a feature that is also associated with verbs in relative clauses (Hayward 1984: 315).

5 Emphatic subjects

(8) Arbore (Eastern Cushitic; Ethiopia; Hayward 1984: 113, 114)
   a. *farawa   zéħe*
      horse.PRED died
      '(A) horse died.' (answer to the constituent question 'What died?')
   b. *farawé   ʔí-y   zaħate*
      horse.NOM PVS-3SG die.3SG.F
      '(A) horse died.'

A more general structural explanation for the lack of case-marking on emphatic S-arguments is provided by Donohue & Brown (1999: 60) based on Nias. They state that "when an argument receives a degree of pragmatic salience, and appears focused or topicalized, then it is beyond the scope of the case-marking system." The argument that emphatic subjects are outside of the domain in which they can be assigned case by the verb (or any other node that in a given syntactic theory would assign case to the subject argument) also comprises the cleft-construction analysis, since in a biclausal structure an element in the first clause (i.e. the cleft) is outside of the domain in which the verb of the second clause can assign any case to it. However, it is not necessary to assume that the verb and logical subject are in different clauses for this more general analysis. It is sufficient for the emphatic subject to be located on a higher level of projection. However, because a claim like this presents a very abstract explanation, it is hard to confirm or disprove.

At least for Tennet, there can be made a clear case that it is not simply the pre-verbal position that prohibits Nominative case-marking on an argument, since there are also pre-verbal arguments with Nominative case-marking, as example (9b) illustrates. Other languages may of course behave differently in this respect, and one could still argue that the logical subject in (9a) and (b) are located in different structural positions.

(9) Tennet (Surmic; Sudan; Randal 1998: 261)
   a. *lokúli cí á-rúh lohâm*
      Lokuli AM IPFV-beat Loham
      'It is Lokuli who is beating Loham.'
   b. *íjja zin wála-i í-kíya*
      and then PN-NOM IPFV-come
      'And then Crow came.'

Further, there is a whole different line of argumentation to explain the lack of S-case-marking on emphatic subjects that could be used in some languages.

Instead of disallowing S-case-marking for structural (i.e. syntactic) reasons, morphology seems to be the important factor in this scenario. In the languages to which this explanation applies, the emphatic status of the subject argument is not only encoded by its position in the clause but by a special marker of discourse structure. The occurrence of this marker apparently blocks other markers such as overt S-case-markers. However, these languages do not have zero-coded emphatic subjects in the same sense as the languages previously discussed since emphatic subjects are overtly marked, though not for their role as the subject argument of a clause. The Savosavo example in (10) illustrates this pattern (also see the discussion of Savosavo in Section 5.8).

(10) Savosavo (Solomons East Papuan; Solomon Islands; Wegener 2008: 221)
pa poi=e te lo *mane=la*
one thing=EMPH EMPH 3SG.M.GEN/DET.SG.M side=LOC.M
'One thing (is) at its/the side.'

5.4 Overtly coded emphatic subjects

The phenomenon of optional case-marking and more specifically optional ergativity has gained recent prominence in linguistic work (see McGregor & Verstraete 2010). It has been noted that case-markers are sometimes dropped in syntactic context in which they normally would be expected in a language.[3] The conditions for the dropping of overt case-marking often relate to information structure. Many languages which show this optional type of case-marking only employ the overt marking when the relevant constituent is in focus, while the marker is usually omitted otherwise. However, often there are additional contexts in which the markers can occur. Special reference has been made to the optional nature of ergative case-marking in particular. For some languages it is noted that the optional ergative case is sometimes also used for intransitive S arguments. Thus, the languages would be better described as having optional marked-nominative case-marking. However, because of the strong association between overt marking of agents and the label 'ergative' that has been put forward by Dixon (1979), the term 'optional ergative' has stuck. Another reason might be that the overt markers are only rarely found in intransitive clauses because in these contexts a need for disambiguation of the participants arises far

---

[3] The influence of optional case-marking on the overall frequency of individual case-forms have already been briefly discussed in Section 2.6.3.

5 Emphatic subjects

less frequently. It is in such contexts that optional ergative markers are often found in. This practice is for example expressed in the following quote:

> I have labeled the affix -*ro* [...] as an ergative marker. It is true that it only occurs on subjects of transitive verbs. However, it does not occur on all subjects of transitive verbs [...]. As in many PNG languages, it seems to occur most commonly where there is potential ambiguity as to which noun phrase is the subject. (Clifton 1997: 22)

Despite this claim that in Kaki Ae the relevant marker occurs only on transitive subjects, Clifton (1997) provides some examples in which the same marker occurs on intransitive subjects as will be demonstrated in the following.

Languages that have a marked-nominative system only in specific contexts, such as focusing or disambiguation, are especially common in the Pacific region. In his survey on participant marking in the so-called Papuan languages (a cover term for non-Austronesian languages of Oceania),Whitehead (1981) lists Siroi, Waskia, Kunimaipa, and Nabak as having an optional S+A marker in combination with zero-coded P arguments.[4] Further, the descriptions of Kaki Ae, Eipo and Yawuru suggest these languages are also of this special type marked-nominative languages that employ overt marking only for emphatic subjects. The pattern is exemplified in the following. The Waskia sentences in (11) demonstrate the alternation between emphatic contexts, in which the marker *ke* follows the subject (11a), and non-emphatic contexts, which lack this marker (11b). The Kaki Ae clause chain in (12) demonstrates the marking of emphatic and non-emphatic subjects. While the mother is marked with the marker -*ro* (glossed as Ergative by Clifton) the noun *aua* 'children' that is the subject in the following clauses does not receive this marking. Thus, the status of the mother is marked as a participant that has not been present in the previous discourse.

(11) Waskia (Kowan; Papua New Guinea, Karkar Island; Ross 1978: 37, 17)

    a. ***nu**   **ke**   taleng duap*
       3SG.PRO NOM policeman
       'He is a policemen (i.e. not someone else)'

    b. ***aga bawa**   taleng duap*
       my brother policeman
       'My brother is a policeman.'

---

[4] Instead of the labels S and A, Whitehead (1981) uses the terms 'actor' and 'agent'.

(12) Kaki Ae (Eleman; Papua New Guinea; Clifton 1997: 52)
naora-**ro** loea-ra-kape naora-**ro** u-ra-ha luera-ma aua
mother-ERG return-IRR-and mother-ERG call-IRR-3SSBJ then-LOC child
erahe uriri-RDP-isani naora kai wä'ï-isani-pe ko"ara oporo hu'a
3PL run-CONT-and mother to go_down-and-? another wood block
fua-isani koi'ara ë'a rea-vere katlain   ekakau   himiri fua-isani
carry-and another that 3SG-POSS fishing_line something many carry-and
a-isani-pe ava-isani
get-and-? go_up-and

'The mother returns, the mother calls, and the children run down to the mother, some carry blocks of wood, some carry fishing line and many other things, they get them and go up.'

While this general pattern of marking (intransitive) subjects only in contrastive or emphatic contexts is quite widespread in the Pacific region (also extending to some Australian languages), the system is analyzed quite differently by different linguists. For all languages for which I could get information on, this structure, the variation between absence and presence of the marker is influenced by information structure. The languages exhibiting the system described in this section employ markers that have both discourse structure and case-marking properties. The linguists working on the relevant languages vary in assigning the pattern to either the domain of grammatical relations or pragmatic discourse relations. These two domains of grammatical marking are often difficult to tease apart (Payne 1997: 276). Furthermore, there is often a strong correlation between a certain discourse status with a certain syntactic role. Therefore, it is no surprise that historical relations between the two types of markers are pretty common. It has already been discussed that markers of discourse relations have been proposed as a source for marked-S systems (cf. Section 1.5.2). It thus might be the case that the respective markers in the Pacific languages just presented are currently in a transitional phase from one of the domains to the other. Some authors note that the optional (or focal) nominative marker in these languages is cognate to an ergative marker in related languages. However, the direction of change cannot be clearly established on this basis, since the ergative stage of related languages could either be more conservative or more innovative than the pattern of the language that does not use the marker to unambiguously encode grammatical relations. For other languages, both directions of change have been argued for: from discourse marking to case-marking and vice versa. Shibatani (1991) discusses the grammaticalization of marking of a discourse category into

5 Emphatic subjects

the marking of grammatical relations, taking the example of topics and subjects. A change from case-marking to discourse marking, on the other hand, has been suggested, e.g. for the Australian language Jingulu (Pensalfini 1999).

The in-depth investigation of the focal marked-nominative type according to the parameters of this study is particularly difficult. For most languages only a few odd examples of subject arguments receiving overt marking are given. These examples are usually accompanied by a mere impressionistic explanation of the factors leading to the presence of the marker (if any). From these few examples it is not possible to deduce in which of the contexts investigated in this study (other than basic (in)transitive clauses) the marker could or could not occur, given the relevant argument is emphatic. Therefore, the languages of this type will only be discussed in this chapter of the study, due to the missing data on for example emphatic existential subjects.

5.5 Research questions

The subsequent sections will provide an overview of the marking of emphatic subjects in marked-S languages. The languages can be classified as using one of three patterns (or a combination of these patterns). These patterns are the following:

1. Emphatic subjects do not receive S-case-marking.

2. Only emphatic subjects receive a special marker for the S-case.

3. Subjects receive S-case-marking independent of their discourse status.

For each language of the sample, I investigate which of the three patterns are found. Pattern 1 and 2 have been discussed in greater detail in the two previous sections. In this section, I will give examples of the all of these possibilities of encoding emphatic subjects.

Pattern 1 is exemplified by the Boraana Oromo sentence in (13). While the first clause demonstrates the prototypical marking of subjects via Nominative case *jaldees-ii*, the subject of the second clause (*kinniis*) is focused and does not receive the Nominative suffix. Instead the so-called 'linker clitic' follows the emphatic noun.

(13) Oromo (Boraana) (Eastern Cushitic; Ethiopia; Stroomer 1995: 122, 123)
Amm=oo jaldees-ii   hin-dabs-an-ne   kinniis=aa
But=LIN baboon-NOM NEG-win-MID-NEG.PST, bee=LIN
dabs-at-e
win-MID-3.M.PST
'But the baboon did not overcome the bees, it was the bees that won.'

The proposed origin of structures like this as cleft-constructions has been discussed before. Data on the marking of predicate nominals and the possibility of having zero-copulas in nominals predications will be provided in Section 5.10. Also, many of the languages with zero-coded emphatic subjects have in common that while their canonical word order is verb-initial, emphatic subjects (or other element on which special emphasis is put) are placed before the verb. Therefore, in this chapter's summary I will also note the basic word order(s) of each language discussed here. Examples of this strategy have already been discussed in Section 5.3 in some detail.

The second pattern of case-marking on emphatic subjects is only found among the languages of the Pacific region.[5] In some of the languages of this region, emphatic subjects receive a special marker while morphological marking of grammatical relations is absent in other contexts. This pattern is exemplified by Waskia. In this language the marker *ke* follows after subject arguments that are focused among other functions (14a) while non-focused counterparts of these sentences the subject NP does not receive case-marking (14b).

(14) Waskia (Kowan; Papua New Guinea, Karkar Island; Ross 1978: 37, 17)

    a. *nu   ke   taleng duap*
        3SG.PRO NOM policeman

       'He is a policemen (i.e. not someone else)'

    b. *aga bawa   taleng duap*
       my brother policeman

       'My brother is a policeman.'

---

[5] Special forms only found with emphatic subjects are more widespread. Bruil (2014: 158–163) discusses the subject-marker *-bi* in Ecuadorian Siona (Tucanoan). The marker is used with focused subjects, but there might be additional uses, such as the disambiguation of arguments. Similar systems can be found in other languages of the same area. However, Ecuadorian Siona also has overt case-markers for (some types of) objects (Bruil 2014: 163–169), and thus does not fall under the definition of a marked-S language. Yet it is very likely that languages with a pattern similar to the one found in the Pacific languages discussed in this section can be found elswhere.

5 Emphatic subjects

The final pattern of interaction between case-marking and discourse structure is the absence of any interaction between the two systems. In other words subject-like arguments are marked with the overt S-case irrespective of their discourse structure relation.

This pattern is found in a number of languages of my sample. In Wappo, focused as well as non-focused subjects receive the Nominative ending in -*i*. When the subject is focused the case-marked noun is followed by the focus-marker *lakhuh* (15a). In sentences with non-focused subjects, this marker is not found (15b).

(15) Wappo (Wappo-Yukian; California; Thompson, Park & Li 2006: 79, Li et al. 1977: 92)

    a. *ce šaw-i* **lakhuh** *nuh-kheʔ*
        that bread-NOM FOC steal-PASS
        'It's the bread that got stolen.'

    b. *mayiš-i mačuʔ-kheʔ*
        corn-NOM ash_roast-PASS
        'The corn has been ash-roasted.'

Another language in which the case-marking is identical for emphatic and non-emphatic subjects is K'abeena (Eastern Cushitic). Unlike in Wappo, the discourse prominence of the subject (or other argument or adjunct) is not encoded by overt morphological marking. This is rather achieved by putting a noun phrase into the position immediately preceding the verb.

(16) K'abeena (Eastern Cushitic; Ethiopia; Crass 2005: 327, 104)

    a. *bokku* **womb^u** *'ijaaránu-r^a heccʼi*
        house.ACC K'abeena.NOM build.IPFV.3SG.M-TMP precede.CVB.3SG.M
        gordanna fiilan^u
        tree_trunk_for_wall.ACC split.IPFV.3SG.M
        'When the K'abeena build a house, they first split the tree trunks for the wall.'

    b. *kamaal^i 'adbaareen^i 'ama'nanu-ba*
        Kamal.NOM familiar.LOC believe.IPFV.3SG.M-NEG
        'Kamal does not believe in familiar spirits.'
        original translation: 'Kamal glaubt nicht an Schutzgeister.'

The following sections provide an in-depth study of the marking of emphatic subjects in marked-S languages organized by areal and genealogical grouping into the Nilo-Saharan (5.6), Afro-Asiatic (5.7) Pacific (5.8) and North-West-American languages (5.9). In the final section, the data is summarized and combined with additional information on the marking of nominal predications and basic word order for each language (5.10).

5.6 Nilo-Saharan

Most of the Nilo-Saharan marked-S languages have a verb-initial basic word order. Fronting of an argument to pre-verbal position leads to the loss of any overt case-marking. König (2008) uses the slogan 'no case before the verb' to allude to this property of these languages. The marked-S languages of the Nilo-Saharan stock are almost completely uniform with regard to this expression of emphatic S arguments. Minor variations can be found in the Agar dialect of Dinka, which has a topic-initial rather then verb-initial word order, according to Andersen (1991). Furthermore, in Tennet two types of pre-verbal subjects can be found, one with (zero) Accusative case-marking and the other one with regular Nominative case.

First, I will present the prototypical Nilo-Saharan system in which emphatic S arguments occur in pre-verbal position and are in the zero-coded accusative case, while non-emphatic post-verbal S arguments receive overt nominative case-marking. This system is found in Datooga (17), Turkana (18) and Nandi (20); the (a) examples demonstrate the emphatic construction while the (b) examples are non-emphatic contexts. Maa behaves in the same fashion (19).

(17) Datooga (Nilotic; Tanzania; Kiessling 2007: 183)

  a. *búunèe   súurjá   àa nì-yîm   dàbí tá-ɲàwá*
     people.ACC others.ACC TOP SBJ3.PRF-put_on weapons.ACC.CS-3PL.POSS
     ŋæ̀æɲi̥
     down
     'Other people had put down their weapons.'

  b. *gà-bìıktá* **qáarèemàŋgà sùurjá**   *qòo*
     SBJ3-return youths.NOM   others.NOM home
     'Other youths went home.'

(18) Turkana (Nilotic; Kenya; Dimmendaal 1982: 82)

  a. *ŋa-atuk`    ŋa-arey`   màke`e-yakà-sɪ a-yɔŋ`*
     N_N.PL-cow.ACC N_N.PL-two.ACC self 3-be-PL   1SG.ACC
     'Two cows is all I have.'

5 Emphatic subjects

    b. *a-yɔŋ`  e-yakà-sı ŋa-àtùk      ŋa-àrèy      màke`*
        1SG.ACC 3-be-PL N_N.PL-COW.NOM N_N.PL-two.NOM self
        'I only have two cows.'

(19) Maa (Nilotic; Kenya; König 2006: 667, 666 after Tucker & Mpaayei 1955)
     a. *en-tító   na-dɔ́l   nınyέ*
        F.SG-girl.ACC REL.F.SG-see 3SG.ACC
        'It is the girl who sees him.'
     b. *έ-dɔ́l-íta   ɔl-**kítéŋ**   en-kɔ́ítóí*
        3SG-see-PROG MSG-OX.NOM F.SG-road.ACC
        'The ox sees the road.'

(20) Nandi (Nilotic; Kenya; Creider & Creider 1989: 124, 125)
     a. *kipe:t kó   kê:r-éy   la:kwé:t*
        Kibet PART see-IPFV child.ACC
        'KIBET is looking at the child.'
     b. *kè:r-éy   **kípe:t**   la:kwé:t*
        see-IPFV Kibet.NOM child.ACC
        'Kibet is looking at the child.'

In addition to the structure demonstrated in (20) above, Creider & Creider (1989: 124–125) discuss a second type of topicalization for Nandi, namely topic final sentences. The structure demonstrated above is referred to as 'topic fronting'. However, from Creider & Creider's (1989: 150) description of the use of this topic-final construction, it seems clear that this is rather a focus construction in the terminology introduced in Section 5.2. Unlike in the construction with the fronted S argument, S arguments in the topic-final structure keep their Nominative tonal shape (21).

(21) Nandi (Creider & Creider 1989: 150)
     *kè:r=éy kipe:t   **kípro:no***
     see-IPFV Kibet.ACC Kiprono.NOM
     'Kiprono sees Kibet.'

In the Agar dialect of Dinka, basically the same situation is found as in the other Nilo-Saharan languages. Pre-verbal subjects do not receive Nominative case-marking (22a, b), which they would receive in post-verbal position. The difference from the languages described previously is that there does not seem to be a verb-initial basic word order in Dinka (or at least not anymore). Andersen (1991) analyzes Agar Dinka as a topic-first language. That means that whichever element occurs in clause-initial position is the topic, usually this is the S or A argument. Only if some other argument is the topic of the discourse, like the P argument occurring sentence-initially in example (22c), the subject is marked with the overt Nominative case. In addition, verbal agreement is with the topic rather then the subject (Andersen 1991).

(22) Dinka (Agar Dialect) (Nilotic; Sudan; Andersen 1991: 272, 273)

a. *lḁy   ạ̀-kuḁaŋ*
animal.ACC DECL-swim
'The animal is swimming.'

b. *lḁy   ạ̀-nḁk   raḁan*
animal.ACC DECL-kill person.ACC
'The animal is killing the person.'

c. *raḁan   ạ̀-nḁk   **lạ̀y***
person.ACC DECL-kill animal.NOM
'The animal is killing THE PERSON.'

A different variation of the Nilo-Saharan pattern 'no case before the verb' is found in Tennet. This language distinguishes between two different S-initial emphatic structures. The first construction behaves like the examples discussed before, as the fronted subject is in the zero-coded Accusative case (23a). Randal (1998) explicitly states that this construction is an instance of clefting and the fronted subject is part of a nominal predication. The other construction used to put emphasis on an argument also involves fronting of this argument before the verb. However, this construction is not a cleft, as can be seen by the lack of the Associative Marker (AM), which among other function introduces relative clauses. Also, the Nominative case-marking is retained if the subject is fronted using this construction (23b).

(23) Tennet (Surmic; Sudan; Randal 1998: 261)

a. ***lokúli***   *cí á-rúh   lohâm*
Lokuli.ACC AM IPFV-beat Loham.ACC
'It is Lokuli who is beating Loham.'

b. *íjja zin   **wála-i**   í-kíya*
and then PN-NOM IPFV-come
'And then Crow came.'

Table 5.1 summarizes the marking of emphatic subjects in the Nilo-Saharan marked-S languages. All languages use overt Nominative case-marking for non-emphatic subject arguments. For emphatic subjects, all languages have at least one construction that marks this argument with the zero-coded Accusative case. Tennet and Nandi have different constructions that can be employed to encode emphatic subjects, so that these arguments are either in the zero-coded Accusative or in the overtly coded Nominative case. Further, the marking of the predicate nominal (Chapterřefnompred) coincides with the predominant pattern of marking emphatic subjects for all languages. This supports the cleft-analysis of these structures to some extent.

language	non-emphatic S	emphatic S	predicate nominal
Datooga	NOM	ACC	ACC
Dinka (Agar)	NOM	ACC	-
Nandi	NOM	ACC/NOM	ACC
Tennet	NOM	ACC/NOM	ACC
Turkana	NOM	ACC	ACC

Table 5.1: Marking of emphatic S arguments in the Nilo-Saharan marked-S languages

5.7 Afro-Asiatic

In the Afro-Asiatic languages, there is no uniform pattern for emphatic contexts. There are some languages that use cleft-structures for focusing, and thus use the same case-form on the emphatic S as on predicate nominals, whether this is the zero-coded form or not. In other languages, however, emphatic subjects use the nominative case-form, differently from the case-marking used for predicate nominals.

A cleft-strategy for emphatic subjects is used in Boraana and Harara Oromo as well as in Arbore. In Boraana Oromo, the so-called 'linker' (functioning as a Genitive, among other uses) attaches to focused constituents. The range of functions of this marker is pretty wide; one of them is to introduce relative clauses. This makes a cleft-analysis of this structure very plausible. Subjects which are focused via the linker precede their cleft-sentence and are zero-coded for case (24). Harar Oromo behaves similarly: emphatic A arguments do not receive Nominative case-marking. Instead they receive some other marking, which consists of the lengthening of their final vowel and attaching the (non-obligatory) suffix '-*túu*.[6] In this construction the agreement on the verb is invariably third person masculine (Owens 1985: 108). This indicates that the logical subject does not function as the syntactic subject in these contexts and is possibly located outside of the clause containing the verb.

In Arbore, emphatic S arguments are in the Predicative case (26a). In this language, it is thus clear that those elements are predicate nominals. This in turn strengthens the cleft hypothesis, as already noted in Section 5.3. Also note that the verb does not agree with the subject in this construction (Hayward 1984: 113–114), indicating that those clauses are probably not simply derived from their counterparts with unmarked information structure (26b).

(24) Oromo (Boraana) (Eastern Cushitic; Ethiopia; Stroomer 1995: 122, 123)
 Amm=oo jaldees-ii hin-dabs-an-ne **kinniis=aa**
 But=LIN baboon-NOM NEG-win-MID-NEG.PST, bee=LIN
 dabs-at-e
 win-MID-3M.PST
 'But the baboon did not overcome the bees, it was the bees that won.'

(25) Oromo (Harar) (Eastern Cushitic; Ethiopia; Owens 1985: 108)
 makiináa tiyyá-a díim-tuu
 car my.FOC red-F
 'It is my car that is red.'

(26) Arbore (Eastern Cushitic; Ethiopia; Hayward 1984: 113, 114)
 a. ***farawa*** *zéħe*
  horse.PRED died
  '(A) horse died.' (answer to the constituent question 'What died?')
 b. ***farawé*** *ʔí-y zaħate*
  horse.NOM PVS-3SG die.3SG.F
  '(A) horse died.'

No difference in case-marking of emphatic and non-emphatic subjects seems to exist in Gamo and K'abeena. The details of information-structure marking in Gamo are interpreted differently by different scholars. The main problem is probably the different use of terminology, which is not uncommon in the domain of information structure (Payne 1997: 262). What Hompó (1990: 359–360) refers to

---

[6] The diacritic before the affix indicates a tonal change of the stem.

5 Emphatic subjects

as 'focused elements' are moved to sentence initial position. This position is also the canonical position of the subject. Sentence-initial as well as non-sentence-initial subjects (with other constituents in 'focus') are marked with the Nominative case-marker. In contrast, Taylor (1994: 222) claims that in standard SOV order it is the object that is focused, and that altering the order to OSV results in subject focus. He also finds no case-marking alternations between the different word orders (27). Given that Hompo analyses the clause initial position as the canonical subject position, her focused elements can probably be understood as discourse topics, an analysis that would be compatible with Taylor's analysis.

The situation in K'abeena resembles the one described for Gamo by Taylor. Focused arguments immediately precede the verb, where they receive the same case-marking as in unfocused position (Crass 2005: 327). There is also the emphatic suffix -n^u (Crass 2005: 256), though the interaction between this suffix and the word order alternations is not discussed by Crass. The data shows that both subjects immediately precede the verb (28a) and S arguments marked with the emphatic affix (28b) are in the Nominative case.

(27) Gamo (Omotic; Ethiopia; Taylor 1994: 222)

    a. *para   č'abo-i   yides*
       horse.ACC Chabo-NOM see.PRF.3SG.M
       'It was Chabo who saw a horse.'

    b. *č'abo-i   para   yides*
       Chabo-NOM horse.ACC see.PRF.3SG.M
       'Chabo saw a horse.'

(28) K'abeena (Eastern Cushitic; Ethiopia; Crass 2005: 327, 256)

    a. *diini-'ne   wakk'eeccu **k'aricc^u** mazaaran^u*
       religion.GEN.1PL.POSS path.ACC   god.NOM prepare.IPFV.3SG.M
       'It is God who prepares the path of our religion.'
       original translation: 'Den Weg unserer Religion bereitet Gott.'

    b. *'áni-'n^u gorru   'ataalaamm^i*
       1SG.NOM-EMPH hunger.ACC be_able.IPFV.1SG
       'When it comes to me, I can cope with hunger well.'
       original translation: 'Was mich betrifft, ich kann Hunger gut ertragen.'

An overview of discourse-motivated marking in the Afro-Asiatic marked-S languages is presented in Table 5.2. Gamo and K'abeena do not use any case-marking in the emphatic context that diverges from non-emphatic subjects. They employ the regular Nominative case, and thus a different case-form than with predicate nominals. Another form of overt marking of emphatic subjects is found in Arbore. Instead of using the Nominative case, the Predicative case is employed. This case is otherwise used to encode predicate nominals, and thus Arbore is a good example of the cleft-strategy to encode emphatic subjects. Boraana and Harar Oromo use Accusative nouns to encode emphatic subjects. In both languages the relevant construction attaches additional material to the emphatic noun. In the Boraana dialect, this material (the so-called 'linker') is used to connect nouns to relative clauses that modify them, among other functions. This supports the cleft analysis of this structure.

language	non-emphatic S	emphatic S	predicate nominal
Arbore	NOM	PRED	PRED
Gamo	NOM	NOM	ACC
K'abeena	NOM	NOM	ACC
Oromo (Boraana)	NOM	ACC+LIN	ACC
Oromo (Harar)	NOM	FOC	ACC

Table 5.2: Marking of emphatic S arguments in the Afro-Asiatic marked-S languages

5.8 Pacific

The languages of the Pacific region exhibit the most diversity in the interaction between case-marking and discourse structure in my sample. Ajië and Nias behave similarly to the Nilo-Saharan languages. In both languages, discourse-prominent arguments are fronted to pre-verbal position and do not receive case-marking. In Savosavo, the situation is a bit more complex. Subjects marked with the so-called 'emphatic marker' do not receive their usual Nominative case-marking and also occur in clause initial position. However, there are also instances in which Nominative case-marking is found on subjects that have the same discourse status properties as the emphatically-marked subjects but that lack the emphatic marker. Further, there are a number of languages in this area that only mark subjects that are in some prominent discourse relation with an overt marker. These systems are usually not treated as proper case-marking systems, but most grammar writers acknowledge that the relevant marker is found with subject arguments only (or at least predominantly).

5 Emphatic subjects

Nias basic word order is verb-initial. To put special emphasis on an argument, it can be fronted to pre-verbal position – this construction is analyzed as encoding both topic or focus function by Donohue & Brown (1999: 60). In this position, all arguments take the Unmutated nominal forms. Thus, if the fronted argument corresponds to an argument that would be in the Mutated form of a noun in a basic clause, the case-marking will be dropped in emphatic contexts (29). Ajië is also verb-initial in its basic word order. The preposition *na* marks S and A arguments (30). This marker does not appear on S or A arguments in pre-verbal position.[7]

(29) Nias (Sundic; Indonesia; Brown 2001: 262)

    a. ***si'o*** *hö'ö ma+i-taru-'ö ba danö*
       stick DIST PRF=3SG.RLS-plant-TR LOC ground.MUT
       'That stick he planted in the ground.'

    b. *i-taru-'ö zi'o hö'ö ba danö*
       PRF-3SG.RLS.plant-TR stick.MUT DIST LOC ground.MUT
       'He planted that stick in the ground.'

(30) Ajië (Oceanic; New Caledonia; Lichtenberk 1978: 111 after de la Fontinelle 1976: 313)

    a. *na kuru **na** tawa*
       3SG sleep NOM dog
       'The dog sleeps.'

    b. ***tawa*** *(we) na kuru*
       dog ('pause') 3SG sleep
       'As for the dog, it sleeps.'

In Savosavo, on the other hand, the basic word order is SOV when constituents are realized as full NPs, a situation that, however, seldom occurs in naturalistic data (Wegener 2008: 199–200). The emphatic marker *=e* (and its set of allomorphs used when cliticizing to pronouns) is used very often in Savosavo.[8] The element marked with the emphatic enclitic is fronted. The exact function of this marker does not seem to correspond to any of the categories usually distinguished in the linguistic analysis of information structure. Wegener (2008: 228–229) describes

---

[7] Claire Moyse-Faurie (p.c. at the *Syntax of the World's Languages* conference in Berlin on 25.09.2008) analyzes the marker glossed as 'pause' by Lichtenberk as a focus-marker that she regards as obligatory in this context.

[8] Wegener (2008: 221) states that it is the second most common morpheme in her data.

the marker as having to do with information structure, though it does not occur exclusively on either focused elements or topic expressions. Furthermore, perfectly grammatical sentences with elements that would be analyzed as corresponding to one of these functions without the emphatic marker also occur.

The marker =e is found in non-verbal as well as in verbal clauses. In non-verbal clauses, it attaches either to the subject (31a) or predicate (31b). When attaching to the subject of the clause, Nominative case-marking does not appear on this argument (31a). In verbal clauses, the emphatic marker can also attach to the subject argument (though this seldom occurs) and like in non-verbal clauses, the Nominative-marker does not occur in this case (32a). Nominative case appears to be blocked by the emphatic marker, possibly due to morphological restrictions.

(31) Savosavo (Solomons East Papuan; Solomon Islands; Wegener 2008: 221, 222)

   a. ***pa poi=e***   te   lo   mane=la
      one thing=EMPH EMPH 3SG.M.GEN/DET.SG.M side=LOC.M
      'One thing (is) at its/the side.'

   b. apoi   ata=e   te   lo   ***keva=na***
      because here=EMPH EMPH DET.SG.M path=NOM
      'Because here (is) the road.'

(32) Savosavo (Wegener 2008: 225, 144)

   a. ***ave=ve***   gazu   te   livu-li   Australia
      1PL.EXCL=EMPH.1PL.EXCL ripe_coconut EMPH carry-3SG.M.OBJ Australia
      l-au   bo-i
      3SG.M.OBJ-take go-FIN
      'We shipped ripe coconuts to Australia.'

   b. ***Jeffi=na***, baigho=e   lo-va   ela sua   ko   adaki
      Jeff=NOM NEG.exist=EMPH 3SG.M=GEN.M one ATT.SG.M DET.SG.F woman
      nyuba=ka   sua   pa ghanaghana=na
      child=LOC.F ATT.SG.M one thought.NOM
      'Jeff, he didn't have any thought whatsoever about/because of the woman.'

However, there are instances when an emphatic subject – even in clauses with the emphatic marker – receives Nominative case-marking, as in the following two constructions. Often, the subject is repeated as a pronoun at the end of a clause. In these cases, the Nominative case occurs on this final pronoun even if the preceding noun phrase referring to the subject argument does not receive

5 Emphatic subjects

case-marking due to the occurrence of the emphatic marker (33a). Also, if the full NP referring to the subject argument of a clause is added as an afterthought topic, while the clause internal subject referent is realized as a subject enclitic, the postposed subject is marked with Nominative case (33b).

(33) Savosavo (Wegener 2008: 224, 143)
    a. *ai to edo Fiji sua **mapa=lo=e** to boboragha*
       this DET.DU two Fiji ATT person=DU=EMPH DET.DU black
       mapa=lo=e to=na
       person=DU=EMPH 3DU=NOM
       'These two Fijians, they (were) black people.'

    b. *zu sesepi=la=ti=lo te alu kozi-zu,*
       and Sesepi=LOC.M=PROX=3SG.M.NOM EMPH stand face.PST.IPFV
       lo mapa=na
       DET.SG.M person=NOM
       'and he stands facing close to Sesepi, the man.'

Also in the languages of the Pacific region, a quite different pattern is found, namely, nominative case-marking only with emphatic arguments. This pattern is exemplified by Waskia, for which Ross (1978: 36) notes that "the subject-marker *ke* is intimately related to topicalisation." The following examples demonstrate the usage of this marker and its absence in non-emphatic contexts on the same grammatical relations.[9] Subject arguments are marked by *ke* if they are answers to constituent questions (34) or if the speaker wants to correct a wrong assumption about the subjects of nominal predications (35) or the S argument of any verb (36).

(34) Waskia (Kowan; Papua New Guinea, Karkar Island; Ross 1978: 37, 31)
    a. ***aweri ke** bamban tagiram ? – gagi ke*
       who NOM fish caught Gagi NOM
       'Who caught the fish? – Gagi (did)'

    b. ***gagi** kasili arigam*
       Gagi snake saw
       'Gagi saw the snake.'

---

[9] At least the first two contexts – answers to constituent questions and correction of wrong assumptions – can be considered clear examples of focus constructions, despite Ross' classification as 'topicalisation'.

(35) Waskia (Ross 1978: 17, 11)

    a. ***nu***   ***ke***   *taleng duap*
        3SG.PRO NOM policeman
        'He is a a policemen (i.e. not someone else)'

    b. *aga **bawa** taleng duap*
        my brother policeman
        'My brother is a policeman.'

(36) Waskia (Ross 1978: 37, 11)

    a. *mela, **gagi ke** madang urat biteso*
        NEG   Gagi NOM Madang work does
        'No it is Gagi who works in Madang.

    b. ***gagi*** *madang sule*   *se bage-so,*   *ayi ?*
        Gagi Madang school at stay-PRS.3SG Q
        'Gagi is at school in Madang, isn't he?'

Ross' discussion of Waskia is the only instance in which the emphatic subject-marker is explicitly treated as Nominative case-marking.[10] Other authors treating similar markers as instances of case rather than information structure markers usually analyze the marker as an ergative . As noted in Section 5.4, one reason for this might be the more frequent occurrence of this marker on transitive subjects than on intransitive ones. Also, in some languages, this marker appears on transitive subjects in different sorts of contexts, not only emphatic ones, while intransitive subjects receive this marker exclusively in emphatic contexts. If the marker in question serves to disambiguate argument structure as well as in contrasting functions, the absence of the marker in the first context would be expected for intransitive subjects. Two languages exhibiting this sort of system are Kaki Ae and Yawuru.[11] The Kaki Ae example (37) has already been discussed on page 109. The marker *-ro* marks the S argument in the first two clauses, which is newly introduced in the discourse, while other subjects remain zero-coded. The Australian language Yawuru has a similar structure. It employs the (optional) Ergative marker *-ni* in so-called contrastive uses for encoding intransitive subjects as well such as in (38a), while in other contexts S arguments cannot be marked with it (38b).

---

[10] Ross (1978) uses the term 'subject-marker', including both transitive and intransitive subjects and thus the domain of a typical nominative case-marker.

[11] Following Lynch (1998), I include languages of Australia into the group of Pacific languages.

5 Emphatic subjects

(37) Kaki Ae (Eleman; Papua New Guinea; Clifton 1997: 52)
*naora-**ro**   loea-ra-kape   naora-**ro**   u-ra-ha   luera-ma aua   erahe*
mother-ERG return-IRR-and mother-ERG call-IRR-3sS then-LOC child 3PL
uriri-RDP-isani naora   kai wä'ï-isani-pe   ko"ara oporo hu'a fua-isani
run-RDP-and mother to go_down-and-? another wood block carry-and
koi'ara ë'a rea-vere katlain   ekakau   himiri fua-isani a-isani-pe
another that 3sG-POSS fishing_line something many carry-and get-and-?
ava-isani
go_up-and
'The mother returns, the mother calls, and the children run down to the mother, some carry blocks of wood, some carry fishing line and many other things, they get them and go up.'

(38) Yawuru (Australian, Nyulnyulan; Western Australia; Hosokawa 1991: 254)
   a. *ngayu-**ni** nga-nga-nda mulukula-gadya, dyuyu-**ni** buru-bardu*
      1-ERG   1-AUX-PFV   work-INTENS   2-ERG   time-still
      kari   mi-na-bi-nda
      grog.ABS 2-TR-drink-PFV
      'I was working hard while you were drinking.'
   b. *ngayu(*-ni) mulkula-gadya-nga-nga-rn*
      1.ABS(*-ERG) work-INTENS-1-AUX-IPFV
      'I'm working (hard).'

Other authors, like Fabian et al. (1998) for Nabak, mainly discuss the discourse structure functions of similar markers, while its predominant or even exclusive appearance with subject arguments is not paid much attention. He labels the Nabak marker *-aŋ* as 'focus'. The marker is mainly used to (re-)introduce participants to the discourse. The use of this marker is demonstrated in (39a), while absence on regular subject arguments is shown in (39b). The marker is supposedly cognate to ergative markers in related languages.

(39) Nabak (Finisterre-Huon; Papua New Guinea; Fabian et al. 1998: 80, 95)
   a. **tam-aŋ** *gaki-ye*
      dog-FOC die-3SG.PSTREM
      'The dog died.'
   b. **bo ke** *da-en   met-ge*
      pig DEM over_there-LOC go-3SG.PSTREM
      'That pig went over there.'

The Eipo postposition *arye* appears to have a different diachronic origin. This marker is also used as a semantic case, and is used to encode instrumental, allative and related meanings. However, it is also used to mark the subject noun phrase especially if the subjects are used contrastively.

(40) Eipo (Trans-New-Guinea; Indonesia; Heeschen 1998: 169)
   a. *el ninye sik **do** **arye** a-motokwe nirye*
      he man their ancestor SBJ here-mountain all
      ba-lam-uk
      go-HAB-3SG.PSTREM
      'Man's ancestor used to go to all mountains.'
   b. *ninye **na-arye** kweb-reib-se*
      man 1-SBJ create-put-1SG.PSTREM
      'It was me who created man.'

A summary of the data from the Pacific languages is given in Table 5.3. Two

language	non-emphatic S	emphatic S	predicate nominal
Ajië	NOM	ACC	ACC
Eipo	bare noun	LOC	bare noun
Kaki Ae	ABS	ERG	ABS
Nabak	bare noun	FOC	bare noun
Nias	MUT	unmutated	unmutated
Savosavo	NOM	ACC + EMPH	ACC
Waskia	bare noun	FOC	bare noun
Yawuru	ABS	ERG	ABS

Table 5.3: Marking of emphatic S arguments in the languages of the Pacific area

distinct patterns are found in these languages. Nias, Ajië and Savosavo do not use the overt S-case-marker in emphatic contexts. In Savosavo, blocking of the marker through the emphatic clitic could be analyzed as the reason for this. Similar to the Nilo-Saharan languages, in Nias and Ajië the emphatic subject appears in a position preceding the otherwise initial verb.

The second pattern found in the Pacific is not usually included in the discussion of marked-S languages. It is exclusively found with languages of this region. The languages in question exhibit marked-S properties only with emphatic subjects. In non-emphatic contexts, they either use no marking of the case relations

5 Emphatic subjects

S, A and P at all (Eipo, Nabak, Waskia) or have an ergative-absolutive alignment with an overt ergative case (Kaki Ae, Yawuru), this marker is extended to S contexts for emphatic subjects. For the languages that have neutral alignment in non-emphatic contexts (i.e. they encode S, A and P identically), the origins and properties of the overt S-case-marker found on emphatic subjects vary to some extent. At least two different sources have to be considered. In Eipo the marker is used as a Allative case in other contexts, while for Nabak and Waskia it is considered to be cognate to an ergative marker in related languages.

5.9 North America

The North American marked-S languages show no remarkable patterns with respect to the marking of discourse prominent arguments. For most languages, the discussion of discourse structure is very sparse. The reason for this might be that apart from intonation and possibly word order, there are no dedicated devices to mark the discourse properties of the participants, as Munro (1976: 276) notes for Mojave. The languages that do have information on these constructions mark emphatic S arguments in the same way as non-emphatic S.

In Wappo, special morphology is used to put emphasis on an argument. If the focus-marker *lakhuh* is attached to the S argument of a clause, the Nominative case-marking remains on this argument (41). Similarly in Maidu, the emphasis marker *-ʔas* can follow every element of a sentence except the verb, and the emphasized element is sentence-initial, case-marking stays invariant (42).

(41) Wappo (Wappo-Yukian; California; Thompson et al. 2006: 79; Li et al. 1977: 92)
ce šaw-i lakhuh nuh-kheʔ
that bread-NOM FOC steal-PASS
'It's the bread that got stolen.'

(42) Maidu (Maiduan; California; Dixon 1911: 711)
sü-m has nik doʼkan
dog-NOM EMPH 1SG.ACC bite
'The dog bit me.'

For the Yuman languages, not much information on discourse structure marking is provided. The Mojave situation is probably prototypical for the whole language family. Munro (1976: 276) states that she "has not found any evidence

5.9 North America

that Mojave has any syntactic devices for indicating topic, other than changes in stress or (possibly) word order."

The only special discourse structure elements that are discussed for any Yuman language are afterthought topics (i.e. right-dislocated arguments). S arguments in this position bear the same nominative case-marking as elsewhere in Jamul Tiipay (43) and Yavapai (44), the two languages for which the context is explicitly discussed.

(43) Jamul Tiipay (Yuman; California; Miller 1990: 334)
 puu mesheyaay raw-ch yu **xu'maay-pe-ch**
 that_one be_afraid IPFV-SSBJ be boy-DEM-NOM
 'He was afraid of that (bull), the orphan boy (was).'

(44) Yavapai (Yuman; Arizona; Kendall 1976: 139)
 a. ʔña **ʔ-tal-c** yu ʔña **ʔ-cita-c** yu-eː-k ke
 1 1-father-NOM be 1 1-mother-NOM be-CONJ-ego NEG
 qalyev-c-m ʔ-u: ʔ-om-km **ʔña-c**
 unhappy-PL-ALLO 1-see 1-not-inc 1-NOM
 'My father and mother, never unhappy do I see them, I.'
 b. ñvat ʔmo-ʔhan ʔ-tkay-c-kñ **ña-c-c**
 goat sheep-good 1-mix-PL-COMPL 1-PL-NOM
 '(We) mixed the sheep and the goats.'

Table 5.4 on the next page summarizes the data for the languages of North-America. They behave quite unremarkably concerning the marking of emphatic subjects. In the Yuman languages, no special marking of discourse prominence in subjects is found on a segmental level and these element receive the regular nominative case. Maidu behaves in a parallel fashion, marking emphatic subjects identically to non-emphatic subjects with Nominative case. Only Wappo uses special morphology to mark focused elements. This marking is, however, not restricted to subjects and combines with the regular case-marking, i.e. Nominative case for subjects. Coincidentally, the marking of emphatic subjects and predicate nominals is the same for the marked-S languages of North America except Wappo. However, the emphatic structures do not show any cleft-like properties otherwise (e.g. fronting of the subject).

5 Emphatic subjects

language	non-emphatic S	emphatic S	predicate nominal
Jamul Tiipay	(NOM)	(NOM)	ACC
Mojave	NOM	NOM	NOM
Yavapai	NOM	NOM	NOM
Wappo	NOM	NOM + FOC	ACC
Maidu	NOM	NOM	NOM

Table 5.4: Marking of emphatic S arguments in the marked-S languages of North America

5.10 Summary

In this section, the data on emphatic subjects in marked-S languages are summarized. Table 5.5 on the facing page provides an overview of the different systems of marking emphatic subjects in the languages discussed in this chapter. First of all, for each language the table indicates how it marks emphatic and non-emphatic subject arguments. The table lists the case-form a noun appears in as well as any additional markers occurring on the noun in the given context. Further on, the basic word order (BWO) and the word order in emphatic contexts (emphatic WO) is given. The table also summarizes the case-form a nominal predicate receives in the given language (this data is discussed in more detail in Chapter 3). And finally, I indicate whether a language allows for zero copulas with nominal predications.

An interesting generalization is that all languages of the sample with verb-initial word order in non-emphatic clauses front emphatic subjects (and other emphatic elements). The tendency that languages with a dominant VSO order allow for an alternative SVO order has also been observed by Greenberg (1963) as his Universal 6. In addition, the overt S-case-marking found on post-verbal subjects is not found in this pre-verbal position in all these languages. This pattern holds for the Nilo-Saharan languages Datooga, Nandi, Tennet and Turkana as well as for the Polynesian languages Nias and Ajië. Also, the zero-coded form of emphatic subjects is identical to the form of predicate nominals in these languages, making an analysis of these structures as a cleft-construction likely. Additional support for the cleft hypothesis comes from the fact that all these languages generally allow zero-copulas. Three other languages for which the cleft analysis of emphatic subjects might work out are the Eastern Cushitic languages Arbore, Boraana Oromo, and Harar Oromo. In Arbore, the emphatic subjects are overtly coded, though not with the Nominative case. Instead, the Predicative case is used indicating the status of this element as predicate nominal.

5.10 Summary

language	non-emphatic S	emphatic S	predicate nominal	zero copula	BWO	emph. WO
Ajië	NOM	ACC	ACC	possible	VOS	SVO
Arbore	NOM	PRED	PRED	possible	S(O)V	SV
Datooga	NOM	ACC	ACC	possible	VSO	SVO
Dinka (Agar)	NOM (non-topic)	ACC	-	-	Topic initial (SVO)	Topic initial
Eipo	bare noun	LOC	bare noun	always	SOV	SOV
Gamo	NOM	NOM	ACC	possible	SVO	SVO
Jamul Tiipay	(NOM)	(NOM)	ACC	always	SOV	?/OVS
K'abeena	NOM	NOM	ACC	no	SOV	OSV
Kaki Ae	ABS	ERG	ABS	always	SOV	SOV
Maidu	NOM	NOM	NOM	no(?)	SOV	SOV
Mojave	NOM	NOM	NOM	possible	SOV	SOV
Nabak	bare noun	FOC	bare noun	always	SOV	SOV
Nandi	NOM	ACC/NOM	ACC	always	VSO	SVO/VOS
Nias	ABS	ERG	ERG	always	VOS	SVO
Oromo (Boraana)	NOM	ACC+(GEN) ?	ACC	possible	SOV	SV
Oromo (Harar)	NOM	FOC	ACC	possible	SOV	SOV
Savosavo	NOM	ACC + EMPH	ACC	always	SOV	S
Tennet	NOM	ACC/NOM	ACC	only equat.	VSO	SVO
Turkana	NOM	ACC	ACC	possible	VSO	SVO
Wappo	NOM	NOM + FOC	ACC	only future	SOV	SOV
Waskia	bare noun	FOC	bare noun	most	SOV	SOV/OVS
Yavapai	NOM	NOM	NOM	no ?	SOV	SOV/OVS
Yawuru	ABS	ERG	ABS	possible	SVO/OVS	SV

Table 5.5: Overview on the marking of emphatic S arguments

6 Subjects of non-basic clauses

6.1 Introduction

In this chapter, case-marking in a number of non-basic clauses will be discussed. Under non-basic clauses, I subsume various types of dependent clauses, as well as clauses in which the number of arguments that a verb takes is changed through morphosyntactic processes. For the latter type one can distinguish between processes that decrease the number of arguments – passivization and antipassivization – and those that increase the number of arguments, such as causativation. Since only the processes that decrease the number of arguments show any exceptional patterns (i.e. patterns that do not employ the S-case), only these contexts will be discussed here. Basic clauses in contrast are defined here as consisting of a single predicate which has not undergone any argument-affecting derivation.

Dependent clauses exhibit special marking strategies in many languages, far exceeding the domain of marked-S. The verb-final word order found with German dependent clauses as opposed to verb-second main clauses is one example of such special marking. Deviating patterns of case-marking are also found in this domain. The domain of dependent clauses can be subdivided into smaller domains, such as relative clauses or adverbial clauses. Each of the different clause-types potentially has its own distinct type of encoding. A brief discussion of different types of dependent clauses and their grammar is given in Section 6.2. However, this topic cannot be covered in depth here.

Next, I will discuss valency reducing operations (Section 6.3). The specific labels that are used for these constructions often carry strong implications about their formal encoding. The promotion of the logical object to subject status is usually seen as a prerequisite for labeling a construction as 'passive'. The more neutral term 'valency-decreasing operations' is more readily applicable to a wide range of phenomena that might not be captured by a more specific label such as passive. Apart from formal marking properties, valency-decreasing constructions are also associated with a specific information structure. The passive, for example, puts attention on the patient argument. However, a similar communicative effect can also be achieved by other formal means. So-called 'imper-

6 Subjects of non-basic clauses

sonal constructions' are a prime example of this. I will briefly discuss these in Section 6.3 as well, yet, whether constructions of this type should be considered to be valency-decreasing is at least debatable.

The contexts studied in this chapter are associated with a rather formal register, such as written rather than spoken language. A large number of passive and dependent clauses for example are typical indicators of written texts of an academic nature. For a number of languages of my sample, these types of register are not very elaborate or commonly used. Thus, the contexts of interest are often not well represented in the description of a language or not even discussed at all.

After introducing these different types of non-basic clauses in Sections 6.2 and 6.3, the patterns of case-marking found in these contexts will be outlined in Section 6.4. Subsequently, I will present data on the encoding of these contexts in the individual languages of North America (Section 6.5), the Pacific region (Section 6.6), the Nilo-Saharan (Section 6.7) and Afro-Asiatic (Sectio n6.8) family. Finally, a summary of the data is provided in Section 6.9.

6.2 Dependent clauses

A common distinction between clause-types is the one between independent clauses that can stand on their own and subordinate or dependent clauses. The meaning of the latter clause-type is tied to another clause and thus they cannot be fully interpreted on their own. However, most languages differentiate between a number of different types of dependent clauses, which often differ according to their grammatical encoding. For the present study the marking of subject arguments is the central aspect of grammatical encoding to be investigated.

Instead of making a binary distinction between main and dependent clauses, it is possible to establish a hierarchy of grammatical integration ranging from structures that constitute one fully integrated clause to two completely independent clauses (Payne 1997: 307). Structures which are typically considered to consist of one independent and one (or more) dependent clause(s) are located in the middle section of this continuum with relative clauses being less grammatically integrated than, e.g. adverbial or even complement clauses. Payne's scale of grammatical integration of clauses is given in Figure 6.1, where the parts of the scale commonly referred to as dependent or subordinate clauses are set aside from the rest of the scale by a box in this version of the scale.

The exact ordering of this continuum is not uncontroversial. While Payne locates the relative clause in the position which is closest to the 'two separate clauses' end of the scale and thus adjacent to coordination (i.e. clause combining

6.2 Dependent clauses

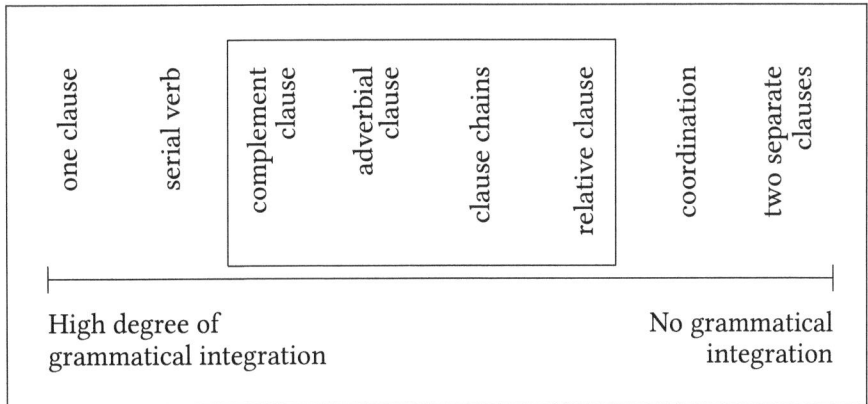

Figure 6.1: Level of integration of clauses (after Payne 1997: 307)

structures), Thompson et al. (2007: 238) state that, unlike relative or complement clauses, adverbial clauses "are viewed as (hypotactic) clause combinations with respect to the main clause." They consider adverbial clauses to be subordinated to a lesser degree than the other two clause-types.

In the following I will briefly introduce the three types of dependent clauses which are relevant for this study, namely relative clauses, adverbial clauses and complement clauses. Since only one of the languages of my sample has clause-chaining, namely Savosavo (Wegener 2008: 286–297), I did not include this structure in my study. The three types of dependent clauses are sometimes also referred to as 'adjectival', 'adverbial' and 'nominal' clauses corresponding to the part of speech that they resemble in function.

RELATIVE CLAUSES modify an argument (and in some languages also other participants) of the main clause. They are often discussed among other nominal modifiers such as adjectives or demonstratives, especially in terms of word order typology (cf. Dryer 2005a). Since the relative clause makes a statement about one of the participants of the main clause this participant is also an argument of the relative clause.[1] Dixon (2010b: 314) refers to the argument shared between main and relative clauses as the COMMON ARGUMENT (CA), a term I will use in the following discussion. Languages differ with respect to whether the common argument is realized in the main clause, in the relative clause or in both. If there is only one instance of the common argument, there can be ambiguity with respect to the question in which clause the argument is located. In this study, I

---

[1] The term participant is used in a very broad sense here and may include the role of location or possessor in a given language.

133

am interested in the realization of the subject element of the relative clause. In situations in which the subject of the relative clause is the common argument, its case-form in the relative clause is often difficult to identify, since it will not be realized as an independent noun phrase in many languages. Therefore, the best example sentences for the purpose of this study are those in which the subject of the relative clause is not the common argument and is represented by a full NP (e.g. *the book that my sister bought*). However, this type of relative clause could not be found in all languages due to lack of data or possibly ungrammaticality of this construction. There is another caveat concerning the study of case-marking found in relative clauses. In some languages, the relative clause construction is actually a nominalization. Instead of having verbal marking – either identical to the marking found in main clauses, or special dependent verb morphology – the verb has nominalizing morphology. Though verbal arguments can be realized in nominalized structures, case-marking is usually not preserved but rather substituted by a genitive, for example.

ADVERBIAL CLAUSES do not modify a single participant of the main clause, but rather modify the verb phrase or entire main clause. They establish a relation in terms of temporal structure or other factors such as presenting the reason for or desired goal of the action in the main clause. Based on their different functions, a large number of subtypes of adverbial clauses can be distinguished, such as temporal, locational, purposive or conditional clauses (for a discussion of these different subtypes see Thompson et al. 2007: 243–265). Main clauses and adverbial clauses do not necessarily share an argument between them, though they might.[2] Therefore instances of full NP subjects within the adverbial clauses are usually easy to find (provided the grammar discusses this type of clause at all).

COMPLEMENT CLAUSES serve as arguments of the main clause – or the matrix clause, as the non-complement clause in this construction is usually referred to.[3] Though there are subject complement clauses, typical complement clauses

---

[2] The following English examples are adverbial clauses having a different (i.a) and co-referential subject (i.b).

(i) a. *John served the meal, after Jack had brought the wine.*
    b. *John$_i$ served the meal, after he$_i$ had brought the wine.*

[3] The term matrix clause is often preferred, since in order to function as a grammatical sentence, the argument position filled by the complement clause would have to be filled first in most cases. Some complement verbs, however, still form grammatical utterances when the complement is deleted, as illustrated in (i.b) for English.

function as the P argument of a complement taking verb. Such verbs can be subdivided into several semantic types such as verbs of utterance or desideratives (an extensive discussion of the different types of complement verbs can be found in Noonan 2007: 120–145). A language may distinguish between different types of complements. This type of dependent clause has its own argument structure and in many cases one of its arguments is co-referential with an argument of the main clause. The co-referential argument is often not realized in the complement clause. Case-marking in complement clauses is often special, and may also vary between different types. The English examples in (1) demonstrate the different case-marking of the complement-internal subject in non-finite (1a) and finite (1b) complement clauses.

(1) a. *She wants [**him** to leave.]*
    b. *She hopes [(that) **he** has already left.]*

Complex syntactic structures like dependent clauses are a feature found more often in written than in spoken language. Many of the languages of my sample (and in fact the majority of the languages in the world) do not have a long tradition as a written language, if any. Therefore dependent structures are often underdescribed in grammars or lacking at all entirely, since they do not play a significant role in language use. Also a language might not have a distinct grammaticalized construction for encoding these structures. Relative clauses and adverbial clauses are the two types of dependent clauses most likely to be treated in a grammar.

Taking a closer look at the token frequency of dependent clauses in written versus spoken language, it becomes clear that the assumption formulated above (i.e. dependent structures are a characteristic feature of written language) is an oversimplification. Biber et al. (1998: 139–141) demonstrate, based on English corpus data, that the distribution of different types of dependent clauses varies greatly between different registers. While relative clauses are most frequently found in academic prose, causative adverbial clauses are for instance most commonly used in conversations. However, the basic observation that data on dependent clauses of all types are scarce in grammars of most under-described languages still remains valid.

(i) a. *John is scared [that he might lose his job].*
    b. *John is scared.*

6.3 Valency-decreasing operations

Under the term 'valency-decreasing operations', a variety of constructions is subsumed. All these operations have in common that fewer grammatical arguments are realized than in the corresponding basic clause. Passive, antipassive, and middle are typical instances of this type of operation. Both formal and functional criteria are of interest when analyzing these voice alternations. A crucial formal aspect is the case-marking of arguments in these constructions (which is also the main focus of the present study), but also the pragmatic implications of these structures are taken into account. Especially if on formal criteria no passive structure can be identified in a language, functional criteria are often considered in order to identify the equivalent construction in a language. So-called 'impersonal constructions' often have functions similar to those of prototypical passives. I will briefly discuss impersonal constructions, though their status as valency-decreasing operations is not unambiguous in languages with verbal person agreement. In the following, the different grammatical categories and constructions that are involved in the reduction of verbal valency will be introduced.

The most common valency-decreasing operation from a cross-linguistic perspective is the PASSIVE. Passive constructions realize non-agent arguments as the grammatical subject of logically transitive verbs. All languages with passive constructions allow for patients to be promoted to grammatical subject status, but languages vary with respect to whether other semantic roles such as ditransitive recipients can be promoted as well. Prototypical passives have a number of formal properties which are not necessarily met by voice operations serving the same pragmatic functions as typical passives in a given language. If a construction meets all of the three following criteria, it constitutes a prototypical instance of a passive (Siewierska 2005b; Payne 1997: 205).

1. Demotion of the A argument of the active counterpart to non-argument status.

2. Promotion of the P argument of the active counterpart to subject.

3. Morphosyntactic marking of the voice alternation on the verb or in the verb phrase (either through affixation of periphrastic means).

If a construction does not meet all of these criteria, linguists differ strongly in whether they call a construction a passive or not. The last criterion – verbal marking of the voice alternation – is quite unproblematic in this respect. A deviation from the active clause in terms of verbal morphosyntax is considered a crucial criterion for identifying a distinct passive voice in a language by some (Siewierska 2005b), while others (Haspelmath 1990; Dryer 1982) do not include morphosyntactic marking of passives as a necessary condition. The two criteria relating to the status of S and P arguments in passives as compared to basic clauses are more problematic. The subjecthood of the logical object is taken as a hard criterion for identifying passives by many linguists – for instance by Munro (1976) on Mojave. Subjecthood is identified via case-marking and/or verbal agreement. In languages in which passive 'subjects' deviate from the standard subject-marking, such constructions can still unproblematically be included under the term valency-decreasing operation, however.

Apart from passives, there are two other voice operations that reduce the number of syntactic arguments in a clause: ANTIPASSIVE and MIDDLE. The antipassive is a structure most commonly associated with languages of the ergative-absolutive type. In antipassive sentences a verb that has two semantic arguments only realizes the A argument of its usual argument structure. The P argument is not realized and the verb treats the remaining A argument syntactically like an S argument, marking it with absolutive rather than ergative case for instance.[4] However, the same label is nowadays applied to parallel constructions in languages with other alignment systems. For example, the Surmic language Tennet has both a passive (2) and an antipassive construction (3).

(2) Tennet (Surmic; Sudan; Randal 1998: 245)

    a. á̰-rṹh-w-ḛ   ido̰ng   íyóko̰
       IPFV-beat-EPEN-PASS drum.NOM now

       'The drum is being beaten now.'

    b. á-rṹh   enné   ídóng   íyóko̰
       IPFV-beat 3SG.NOM drum.ACC now

       'He is beating the drum now.'

(3) Tennet (Randal 1998: 245)

    a. á-dáh-ye   do̰lḛc
       IPFV-eat-ANTIP child.NOM

       'The child is eating.'

---

[4] As with passive agents, the P argument can be overtly realized in some languages as a non-argument phrase, for example with a special oblique case.

6 Subjects of non-basic clauses

b. *á-dáh   do̧lę́c   áhát*
   IPFV-eat child.NOM asida.ACC
   'The child is eating asida.'

The last valency-decreasing operation that is relevant here is the middle. The middle is often interpreted as the voice in between active and passive (Klaiman 1991: 3–4). In this construction, the role of the agent is not exactly downplayed, but rather the fact that an agent is involved is not considered. The semantic difference between active (4a), passive (4b) and middle (4c) sentences is tentatively illustrated by the following English examples. Note, however, that the middle as a distinct voice is only identified in a small set of languages and in the English context the construction in (4c) is rather described as an inchoative (Levin 1993: 2–3).

(4) a. *The ball broke the vase.*
     b. *The vase was broken (by the ball).*
     c. *The vase broke.*

A functionally less restrictive argument-reducing voice operation is usually referred to as a general DETRANSITIVIZING operation. Such an operation adds a special marker to a semantically transitive verb indicating that the verb is used as a syntactically intransitive verb. One of the arguments of the verb is deleted, but there are no syntactic restrictions regarding which argument of a transitive verb is not realized. Thus, basically any of the two arguments of a transitive verb could be deleted in a detransitivizing operation. However, there can be semantic restrictions or at least general tendencies for an individual verb on whether the A or P argument is deleted in this type of operation.

Apart from the formal criteria listed above, the pragmatics of a construction are often also taken into account when identifying valency-decreasing operations. Pragmatic criteria are for instance a central factor in the discussion of passives by Keenan & Dryer (2007). Even if a language does not have a passive construction (or any of the other voice operations discussed in this chapter), it will still have means to encode the same discourse functions associated with passives. Syntactically transitive constructions can have an unspecified A argument in many languages. The German 'man'-construction as in *man spricht deutsch.* 'one speaks German (here)' is an instance of this. Such constructions are often referred to as 'impersonal constructions'. In this type of construction the role of the agent is downplayed. The logical P argument of the construction remains in this position syntactically, but pragmatically it is the most salient argument. The logical A argument of this construction is unknown or irrelevant in the given situation. Therefore, the A argument is not realized lexically. From a syntactic point of view, these constructions are transitive, and thus do not decrease the number of arguments of a verb. Therefore such constructions are not relevant for the further discussion in this chapter.

6.4 Research questions

Case-marking in non-basic clauses does differ in a number of languages of the marked-S type. However, this is not an exclusive feature of the languages studied here. Deviating patterns of case-assignment in non-basic clauses are also commonly found in other languages (i.e. non-marked-S languages). In this section I will demonstrate (with examples from languages of the marked-S type) how subjects of non-basic clauses behave differently from prototypical subjects of basic clauses. In most instances, the factor that differentiates between the clauses is the assignment of S-case to basic clause subjects, while non-basic subjects receive some other case-marking, usually the zero-case. However, there are often some other structural differences between the two types of structures such as in word order, or verbal indexing. I will note these differences when discussing the data. However, the main focus of this chapter is on the case-marking.

In the following sections, I will discuss how marked-S languages mark the case of the subject element of non-basic clauses. This includes the following:

- case-marking of subjects in all types of dependent clauses (i.e. relative clauses, adverbial clauses, complement clauses)

- (promoted) subjects of valency-decreasing operations

A number of marked-S languages do not mark subjects of dependent clauses in the same way they mark subjects of main clauses. Wappo relative clauses, for example, leave the internal subject of the relative clause zero-coded (5b). It never receives Nominative case like it would in main clauses (5a). Similarly, in adverbial (5c) and complement clauses (5d) the subject remains zero-coded.

(5) Wappo (Wappo-Yukian; California; Thompson et al. 2006: 4, 117, 77, Thompson et al. 2007: 239)

    a. ce   ew   ce   k'ew-i   t'um-taʔ
       DEM fish DEM man-NOM buy-PST
       'That fish, the man bought (it).'

6 *Subjects of non-basic clauses*

b. [ce **k'ew** ew t'um-ta]   cephi   i   naw-ta?
   DEM man fish buy-PST.DEP 3SG.NOM 1SG.ACC see-PST
   'The man who bought the fish saw me.'

c. [**te**   ce ew t'ume cel'] keye ah   ce pa?eh   'If he had
   3SG.ACC DEM fish buy.DEP COND OPT 1SG.NOM DEM eat.HYP
   bought the fish, I would have eaten it'

d. ah   [**te**   šawo   pa?-tah] hais-khi?
   1SG.NOM 3SG.ACC bread.ACC eat-PST know-N_FUT
   'I know that he ate bread.'

In other languages, however, subjects in different types of dependent clauses receive different kinds of case-marking. While Murle relative clauses mark their subjects in Nominative case (6a), complement clauses have zero-coded subjects (6b). Mojave exhibits yet another pattern: subjects of relative clauses are zero-coded (7a) but subjects of adverbial clauses are in the Nominative case (7b).

(6) Murle (Surmic; Sudan; Arensen 1982: 112, 113)

   a. kɛɛti   naana   kiziwan   [o   or   **niina**]
      skin.1SG 1SG.NOM buffalo.ACC which shoot.PST 2SG.NOM
      'I am skinning the buffalo which you shot.'

   b. kaga naana [nɔnnɔ aak idiŋ]
      know 1SG.NOM 3SG.ACC cook meat.ACC
      'I know that she is cooking meat.'

(7) Mojave (Yuman; Arizona; Munro 1976: 188, Munro 1980: 144)

   a. [θinʸaʔa:k mat=kəhʷelʸ kʷ-nʸavay]-nʸ-č   ʔ-ahvay-nʸ ičo:-k
      woman   Parker   REL-live-DEM-NOM 1-dress-DEM make-TNS
      'The woman who lives in Parker made my dress.'

   b. [ʔinye-č pap   ʔ-akchoor-m] judyč   salyii-k
      1SG-NOM potato 1-peel-DSBJ   Judy-NOM fry-TNS
      'After I peeled the potatoes, Judy fried them.'

Still other marked-S languages do not show any difference in the case-marking of subjects of main and dependent clauses. In the Harar dialect of Oromo, subjects receive the regular Nominative case-marking in relative (8a) as well as adverbial clauses (8b).

(8) Oromo (Harar) (Eastern Cushitic; Ethiopia; Owens 1985: 131, 143)
    a. *namicc-íi* [(xan) *intal-tíi isá baréed-dúu*] *ác jira*
        man-NOM as girl-NOM 3SG.M.ACC pretty-F there exist.3SG.M
        'The man whose daughter is pretty is there.'
    b. [*hagá isíin d'uf-t-ú*] *taa'-e*
        until 3.SG.F.NOM come-F-DEP stay-PST
        'He stayed until she came.'

I will now turn to the different patterns of marking subjects in valency-decreasing constructions. As already noted in Section 6.3, Tennet has both a passive (9a) and an antipassive (9b). In both constructions the subject receives Nominative case-marking.

(9) Tennet (Surmic; Sudan; Randal 1998: 245)
    a. *á-rúh-w-e idong íyóko*
        IPFV-beat-EPEN-PASS drum.NOM now
        'The drum is being beaten now.'
    b. *á-dáh-ye doléc*
        IPFV-eat-ANTIP child.NOM
        'The child is eating.'

In Maa, three grammatical voices are distinguished: middle, antipassive, and the so-called impersonal passive. In the middle (10a) and antipassive (10b) the subject is in the Nominative case. In the impersonal passive (10c) on the other hand the subject is in the Accusative (i.e. zero-coded case)

(10) Maa (Nilotic; Kenya; Payne 2007: ex. 11, ex. 13, ex. 16, ex. 15)
    a. *ŋ-é-duŋ-o ɛn-ámʊ̀kɛ̀*
        CON-3-cut-MID.N_PFV F.SG-sandal.NOM
        'The shoe was cut.'
    b. *n-é-ramat-íshò ɔl-mʊrraní*
        CON-3-tend_livestock-ANTIP M.SG-warrior.NOM
        'The warrior herds [e.g. cows].'
    c. *ɛ-tɛ-ɛn-ák-ì ɔl-apúrrònì*
        3-PRF-tie-PRF-PASS M.SG-thief.ACC
        'The thief was arrested.'
    d. *ɛ-ɪbʊ́ŋ-á ɪ-s'ɪkarɪní ɔl-apúrrònì*
        3-catch-PRF PL-police.NOM M.SG-thief.ACC
        'The policemen have arrested the thief.'

6 Subjects of non-basic clauses

Other than with the contexts of existential and locational predication (see Chapter 4), which were encoded via identical constructions in most languages of my sample, the contexts studied in this chapter are typically encoded by a construction not shared with the other contexts. Therefore the data in the following sections will be organized by the contexts rather than discussing all contexts for each language at the same time. As in the previous chapters, the data are organized by geographical and genealogical groupings. Section 6.5 discusses the languages of North America. Data from the languages of the Pacific are given in Section 6.6. And the languages of Africa are presented in Sections 6.7 (Nilo-Saharan) and 6.8 (Afro-Asiatic) respectively.

6.5 North America

In a number of North American marked-S languages, dependent clauses, and especially relative clauses, do not mark their subjects with nominative case but leave them zero-coded. In Mojave, S arguments in valency-decreasing constructions are also left zero-coded. However, most languages of the region use the nominative case in this context. Generally, the voice systems of the North American languages in my sample are not highly complex, judging from the available data.

In Wappo, S (11a) and A arguments (as demonstrated in example (5b) above) in relative clauses have the zero-coded form. In main clauses these arguments are marked with the Nominative case-suffix -*i* in contrast (11b). Note that it is only subject case-marking via Nominative case which is absent from relative clauses. Case-marking of recipient arguments via Dative case is preserved in relative clauses (12).

(11) Wappo (Wappo-Yukian; California; Thompson et al. 2006: 117, 41)
    a. [*ce* **k'ew** *kat'akh*]   *cephi*   *k'ešu peh-khiʔ*
       DEM man laugh.STAT.DEP 3SG.NOM deer look_at-STAT
       'The man who laughed is looking at the deer.'
    b. *hay-i*   *hoʔ-taʔ*
       dog-NOM bark-PST
       'The dog barked.'

(12) Wappo (Thompson et al. 2006: 117, 12)
    a. [*mi ce* *k'ew-**thu** takaʔ ma-hes-ta*]   (*ce*) *ah*   *naw-taʔ*
       2SG DEM man-DAT basket DIR-give-PST.DEP DEM 1SG.NOM see-PST
       'I saw the man you gave the basket to.'

b. *ce   k'ew-i   chica-**thu** ew ma-hes-ta?*
   DEM man-NOM bear-DAT fish DIR-give-PST
   'The man gave the fish to the bear.'

But not only subjects of relative clauses are left without overt case-marking in this language. Adverbial clauses exhibit the same pattern, as exemplified by the following temporal (13a) and conditional clauses (13b). Complement clauses (13c) have zero-coded subjects as well.

(13) Wappo (Thompson et al. 2006: 71, 77, Thompson et al. 2007: 239)
   a. [*ce* **layh**   *tu-le?a-cel'*]   *okal'te-lahkhi?*
      DEM white_person DIR-arrive-when talk.IPFV-NEG
      'When the white man comes, don't talk'
   b. [***mi*** *te*   *o-me?-is*   *cel'*] *keye čho?e-lahkhih*
      2SG.ACC 3SG.ACC UOP-feed-CAUS COND OPT die.IMP-NEG.HYP
      'If you had fed it, it wouldn't have died'
   c. *ah*   [***te***   *šawo*   *pa?-tah*] *hais-khi?*
      1SG.NOM 3SG.ACC bread.ACC eat-PST know-N_FUT
      'I know that he ate bread.'

With respect to relative clauses the languages of the Yuman family exhibit a similar pattern. In Mojave, for example, nouns serving as S (14) or A argument (15) of a relative clause are in the zero-coded form according to Munro (1976: 187–190).

(14) Mojave (Yuman; Arizona; Munro 1976: 188)
   a. [*?ava: k^w-n^yəməsavc*]-*l^y ?-iva-m*
      house REL-white-LOC   1-sit-TNS
      'I am in the white house.'
   b. *?ava:-č*   *n^yəməsa:-m*
      house-NOM white-TNS
      'The house is white.'

(15) Mojave (Munro 1976: 188)
   a. [*hatčoq poš k^w-taver*] *?-iyu:-pč*
      dog.ACC cat.ACC REL-chase 1-see-TNS
      'I saw the dog that chased the cat.'

6 Subjects of non-basic clauses

b. *hatčoq-č poš taver-m*
   dog-NOM cat.ACC chase-TNS
   'The dog chased the cat.'

Dixon (2010b: 333–334) discusses relative clauses in Mojave based on Munro's data with a slightly different interpretation. Following Munro, he distinguishes between relative clauses in which the common argument is the subject of the relative clause and those in which it is not. In the former type, the verb of the relative clause is marked by the prefix k^w- and according to Dixon's analysis the common argument is stated in the main clause and not realized as independent NP in this type of relative clause. Accordingly, the CA is case-marked for its function in the main clause and not the relative clause. If the common argument does not function as the relative clause's subject, then the verb prefix is missing and the common argument is realized in the relative clause. In example (15a) above, according to his analysis, the noun *hatčoq* 'dog' is the P argument of the main clause's predicate ('to see') and the Accusative form is thus expected.

In the following example (16), the CA serves as the subject of both main and relative clause. As is to be expected for subject relative clauses, the verb of the relative clause is marked by the prefix k^w- (just like in (15a)). However, the Nominative case is missing from the noun phrase *ɔin^yaʔa:k-n^y* 'that woman'. Instead, the relative clauses as a whole is case-marked for the role. It is not clear to me how this can be explained in Dixon's analysis, which holds that in subject relative clauses the common argument is not realized in the main clause. This behavior of marking the relative clause for the function the common argument bears in the main clause is also found in example (17), in which the relative clause is marked with Locative case. This example is a non-subject relative clause. Accordingly, the subject of the relative clause is realized inside the relative clause since it is not an argument of the main clause. As in the examples of subject relative clauses above, the subject is zero-coded.[5]

(16) Mojave (Munro 1976: 188)
   a. [*θin^yaʔa:k mat=kəh^wel^y k^w-n^yavay*]-*n^y-č ʔ-ahvay-n^y ičo:-k*
      woman Parker REL-live-DEM-NOM 1-dress-DEM make-TNS
      'The woman who lives in Parker made my dress.'
   b. *θin^yaʔa:k-n^y-č mat=kəh^wel^y n^yavay-n^y-k*
      woman-DEM-NOM Parker live-TNS
      'The woman lives in Parker.'

---

[5] The relative clause in (14) is also marked with Locative case. It functions as location in the main clause, but bears the subject relative prefix k^w-. Munro (1976) does not comment on this.

(17) Mojave (Munro 1977: 451, Munro 1976: 221)
   a. [ʔ-nakut ʔava u:čo:]-lʸ ʔ-navay-k
      1-father house make-LOC 1-live-TNS
      'I live in the house my father built.'
   b. ʔinʸep ʔ-nakut-č ʔava: vidanʸ ičo:-k
      me 1-father-NOM house this make-TNS
      'My father built this house.'

Other than relative clauses, Mojave adverbial clauses straightforwardly mark their subjects with the Nominative. Case-marking of subjects of temporal clauses is illustrated by the examples in (18).

(18) Mojave (Munro 1980: 12, Langdon & Munro 1979: 322)
   a. [ʔiipa iiwa-ny-č nya-chalahop-m] isma-mot-e
      man heart-DEM-NOM when-empty-DSBJ sleep-NEG-FUT
      'When a man is lonely, he can't sleep.'
      lit.: 'When a man's heart is empty, he can't sleep.'
   b. [ʔi:kʷi:č-və-č nəkəmič-m] ʔə-taly-č zu:pa:
      men-DEM-NOM return.PL-DSBJ 1-mother-NOM crack_acorns
      'When the men came back, my mother cracked acorns.'

Complement clauses are not discussed in any detail in the Mojave literature. Munro (1976: 232–234) notes that subordinate clauses with nʸa- 'when'/'if' and the switch reference/tense marker -k and -m have Nominative subjects. While the when-and-if-clauses are of the adverbial type discussed above, the switch reference markers apparently are used in complementation, as in the following examples. Example (19a) marks the subjects of main (inʸeč 'I') and complement clause (Judy) with Nominative case. In the second example, the switch reference marker is missing, however. Judging from the translation, this is an instance of complementation. In this example, the subject iču:ra:v 'man' is not marked with the Nominative case (19b), which it receives when the complement is realized as an independent main clause (19c). But this might be explained by the general possibility of Nominative case-marking to be dropped in Mojave, especially in fast speech.

(19) Mojave (Munro 1976: 274, 220)
   a. ʔinʸ eč [judy-č iva:-p-m] ʔ-su:paw-č
      1SG.NOM Judy-NOM arrive-p-DSBJ 1-know-?
      'I know that Judy has arrived.'

145

b. [*pa   ʔič   u:ra:v*]-*nʸ ʔ-aʔa:v-k-e*
   man something hurt-DEM 1-hear-TNS-AUGV
   'I know the man is sick.'

c. *pa-č   ʔič   ira:v-k*
   man-NOM something hurt-TNS
   'The man is sick.'

In general, the case-marking of dependent clauses exhibits parallel structures across the languages of the Yuman family. For Jamul Tiipay, Miller (2001: 210) states that within a relative clause subjects always appear in the Accusative case (20a, b) while oblique noun phrases might be case-marked. Similarly to Mojave, adverbial clauses show a different pattern, cf. the purpose clause in (20c) that overtly marks its subject with Nominative case. In Yavapai as well, subjects of relative clauses are zero-coded (21a, b), while adverbial clauses mark their subjects with Nominative case as exemplified by the conditionals in (21c). The same discussion as for Mojave could be held about the location of the common argument, i.e. whether it is in or outside the relative clause. In example (21a), the cat serves as the subject of the relative as well as main clause and thus the absence of case-marking cannot be explained on account of its role in the main clause (as proposed by Dixon for Mojave). Example (21b), on the other hand, is ambiguous since the coyote is the object of the main clause and as such would be expected to be zero-coded. Also, there is an alternative construction which is often translated as a relative clause into English (21d), in which the subject receives Nominative case. Kendall (1976: 221) treats it as some kind of topicalization construction.

(20) Jamul Tiipay (Yuman; California; Miller 2001: 207, 210, 259)

a. [*'iipay peya nye-kwe-'iny-pe*]-*ch   mespa*
   man this 3>1-SBJ.REL-give-DEM-NOM die
   'The man who gave me this died.'

b. [*leech Marii chshaak-pu*]   *mamwi-aa*
   milk Maria bring_towards-DEM 2.do_what-Q
   'What did you do with the milk Maria brought?'

c. [***maach*** *kaavaay peya me-llywa-x-ich*] *uukwii*
   2SG.NOM horse   this 2-ride-IRR-PURP buy
   'I bought this horse for you to ride.'

(21) Yavapai (Yuman; Arizona; Kendall 1976: 51, 213, 24, 221)
    a. [ñmi vqi   hmañ k-ttmo:-c]   hmañ hme-ha   ck^{y}o:-kñ
       cat female child REL-scratch-NOM child male_that bite-COMPL
       'The cat that scratched the girl bit the boy.'
    b. [kiθar q^{w}ar qoleyaw k-ne:h-a]   ʔ-u:-kñ
       coyote   chicken REL-kill-TNS 1-see-COMPL
       'I saw the coyote that killed the chicken.'
    c. [vqi   hmañ-c   ñmi vhe: syo:m-kiθo] ñmi-c   ttmo:-ha
       woman child-NOM cat tail pull-COND cat-NOM scratch-FUT
       'If the girl pulls the cat's tail, it will scratch (her).'
    d. can-c   k^{w}e civiam-l wa-m   [ñθaʔa   pil-c   kkav-k
       John-NOM car-INESS   sit-ALLO that_one_visible Bill-NOM buy-EGO
       no:-km]
       FUT-ICML
       'John is sitting in the car that Bill is going to buy.

For other Yuman languages, there is only sparse information on dependent clauses, usually consisting of just one or two odd examples without any discussion of their structure. Among these languages is Cocopa. The example in (22a) clearly contains a dependent clause. However, its internal structure and type are relatively unclear. The literal translation is probably something along the lines of 'where the king's house is, he arrived at it', which could be interpreted as an adverbial locational clause. Whatever the exact semantic type of this clause is, the subject of the dependent clause is in the Nominative case. Likewise, the subject is marked with the Nominative in the temporal adverbial clause in (22b). The Mesa Grande Diegueño example in (23) could likewise be interpreted as an adverbial clause, or maybe a relative clause. Gorbet (1976: 135) analyzes it as adverbial, but he notes that others might analyze it as a relative clause. The subject of this dependent clause is zero-coded.

(22) Cocopa (Yuman; California; Crawford 1966: 191, Langdon & Munro 1979: 325)
    a. [ré   n^{y}awá-c   ṣayá-m],   n^{y}ṣá-ƚ^y p-wámca
       king 3SG.house-NOM be_there-DSBJ it-LOC 3-arrive
       'He arrived there at the king's house.'

6 Subjects of non-basic clauses

> b. [ʔnʸa:-č lča:š-m] sa:m-tʸ nʸ-əwa:ča
> 1SG-NOM little-DSBJ Somerton-LOC 1-live
> 'When I was little, we lived in Somerton.'

(23) Diegueño (Mesa Grande) (Yuman; California; Gorbet 1976: 135)
['xat nʸ-cu:kuw]-pu-i nʸi: w-Lic-x w-ma:w
dog 3>1-bite-DEM-LOC at_all 3-bad-IRR 3-NEG
'the bite wasn't bad at all' (lit: 'where the dog bit me, it wasn't bad at all')

In Maidu, the discussion of complex sentences, i.e. those containing more than one clause, is very brief (Shipley 1964: 69–70). None of the given examples has an overt subject argument in the dependent clause and the case-marking on such arguments, should they occur, is not discussed.

Turning to the investigation of valency-decreasing constructions, Mojave has an operation in which the logical subject is deleted. The single argument of the resulting clause (i.e. the logical object) remains in the zero-coded form. Munro (1976) therefore does not consider them to be subjects, although she still glosses the verbal marker that is found in this construction as passive. In addition 'passive' verbs take the 1st and 2nd person object-agreement suffixes, and as such, agree with their subjects (24a), third person objects do not agree with the verb in any context in Mojave. Comparing the 'passive' clauses in example (24b) with (24c), in which the logical subject is not realized either, the 'passive' morpheme on the verb appears to make the logical object more central in the clause.

(24) Mojave (Munro 1976: 241, 220)

> a. nʸ-tapiʔipay-č-m
> 1.OBJ-save-PASS-TNS
> 'I was saved.'
>
> b. masahay-nʸ əta:v-č-m
> girl-DEM hit-PASS-TNS
> 'The girl got hit.'
>
> c. masahay-nʸ əta:v-k
> girl-DEM hit-TNS
> '(Someone) hit the girl.'

Two other Yuman languages, namely Yavapai (25) and Havasupai (26), on the other hand, have clear passive constructions in which the logical object is promoted to syntactic Nominative-marked subject. As in Wappo, A arguments of passive clauses bear Nominative case-marking (27a, 28a).

(25) Yavapai (Kendall 1976: 127)

    a. *hlo-v-c*   *si:l-v-kñ*
       rabbit-DEM-NOM fry-PASS-COMPL
       'The rabbit was fried.'

    b. *θala-c*   *hlo*   *si:l-kñ*
       Thala-NOM rabbit fry-COMPL
       'Thala fried the rabbit.'

(26) Havasupai (Yuman; Arizona; Kozlowski 1972: 60, 61)

    a. *wa-ha-c*   *wi-v-m*   *yo-v-c-a*
       house-DEM-NOM stone-DEM-PRTV make-PASS-PL-MODAL
       'The house is made of stone.'

    b. *ah-ñu-c*   *mat-ñu-m*   *pay vtil-v-k-yu*
       water-DEM-NOM earth-DEM-on all   lay-PASS-IND-AUX
       'The water is lying all over the ground (over there).

(27) Wappo (Thompson et al. 2006: 79, 40)

    a. *šiʔay-i*   *mot'-kheʔ*
       stalk-NOM pile_up-PASS
       'The stalks have been piled up'

    b. **ah**   *hol koṭo:mela te-k'eč'-taʔ*
       1SG.NOM tree big.PL   DIR-chop-PST
       'I chopped down the big trees.'

(28) Wappo (Thompson et al. 2006: 79, 46)

    a. ***cephi***   *ošay'-kheʔ*
       3SG.NOM pay-PASS
       'S/he got paid'

    b. **ah**   *mi*   *o-šay'i-ya:miʔ*
       1SG.NOM 2SG.ACC UOP-pay-FUT
       'I'm going to pay you.'

Shipley (1964) does not discuss any passive or passive-like constructions in his grammar of Maidu. Also, Siewierska (2005b) lists Maidu as one of the languages in which a passive is absent, giving Shipley's work as reference.

6 Subjects of non-basic clauses

language	S rel	S adv	S compl	S VDC
Cocopa	-	NOM	-	-
Diegueño (Mesa Grande)	ACC	ACC	-	-
Havasupai	-	-	-	NOM
Jamul Tiipay	ACC	NOM	-	-
Mojave	ACC	NOM	NOM	ACC
Wappo	ACC	ACC	ACC	NOM
Yavapai	ACC	NOM	-	NOM

Table 6.1: Marking of subjects in non-basic clauses in the marked-S languages of North America

An overview of the marking of subjects in non-basic clauses is provided in Table 6.1 for the languages of North America.[6] The most remarkable feature is the consistent absence of nominative case-marking for subjects of relative clauses.

6.6 Pacific

Dependent clauses in the marked-S languages of the Pacific exhibit quite a few interesting patterns with respect to case-marking. The other non-basic clauses are not remarkable, though more detailed data on the Nias passive could possibly be very interesting.

Main clauses and relative clauses in Nias show opposite properties, with respect to the Mutated and Unmutated forms. Compare the relativized S in (29a) with the main clause S in (29b). The same is true for the P argument, as can be seen by comparing the (a) and (b) sentences in examples (30–31).

(29) Nias (Sundic; Indonesia; Brown 2001: 414, 559)

    a. nihs [si=ma=mate fo'omo meneßi]
        person REL=COMPL=die wife yesterday

        'the man whose wife died yesterday.'

    b. mate *zibaya*-nia meneßi
        die uncle.MUT-3SG.POSS yesterday

        'His uncle died yesterday.'

---

[6] In the column headings the following abbreviations are used: S = S-like/subject argument; rel = relative clause; adv = adverbial clause; compl = complement clause; VDC = valency-decreasing construction

(30) Nias (Brown 2001: 414)

    a. *Andrehe'e nasu*   [*si=usu*   ***ya'o***]
       DIST   dog.MUT REL=bite 1SG
       'That's the dog that bit me.'

    b. *i-usu*   ***ndrao*** *asu*
       3SG.RLS-bite 1SG.MUT dog
       'The dog bit me.'

(31) Nias (Brown 2001: 415)

    a. *Andrehe'e mbua*   [*si=ma*   *i-halö*   ***bua mbala*** *andre*]
       DIST   fruit_tree.MUT REL=PFV 3SG.RLS-take fruit papaya DIST
       'That is the tree that he took those papaya from.'

    b. *i-halö*   ***mbua***   ***mbala***   *moroi*   *ba mbua*
       3SG.RLS-take fruit.MUT papaya.MUT come.from LOC fruit_tree.MUT
       hö'ö
       DIST
       'He took the papapya from the tree.'

The A argument of a relative clause is realized as a noun in the Mutated form (32a), while in main clauses it would be Unmutated.[7] The status of relative clause A arguments, however, is somewhat unclear. In relative clauses that have the internal A argument realized as an overt noun phrase, the verb usually bears the prefix *ni* glossed as passive (cf. 32a). The status of this passive is not completely clear. The passive morpheme appears predominantly within relative clauses, yet in some rare instances, is also used in independent main clauses according to Lea Brown (p.c.). I will return to this issue when discussing valency-reducing operations.

---

[7] Another strategy for realizing the A argument of a relative clause is to have the A as a possessor (Brown 2001: 420).

  (i) a. *u-fake*   *zekhula*   *ni-rökhi-**nia***
        1SG.RLS-use coconut.MUT PASS-grate-3SG.POSS
        'I used the coconut which she grated.'

     b. *i-rökhi*   *zekhula*
        3SG.RLS-grate coconut.MUT
        'She grated the coconut.'

6 Subjects of non-basic clauses

(32) Nias (Brown 2001: 422)

    a. *Andrehe'e nohi* [*si=löna ni-lau **nono** matua*]
       DIST   coconut_tree.MUT REL=NEG PASS-climb child.MUT male
       'That is the coconut tree the boy did not climb.'

    b. *Ma=i-bözi   nasu   **ono** matua ba   ma=m-oloi   ya*
       PERF=3SG.RLS-hit dog.MUT child male   CONJ PFV=DYN-run 3SG.MUT
       'The boy hit the dog and ran away.'

In Ajië, subjects of purpose clauses (33a) and reason clauses (33b) are in the Nominative case. De la Fontinelle (1976: 330) gives this example with parentheses around the Nominative marker indicating its optionality, but she does not comment on this any further.

(33) Ajië (Oceanic; New Caledonia; Lichtenberk 1978: 113 after de la Fontinelle 1976: 330 and Kasarhérou (née de la Fontinelle) 1961: 189, 190)

    a. *na uu   kwaʔ* [*cɛ   ki   dii   **na**   neɟʌʔ*]
       3SG call_for rain   PURP HYP wet NOM ground
       'He calls for rain so that the ground may be wet.'

    b. *gwe   daa tuwiri* [*wɛ   wi   bomu **na**   kɔwi-ɲ*] [*wɛ   wi   ɔi*
       1SG.PROSP NEG touch REAS DUBT smell NOM hand-1SG REAS DUBT eat
       *ne-lə?   ɣi-ɲa   **na**   yiipu*]
       COLL-braid POSS-1SG NOM rat
       'I am not going to touch it because my hand might smell (and) because the rat might eat my braids.'

For Savosavo, information is provided for a large number of different types of dependent clauses (Wegener 2008: 254–286). Several of these types allow for the optional or obligatory realization of their subjects in the Genitive rather than the Nominative case. Relative clauses always encode their subjects in the Genitive case. Other constituents of the relative clause are encoded like in independent clauses. The examples in (34) illustrate this pattern. Adverbial clauses, on the other hand, use either the Nominative or Genitive case to mark their subjects, as seen in (35).

(34) Savosavo (Solomons East Papuan; Solomon Islands; Wegener 2008: 257, 258)

    a. [*lo   fomu=gha ze   pale-tu*] *lo   mavutu*
       DET.PL form=PL 3.PL.GEN stay-REL DET.SG place
       'The place where the forms are.'

b. [*lo   lo-ma   nyuba ko-va   Honiara bo-tu*] *lo*
   DET.SG.M 3SG.M-GEN.SG.F child 3SG.F-GEN.M Honiara go-REL DET.SG.M
   mapa
   person
   'the man whose daughter went to Honiara'

(35) Savosavo (Wegener 2008: 275, 272)
   a. [*kokoroko=**na** ngia*] *ze   ka   gholigholi tete=ghu=e*
      chicken=NOM cry.SIM 3PL.GEN already scrape   balance=NMLZ=EMPH
      lo   tada=gha=na
      DET=PL man=PL=NOM
      'As the rooster crowed, they already scraped (coconuts), the men.'
   b. *pa muzi=la*   [*ko-**va**   elu   epi-atu*] *lo   sua=gha=na*
      one night=LOC.M 3SG.F-GEN.M wake sit-BG.IPFV DET.PL giant=PL=NOM
      ngori-ngori(-i)
      RDP-snore(-FIN)
      'One night as she was still awake sitting there, the giants snored.'
   c. *te=lo   ai   mau=na   zua* [*tulola=**ze**   tei(-i)*...]
      CONJ=3SG.M.NOM 1SG.GEN father=NOM ask   then=3PL.NOM say(-FIN)
      'Then my father asked and then they said ...'

I will now turn to the discussion of valency-decreasing constructions. None of the existing descriptions of Nias gives an extensive discussion of the passive. The passive morpheme appears predominantly within relative clauses. The passive subject is in the mutated form in (36). In some rare instances, the passive is also used in independent main clauses according to Lea Brown (p.c.), though unfortunately, I have no example sentence to demonstrate this behavior.

(36) Nias (Brown 2001: 573)
   *ma=oya=ae   **mbalatu** ni-nößö-i-nia*
   PFV=many=already knife.MUT PASS-make-TR-3SG.POSS
   'He had already made a lot of knifes' (lit. 'The knifes made by him were already a lot')

The 3rd person possessive suffix on the passivized verb could indicate that this is an impersonal construction rather than a true passive. Further, some passivized verbs have a transitivizer (TR) affixed to their stem (37a), which makes the whole

6 Subjects of non-basic clauses

situation even less transparent. But compare also (37b), where the TR-marker occurs also with the non-passivized form of the same verb.

(37) Nias (Brown 2001: 556, 555)

    a. *ya'ia ni-bali-'ö-ra   saßuyu*
       3SG PASS-turn-TR-3PL.POSS slave

       'He was made a slave.'

    b. *la-bali-'ö   ya   saßuyu*
       3PL.RLS-turn-TR 3SG.MUT slave

       'They made him a slave.'

There is no specialized passive or antipassive construction in Savosavo, but the detransitivizer -*za* serves similar functions to those associated with passives and antipassives in other languages. When it is attached to transitive verbs, this results in a change in the argument structure of the verb. There are three possibilities for the nature of change in argument structure, the first (corresponding to a passive reading) being the most common (Wegener 2008: 171):

1. The subject is demoted and removed, the object is promoted to subject position.

2. The subject is unchanged, only the object is removed.

3. Both subject and object are removed and are replaced by a subject that is a semantic cognate of the verb, e.g. 'a shout' in case of a verb 'to shout'

The following example illustrates the passive use of the detransitivizer. In this example the subject is in the Nominative case (38).

(38) Savosavo (Wegener 2008: 171)

    a. *lo   karoti=**na**   tozo-za-i*
       DET.SG.M carrot=NOM cut-DETR-FIN

       'The carrot is cut.'

    b. *karoti=lo   te   tozo-li(-i)*
       carrot=3.SG.M.NOM EMPH cut-3SG.M.OBJ(-FIN)

       'He cut (a) carrot.'

Table 6.2 summarizes the data just discussed. Similar to the North American languages, case-marking of subjects in relative clauses is most interesting, although the patterns found in the Pacific are quite distinct from those found in North America.

language	S rel	S adv	S compl	S VDC
Ajië	-	NOM	-	-
Nias	ERG	-	-	ABS
Savosavo	GEN	NOM/GEN	-	NOM

Table 6.2: Subjects marking for non-basic clauses in the marked-S languages of the Pacific

6.7 Nilo-Saharan

The subject arguments of non-basic clauses are typically marked with the nominative case in the Nilo-Saharan languages, though for each context there is at least one language behaving in an exceptional way. Another interesting phenomenon is attested in Päri, a language with a marked-nominative system only with dependent clauses.

The Päri system exhibits a split within its alignment type, as defined in Chapter 2. More precisely, it is split between different clause-types. In main clauses, Päri has an ergative-pattern, yet in imperatives and most dependent clause-types the overt Ergative marker is also used for intransitive S (Andersen 1988: 316–319). Those clauses thus exhibit a marked-nominative pattern, which Andersen (1988: 316) believes to be the source for the ergative pattern of main clauses in Päri. This split is not only limited to case-marking, but it is also found with the verbal indexing-system and word order. The examples in (39) illustrate the marked-nominative pattern. The questions in (39a, b) are listed among the class of dependent clauses. Unfortunately, Andersen does not analyze the structure of the item glossed as 'why'. Its complex structure and the fact that the whole structure is identified as a complex clause suggest that this item constitutes the main or matrix clause to the following subordinate clause. In the main clauses (39c,cd), this marking is indeed restricted to A arguments and not found on S arguments.

(39) Päri (Nilotic; Sudan; Andersen 1988: 319, 318, 292)

a. *pìr ŋɔ́ dháagɔ́ icɔ̀ɔl-yí ɲìpɔ̀nd´-ὲ*
why woman call-3SG child-ERG
'Why did the child call the woman?'

b. *pìr ŋɔ́ ìpʌ̀ʌr cícɔ̀-ê*
why jump man-ERG
'Why did the man jump?'

6 Subjects of non-basic clauses

    c. *ùbúr á-túuk`*
       Ubur COMPL-play
       'Ubur played.'

    d. *dháagɔ́ á-yàaɲ   ùbúr-ì*
       woman COMPL-insult Ubur-ERG
       'Ubur insulted the woman.'

Among the subordinate clause-types that Andersen lists as having marked-nominative coding are purposive clauses. This fits Dixon's expectations about this type of splits:

> [...] 'purposive (= infinitival) clauses' normally refer to some attempt at controlled action; clauses of this kind generally have an A or S 'agent' NP that is co-referential with some NP in their main clause [...] for this type of subordinate construction, we would surely expect S and A to be treated in the same way within the complement clause. (Dixon 1994: 101–102)

Now I will return to the Nilo-Saharan languages which do exhibit marked-nominative coding in main clauses. In Tennet, relative clause-internal subjects are in the Nominative case (40). Similarly in Nandi, subjects of relative clauses are marked with the Nominative (41). Maa relative clauses, which have the structure V-AGR N [V-REL N], also employ the Nominative case for subject-marking according to Tucker & Mpaayei (1955: chapter 12).

(40) Tennet (Surmic; Sudan; Randal 1998: 259, 255)

    a. *k-í-cín-a   anná   dhṹnọc   [cí bạlị ákáti   lọhám-i]*
       1-PFV-see-1SG 1SG.NOM waterbuck AM PST PFV.spear Loham-NOM
       'I saw the waterbuck that Loham speared.'

    b. *elegyé [cí-k úk   **enné**   á-kát-a]*
       animals AM-PL PFV.go 3SG.NOM PFV-spear-(pause)
       'the animals that he went and speared'

(41) Nandi (Nilotic; Kenya; Creider & Creider 1989: 134, 133)

    a. *á-mác-é   ci:tà   [ne kè:r-éy   **te:ta**]*
       1SG-want-IPFV person REL 3-see-IPFV COW.NOM
       'I want the person that the cow is looking at.'

    b. *á-mác-é   ci:tà   [ne kè:r-éy   te:tà]*
       1SG-want-IPFV person REL 3-see-IPFV cow
       'I want the person that is looking at the cow.'

6.7 Nilo-Saharan

Arensen (1982: 112–114) distinguishes between what he calls 'dependent' and 'subordinate' clauses in his description of Murle. All examples he lists as dependent clauses are relative clauses. Subjects inside the relative clause are in the Nominative case (42a). The clauses referred to as subordinate clauses by Arensen on the other hand mark their subjects with Accusative case (42b, c). All examples he presents are of the complement clause-type.

(42) Murle (Surmic; Sudan; Arensen 1982: 112, 113, 114)

    a. kɛɛti naana kiziwan [o or **niina**]
       skin.1SG 1SG.NOM buffalo.ACC which shoot.PST 2SG.NOM
       'I am skinning the buffalo which you shot.'

    b. kaga naana [**nɔnnɔ** aak idiŋ]
       Know 1SG.NOM 3SG.ACC cook meat.ACC
       'I know that she is cooking meat.'

    c. karɔɔŋ naana [**ɔl** kiliŋliŋit]
       want.1SG 1SG.NOM people.ACC work
       'I want the people to work.'

Turkana relative clauses mark their subjects, when clause internal, in Nominative case (43). However, the subject is only realized in the relative clause if it is not the common argument (43b).

(43) Turkana (Nilotic; Kenya; Dimmendaal 1982: 309, 314)

    a. e-dya` [lo-wɔ̀ɔnɪ-k-a-ɪdɛs-ɪ̀ a-yɔŋ]
       boy.ACC that-other_day-TR-1SG-hit-ASP 1SG.ACC
       'The boy that hit me the other day.'

    b. e-dya` [ŋolo`ŋwɔ̀ɔnɪ̣ a-ɪdɛ̀s-ɪ **a-yɔ̀ŋ**]
       boy.ACC that other_day 1SG-hit-ASP 1SG.NOM
       'The boy that I hit the other day.'

    c. k-à-ɪdɛ̀s-ɪ` e-dyà a-yɔŋ` ŋwòonɪ̣
       TR-1SG-hit-ASP boy.NOM 1SG.ACC other_day
       'The boy hit me the other day.'

    d. nà-mɔnɪ`[na-e-yà ŋi-còm-in ka` ŋɪ-tɔm-ɛ]
       in-forest that-3-be baboons.NOM with elephants.ACC
       'In the forest where there are baboons and elephants.'

6 Subjects of non-basic clauses

Other dependent clauses behave differently from relative clauses with respect to case-marking. Most examples listed are of the complement clause type. Like in relative clauses, the subject is only overtly realized in the complement clause when it is not identical to the subject of the matrix clause. Otherwise, the subject argument is only realized in the main clause in Turkana (44a). When occurring inside the complement clause, the subject is in topicalized position (i.e. before the verb of the dependent clause) and thus is in the Accusative case. Dimmendaal (1982: 374) argues that they are nonetheless part of the dependent rather than the matrix clause, since the matrix verb does not show any object agreement (44b).[8]

(44) Turkana (Dimmendaal 1982: 374)

    a. *à-sak-ì*   *a-yɔ̀ŋ*   *i-yoŋ`*   *akɪ-ar`*
        1SG-want-ASP 1SG.NOM 2SG.ACC INF-kill
        'I want to kill you.'

    b. *à-sak-ì*   *a-yɔ̀ŋ*   *i-yoŋ`*   *ɪ-ar-ì*
        1SG-want-ASP 1SG.NOM 2SG.ACC 2SG-kill-ASP
        'I want you to kill it.'

    c. *to-ryam-ʊ̀ ŋesì*   *à-pa`*        *kɛŋ`*   *ɛ-maʊ̀*
        3-find-VEN 3SG.NOM NC-father.ACC 3SG.POSS 3-lack
        'He found his father was not there.'

In the following paragraphs, valency-decreasing operations are discussed. The single argument of the Turkana 'impersonal active voice' (as Dimmendaal refers to the most passive-like construction) has Nominative marking (Dimmendaal 1982: 132–133). In Murle, the subject of passive sentences is in Nominative case (45a). And as seen already in Section 6.4, Tennet passive (46a) and antipassive subjects (46b) also are in the Nominative case.

(45) Murle (Arensen 1982: 140, 137)

    a. *ajuk-ɛ*   *ɛɛt-i*
        trow-PASS man-NOM
        'The man is thrown.'

    b. *ajuk ɛɛt-i*   *dila*
        trow man-NOM spear.ACC
        'The man throws a spear.'

---

[8] In Turkana the marker *k-* precedes the subject agreement affix if there is a first or second person object (Dimmendaal 1982: 122).

(46) Tennet (Randal 1998: 245)

    a. *á̰-rṵ́h-w-ḛ*   *ḭ́yóko̰*
       IPFV-beat-EPEN-PASS drum.NOM now

      'The drum is being beaten now.'

    b. *á-dáh-ye*   **do̰lḛ́c**
       IPFV-eat-ANTIP child.NOM

      'The child is eating.'

There are two processes which delete the logical subject of a sentence in Nandi. The first – termed 'stativization' by Creider & Creider – has the logical object as the surface (Nominative) subject and expression of an agent is not permitted (47a). In the other process, which is actually referred to as 'passivization', the agent is obligatorily deleted but the object gains no Nominative case-marking (Creider & Creider 1989: 125–126), as illustrated in (47b, c). In this construction, the verb receives invariant first person plural agreement, while the 3rd person stem form of the verb is chosen (Creider & Creider 1989: 100). 'Impersonal construction' would probably be a better label for this construction, while the 'stative' actually meets all criteria usually employed for a construction to be classified as a passive. Creider & Creider (1989) claim that the lack of an optional oblique phrase representing the logical subject disqualifies the construction from being considered a passive. However, this criterion is not widely used in cross-linguistic work on passives.[9]

(47) Nandi (Creider & Creider 1989: 125, 126)

    a. *ká:-ko-yà:t-ák*   **ka:ri:k**
       PST-3-open-STAT/PASS houses.NOM

      'The houses have been opened.'

    b. *kí:-ke:-sìc*   *kipe:t kény*
       PST-1PL-bear.3 Kibet ago

      'Kibet was born long ago.'

    c. *kí-yâ:t-éy*   *kúrké:t*
       1PL-open-IPFV.3 door

      'The door is being opened.'

---

[9] As Creider & Creider (1989: 100) note they chose the English passive, which allows for the oblique realization of logical subjects in passive clauses, as their model for a passive construction.

6 Subjects of non-basic clauses

Subjects of passive sentences are in the Accusative form in Maa (Tucker & Mpaayei 1955: 175). Payne (2007) lists three kinds of verbal diathesis: middle, antipassive and impersonal passive. In the middle (48a) and antipassive (48b), the subject is in the Nominative case. In the impersonal passive on the other hand the subject is in the Accusative (i.e. zero-coded case), as shown in (48c). Compare this with the active counterpart of the sentence (48d).

(48) Maa (Payne 2007: ex.11, ex.13, ex.16, ex.15)
    a. ŋ-é-duŋ-o   ɛn-**ámʊ̀kɛ̀**
       CON-3-cut-MID.N_PFV F.SG-sandal.NOM
       'The shoe was cut.'
    b. n-é-ramat-íshò   ɔl-**mʊrraní**
       CON-3-tend.livestock-ANTIP M.SG-warrior.NOM
       'The warrior herds [e.g. cows].'
    c. ɛ-tɛ-ɛn-ák-ì   ɔl-apúrrònì
       3-PFV-tie-PFV-PASS M.SG-thief.ACC
       'The thief was arrested.'
    d. ɛ-ɪbʊ́ŋ-á   ɪ-s'ɪkarɪní   ɔl-apúrrònì
       3-catch-PFV PL-police.NOM M.SG-thief.ACC
       'The policemen have arrested the thief.'

All these findings are summarized in Table 6.3. Unlike from the previous sections, relative clauses in the Nilo-Saharan languages always employ the nominative case to mark subjects. If any variation is found among dependent clauses, it is with complement clauses.

language	S rel	S adv	S compl	S VDC
Maa	NOM	-	-	ACC/NOM
Murle	NOM	-	ACC	NOM
Nandi	NOM	-	-	NOM
Päri	-	NOM	NOM	-
Tennet	NOM	-	-	NOM
Turkana	NOM	-	ACC (topic)	NOM

Table 6.3: The marking of subjects in non-basic clauses in Nilo-Saharan

6.8 Afro-Asiatic

Non-basic clauses in the Afro-Asiatic languages exhibit little, if any, deviation from the general pattern of marking subjects with nominative case. Only the passive construction in Boraana Oromo might be different in this respect. Unfortunately, quite a few questions about the grammar of this construction remain unanswered. In general, more detailed information on non-basic clauses in the Afro-Asiatic languages would be very desirable. Especially lacking is information about dependent clauses other than relative clauses, since only few grammars treat this topic.

Relative clauses in the Boraana dialect of Oromo mark subjects with Nominative case (49). In the Harar dialect, the subject in dependent clauses is marked with Nominative case as well. This is true for relative clauses (50a, b) as well as adverbial clauses (50c). The latter, however, do not have an overt subject inside the dependent clause in most cases.

(49) Oromo (Boraana) (Eastern Cushitic; Ethiopia; Stroomer 1995: 104, Andrzejewski 1962: 125)

    a. *nam-ii*   beesee hat-e   is=aa
        man-NOM money steal-3SG.M.PST him=LIN(Q)
        'Is he the one that stole the money?'

    b. *Nam-i*   Diido ijeese Jaanjamtu'
        person-NOM Diido killed Jaanjamtu
        'The people who killed Diido were the Janjamtu.'

(50) Oromo (Harar) (Eastern Cushitic; Ethiopia; Owens 1985: 131, 143)

    a. *intal-tíi* (taan) *inníi*   arke ác   jirti
        girl-NOM (as)   3SG.M.NOM saw there exist.3SG.F
        'The girl he saw in there.'

    b. *namicc-íi* (xan) *intal-tíi* isá   baréed-dúu ác   jira
        man-NOM (as)   girl-NOM 3SG.M.ACC pretty-F   there exist.3SG.M
        'The man whose daughter is pretty is there.'

    c. *hagá isíin*   d'uf-t-ú   taa'-e
        until 3.SG.F.NOM come-F-DEP stay-PST
        'He stayed until she came.'

Arbore relative clauses are discussed by Hayward (1984: 314). In most of his examples there is no independent NP functioning as the subject of the relative clause. One of the few examples in which a subject is realized within the relative clause is given in (51a). The subject is in the Nominative case. Example (51b) appears to be a complement clause according to the translation. However, the structure of this example is not discussed by Hayward. In this case, the subject of the complement clause *saal-t-átto* 'that woman' is zero-coded. However, the referent coded by 'that woman' is apparently topicalised in this construction. This fact could account for the absence of Nominative case-marking.

(51) Arbore (Eastern Cushitic; Ethiopia; Hayward 1984: 318, 321)
    a. *maar-t-á* **s[eʔẹ]** *ḍa[l:-]e*   *hunna ma ká[ṭːʰ]o*
       calf.F.NOM COW.NOM give_birth-3SG.PFV ?   who ?
       'The calf which the cow gave birth to has no strength.'
    b. **saal-t-átto,** *hatt-áy zaHate k'ub-áŋ*   *k'ab-a*
       woman-F-DIST that-3SG die.3SG hand-INST have-?
       'That woman, I know that she died.'

In K'abeena relative clauses, the common argument is always realized in the main clause and is marked for its function there. There is no resumptive or relative pronoun, and as such, the common argument is gaped in the relative clause. Other arguments within the relative clause get the same marking which they would receive in a main clause. This means that subjects inside the relative clause are in the Nominative case (52a). Adverbial clauses mark their subjects via Nominative case as well (52b).

(52) K'abeena (Eastern Cushitic; Ethiopia; Crass 2005: 287)
    a. **ná'u-n^i**   *nassinoon-si*   *c'uul^u*
       1PL.NOM-EMPH raise.PFV.1PL-3SG.M.OBJ.REL child.NOM
       laga'yo-'n^e
       leave.PFV.3SG.M-1PL.OBJ
       'The child which we raised has left us.'
       original translation: 'Das Kind, das wir selbst aufgezogen haben, hat uns verlassen.'
    b. **got^u**   *wajjo-r^a*   *hilikk'^{i}*
       hyena.NOM scream.PFV.3SG.M-TMP be_shocked.CVB.1SG
       ke'yoomm^i
       stand_up.PFV.1SG
       'When/After/Because a hyena (had) shrieked, I was shocked and stood up.'
       original translation: 'Als/Nachdem/Weil eine Hyäne schrie/geschriehen hatte, erschrak ich und stand auf.'

Finally, for Gamo, the two types of dependent clause on which information is provided are relative clauses (53a) and complement clauses (53b). Both mark subjects in the Nominative case.

(53) Gamo (Omotic; Ethiopia; Hompó 1990: 400, 361)

    a. [*nun-i*   *beʔ-i-d-a*]   *misiri-y-aa*   *pisa*
        1PL-NOM see-PM-TNS-COMPLX woman-DEF-NOM basket.ACC
        os̀-a-us
        make-PM-TNS.COMPLX
        'The woman whom we saw makes baskets.'

    b. *tan-i*   [*nen-i*   *oras̀-a*   *oič-onta*   *malaa*]
        1SG-NOM   2SG-NOM Oratsi-ACC ask-NEG-INF that
        yotadis-šin
        tell-PM.TNS.COMPLX.AUX
        'I have told you not to ask Oratsi.'

Most Afro-Asiatic languages for which voice alternations are discussed in the grammar have a construction labeled as passive. However, these passive constructions do not exhibit identical properties across the languages, especially concerning the passivisation of non-P arguments. Passive subjects that correspond to direct objects in the active counterpart of a clause are marked with Nominative case in K'abeena (54, 55), Gamo (56a, b), and Harar Oromo (57a, b). For Gamo and Harar Oromo, the grammars provide additional information on the passivisation of ditransitive clauses. Gamo recipients or oblique marked participants which get promoted to subject of a passive sentence keep their original case-marking but gain verbal agreement (Hompó 1990: 394), as demonstrated in (56c). In Harar Oromo both objects of ditransitives can be promoted to Nominative marked subject (57b, c). Passive agents cannot be expressed in Harar Oromo, while they can be realized as Locative phrases in K'abeena (55). For Gamo, no information on this topic is provided in the grammar.

(54) K'abeena (Crass 2005: 275)

    a. *'daliil^i*   *'osa'lanto*
        Dalil.NOM laugh.PASS.PFV.3SG.F
        'Dalil was laughed at.'
        original translation: 'Dalil wurde ausgelacht.'

    b. *'ilf^u*   *'osa'lito*
        Ilfu.NOM laugh.PFV.3SG.F
        'Ilfu laughed (at Dalil).'
        original translation: 'Ilfu lachte.' or 'Ilfu lachte (Dalil) aus.'

6 *Subjects of non-basic clauses*

(55) K'abeena (Crass 2005: 275)

    a. ***lal^u***   *faangaan^i 'aa'ammo*
       cattle.NOM thief.LOC take.PASS.PFV.3SG.M
       'The cattle was stolen by thieves.'
       original translation: 'Die Rinder wurden von Dieben gestohlen.'

    b. ***faangoo*** *lalu*   *'aa'ito*
       thief.NOM cattle.ACC take.PFV.3PL
       'Thieves have stolen the cattle.'
       original translation: 'Diebe haben die Rinder gestohlen.'

(56) Gamo (Hompó 1990: 378, 394)

    a. *deša-z-**ii***   *danna-z-a-s*   *imme-ett-i-d-es*
       goat-DEF-NOM judge-DEF-GEN-REC give-PASS-PM-TNS-COMPLX
       'The goat was given to the judge.'

    b. *kawo-z-ii*   *zallʔanča-t-a-n*   *wod'-ett-i-d-es*
       king-DEF-NOM merchant-PL-ACC-LOC kill-PASS-PM-TNS-COMPLX
       'The king was killed by merchants.'

    c. *ta-s*   *zar-ett-a-d-is*
       1SG-REC answer-PASS-PM-TNS-COMPLX
       'I was answered.'

(57) Oromo (Harar) (Owens 1985: 172, 173)

    a. *makiináa-n ní* *tolf-am-t-a*
       car-NOM   FOC repair-PASS-F-IPFV
       'The car will be repaired.'

    b. *an*   *hucc'ú-n*   *d'owwat-am-e*
       1SG.NOM clothes-1SG deny-PASS-PST
       'I was denied the clothes.'

    c. *hucc'úu-n*   *ná*   *d'owwat-am-t-e*
       clothes-NOM 1SG.ACC deny-PASS-F-PST
       'The clothes were denied me.'

All examples of the passive in the Boraana dialect of Oromo mark their grammatical subject with the focus-marker *yaa* (58a, b, c).[10] Stroomer (1995) does not specify whether focus marking is obligatory for subjects of passives. Therefore,

---

[10] As the following example demonstrates, at least pronouns can be in the Nominative case when

it is not clear whether passive subjects would receive Nominative case-marking in such a context (if the grammar of Boraana Oromo allows for it at all). Compare also the impersonal construction in (58d), in which the the focus-marker is also used.

(58) Oromo (Boraana) (Stroomer 1995: 74, 89, 90)

    a. *fooni yaa d'aab-am-ani*
       meat FOC cook-PASS-3PL.PST
       'The meat has been cooked.'

    b. *mana yaa jaar-am-e*
       house FOC build-PASS-3SG.PST
       'The house has been built.'

    c. *sangaa yaa k'al-am-e*
       ox   FOC slaughter-PASS-3SG.PST
       'The ox has been killed.'

    d. *sangaa yaa ijees-ani*
       ox   FOC kill-3PL.PST
       'They killed the ox'

Table 6.4 on the next page summarizes the data. The Afro-Asiatic marked-S languages make the most regular use of the nominative-case for encoding subjects in non-basic clauses. Only the Boraana Oromo passive seems to have a peculiar pattern. However, very little is known about the structure of this construction.

6.9 Summary

Non-basic clauses mark their subjects with regular S-case-marking[11] in most instances. However, some marked-S languages employ non-standard subject case-

---

    marked by the focus-marker in Boraana Oromo. Stroomer (1995: 74) does not comment any further on case-marking with the focus-marker.

    (i) *aani   yaa kalee   billaa gabayaa bit-ad'd'-e*
        1SG.NOM FOC yesterday knife market buy-MID-1SG.PST
        'Yesterday I bought a knife at the market.'

[11] Remember that in the terminology established in Chapter 1 the label S-case refers to the case-form that is used among other functions for marking the single argument of intransitive verbs (S). It corresponds to the nominative case in languages with nominative-accusative alignment and the absolutive in those with ergative-absolutive alignment.

6 Subjects of non-basic clauses

language	S rel	S adv	S compl	S VDC
Arbore	NOM	-	-	-
Gamo	NOM	-	NOM	NOM
K'abeena	NOM	NOM	-	NOM
Oromo (Boraana)	NOM	-	-	ACC+FOC?
Oromo (Harar)	NOM	NOM	-	NOM

Table 6.4: Subject-marking of non-basic clauses in the Afro-Asiatic marked-S languages

marking for some of the roles discussed in this chapter. If a non-basic subject receives a different case-form than the S-case, this will usually be the zero-case. An overview of the data of all marked-S languages investigated in this chapter is provided in Table 6.5 on the facing page.

Atypical case-marking of subjects is most frequently found with dependent clauses. Within the domain of dependent clauses, relative clauses are the most likely type of dependent clause to employ an exceptional case-form for the subject. This is particular obvious for the languages of North America, especially Wappo and the Yuman languages. While the Yuman languages only use zero-coding for subjects in relative clauses, Wappo does not mark any type of dependent subject with the Nominative. In addition atypical case-marking for dependent subjects is found in Nias, which seems to reverse the marking relations in relative clauses; it is also found in Savosavo, where Genitive marking is obligatorily (relative clauses) or optionally used (adverbial clauses) in dependent clauses. Also in Africa, some special patterns are found in this domain of grammar. Murle uses the Accusative case for subjects of complement clauses. In Turkana, subjects of complement clauses (and all other arguments) obligatorily have to appear in the pre-verbal topic-position and thus receive Accusative case. While the Yuman languages use zero-coding for relative clause subjects and overt marking for other dependent clauses, Murle and Turkana show the reverse. Accordingly, there does not appear to be a close association of any type of dependent clause with the case-marking pattern found in main clauses.

The scale proposed for grammatical integration of clause-types (Payne 1997) discussed in Section 6.2 could serve as an indicator of how different types of clauses might be expected to behave. Payne's scale would suggest that relative clauses should behave more like independent clauses than any other type of dependent clause. The data does not provide clear support for such a relation, al-

language	S rel	S adv	S compl	S VDC
Ajië	-	NOM	-	-
Arbore	NOM	-	-	-
Cocopa	-	NOM	-	-
Diegueño	ACC	ACC	-	-
Gamo	NOM	-	NOM	NOM
Havasupai	-	-	-	NOM
Jamul Tiipay	ACC	NOM	-	-
K'abeena	NOM	NOM	-	NOM
Maa	NOM	-	-	ACC/NOM
Maidu	-	-	-	-
Mojave	ACC	NOM	NOM	ACC
Murle	NOM	-	ACC	NOM
Nandi	NOM	-	-	NOM
Nias	ERG	-	-	ERG
Oromo (Boraana)	NOM	-	-	ACC+FOC
Oromo (Harar)	NOM	NOM	-	NOM
Päri	-	NOM	NOM	-
Savosavo	GEN	NOM/GEN	-	NOM
Tennet	NOM	-	-	NOM
Turkana	NOM	-	ACC (topic)	NOM
Wappo	ACC	ACC	ACC	NOM
Yavapai	ACC	NOM	-	NOM

Table 6.5: Overview of the marking of subjects in non-basic clauses

though more languages would be needed to test for significant correlations. In addition, Päri exhibits a marked-nominative system only in dependent clauses, while other clauses have standard ergative-absolutive alignment.

Subjects in valency-decreasing constructions typically employ the S-case. A notable exception to this general tendency is Maa, where passive employs the Accusative case to mark subjects. Also the 'passive' constructions of Mojave and Boraana Oromo employ idiosyncratic marking of the subjects. However, these constructions (like the Nias Passive) demand better understanding than presently available before drawing any conclusions from this behavior.

7 Non-clause-level case marking

7.1 Introduction

This last chapter in the data-oriented part of this study is dedicated to a number of special contexts. All of these contexts have in common the fact that the case-marking of the noun is not based on its role at the clause level. The contexts studied in the previous chapters were clauses of some kind or even more complex constructions, e.g. the biclausal analysis of focus constructions (Chapter 5). In all these contexts, the encoding of the subject or subject-like elements was investigated, including the marking of one additional role, namely predicate nominals. In this chapter, the contexts are on a lower level, and the roles investigated cannot be considered to be subjects of any sort. Instead, all contexts encode roles that do not relate to verbal argument structure but are defined on a different level. In the first context discussed in this chapter, attributive possession, this level is the noun phrase. The role of interest in this context is that of adnominal possessor. Attributive possession in general and the encoding of possessors are discussed in Section 7.2. The two other roles to be discussed in this chapter are not defined by any syntactic relation at all but are rather defined entirely by the larger meta-linguistic or conversational context. First, I discuss the form of a noun (most often a name) when addressing someone. Some languages have a dedicated case-form, a vocative, to be used in this function. A brief discussion of the grammar of address is provided in Section 7.3. The other extra-syntactic form is the citation form of a noun, which is used in meta-linguistic reference to a noun. It is often associated with the form used in dictionaries, but also for labeling things. This form is discussed in Section 7.4.

After introducing the three roles investigated in this chapter, Section 7.5 addresses the different coding-patterns to be distinguished here. The subsequent sections provide data on the marking of extra-syntactic functions and structures below the level of the clause. As in the previous chapters, the data are divided by area and genealogical groupings. Starting with the African marked-S languages, Section 7.6 discusses the Nilo-Saharan languages and Section 7.7 deals with the Afro-Asiatic ones. Data on the languages of the Pacific area are given in

7 Non-clause-level case marking

Section 7.8, while Section 7.9 provides information on the North American languages. Finally, a summary comparing the encoding strategies of extra-syntactic contexts and attributive possessors in all marked-S languages is given in Section 7.10.

7.2 Attributive possessors

Attributive possessors modify a noun in a way similar to other nominal modifiers such as adjectives or quantifiers.[1] They can be either realized as full nouns or as pronominal elements. If realized as pronominal elements, indicating number, person and/or gender of the possessor, the range of cross-linguistic coding strategies is very large. In many languages, the head-noun is marked with person agreement affixes if the possessor is not realized as an independent noun, either identical to the markers used for indexing on verbs or a different set of markers. Other languages use independent pronouns to encode grammatical features of possessors not realized as independent nouns. These can either be a special set of possessive pronouns or the same forms used in other pronominal contexts. The encoding of full-noun attributive possessors can be very different from the encoding of pronominal attributive possessors. As for the contexts studied here, I will focus on the encoding of possessors as full nouns rather than as pronominals. The pronominal coding properties will only be discussed when relevant.

First, I will discuss the attributive possessive context in general. A possessive contexts contains (at least) two entities, one that will be labeled as the POSSESSOR in the following and one that will be labeled as the POSSESSEE.[2] The semantics of possessive constructions have been discussed extensively (Heine 1997: 143–156). It has been noted that most possessive constructions are not restricted to actual possession in the strict sense of one entity being the legal owner of another entity (Lyons 1977: 722). More often the possessive context expresses a more general association between two entities. Kinship terms and part-whole relations are the

---

[1] Another strategy to encode possessive relationships is via predicative possessive constructions, and thus is analyzed at the level of the clause. This context, studied in much detail by Stassen (2009), has already been discussed to some extent in Chapter 4. In that chapter, I have explained that in the languages of my sample predicative possession is either encoded via a locational strategy, and hence with the same construction as locational predication, or via a transitive possessive verb with regular transitive case-marking on its arguments.

[2] The Latin-derived term 'possessum' is also commonly used in the linguistic literature. Dixon (2010b: 262) introduces the roles R (possessor) and D (possessed) for the two nouns. However, since the label 'R' is also used for ditransitive recipients, I will not use these abbreviations here to avoid confusion.

most common semantic domains to be expressed by possessive constructions, next to actual ownership (Dixon 2010b: 263).

Further, many languages distinguish between so-called alienable possession, involving items that can easily be disposed of, and inalienable possession, involving items that are permanently possessed such as body-parts or kin (Chappell & McGregor 1996). If a language distinguishes between these two types of possessives, each type has a dedicated construction; the two constructions might vary greatly in their means of expression. Due to the tight-knit relation between possessor and possessee in inalienable possession, the relationship is usually expressed using less material than with alienable possession. Strategies often associated with inalienable possession are mere juxtaposition and indexing on the possessee, while alienable possession is often expressed through genitives or free or bound linker morphemes between the two entities (Chappell & McGregor 1996: 4–5).

Croft (2003: 32–40) presents a detailed analysis of the different kinds of marking found in possessive constructions. He distinguishes between three basic types: 'simple strategies', 'relational strategies', and 'indexing strategies'. He further notes that these distinctions might become blurred once a strategy becomes more grammaticalized. Not all the details of Croft's typology are relevant for the present study. Therefore, I will concentrate on the strategies and distinctions which are relevant for the present discussion. Apart from pure positional marking (i.e. juxtaposition of possessor and possessee), head-marking and dependent-marking strategies can be distinguished. The dependent-marking strategy appears to be more common cross-linguistically. In this strategy, the possessor is marked for its role in the possessive construction, for example by a special inflectional case-form, which is often labeled as 'genitive'. This terminology is indeed so common that Payne (1997: 104) refers to adnominal possessors as 'genitive' irrespective of whether they are inflectionally marked or not. Apart from being fully fledged case-forms, the possessor in an attributive possessive construction can also be marked via possessive particles or distinct prepositions (cf. the English *of*-possessive). Head-marking attributive possessive constructions are often associated with inflectional markers on the possessee that agree with the possessor in person, number and the like. These markers are often only used when the possessor is not expressed as an independent noun. However, some languages use these markers in all possessive contexts. Further, in some languages there is a special case-form used on the possessee sometimes called an 'anti-genitive' (Andersen 1991). This marker differs from the affixal possessor agreement-system, since it is not inflected for any properties of the possessor,

7 Non-clause-level case marking

like person or number. Since this type of case-marking appears to be less common and does not occur in any of the traditional case-marking languages (like Latin, Greek or Sanskrit) there is no common term for a case like this. Dixon (2010b: 268) proposes 'pertensive' as a label. However, note that he restricts the use of the term 'case' to clause level marking and thus does not consider the genitive nor his newly coined 'pertensive' to be cases altogether.

7.3 Forms of address

A special purpose form of the noun is the form used in addressing a person (or more seldom a thing). Latin grammar has the Vocative, traditionally regarded as a special case-form, and such a special form exists in a number of other languages. However, if there is no special case-form in this context, the address function is supposed to be passed over to the nominative case, as Jespersen (1992 [1924]: 184) noted.

Daniel & Spencer (2009) discuss the 'vocative' as a member of case paradigms and also consider other means used to achieve the same function. The function of addressing someone is often performed by intonation or other prosodic means. Lengthening of vowels or reduction of the noun stem are also commonly used, as well as vocative particles. These particles combine with the unmarked or nominative case-form of a noun to form a kind of detached vocative according to Daniel & Spencer (2009: 630). They also find that the vocative seems to be derived from the nominative case in most languages (even if other case-forms are not). However, they conclude that it is actually the unmarked form of a noun, which often coincides with the nominative, that serves as a source for the vocative. In some cases, as they note, the vocative "is even less marked than the nominative" (Daniel & Spencer 2009: 631).

By definition, nouns serving as terms of address are not integrated into the argument-structure of a sentence. This is illustrated by the English example in (1) in which the term of address is co-referential with the subject of the sentence expressed via the second person pronoun. Orthographic convention often separates these nouns from the remainder of the sentence by punctuation.

(1) *Do you hear me, John?*

In this study, I will restrict myself to the actual morphological shape of nouns used for address. This topic of research is extremely restricted in its scope. Other factors, especially concerning the prosody of terms of address, certainly need to be taken into account in order to get a full picture of this domain of grammar.

7.4 Citation form

The citation form of a noun is a meta-linguistic concept. However, there are also actual speech situations in which such a form might prove useful. Creissels (2009: 450) lists labeling boxes or the like for their content or identifying persons by means of a passport as such contexts. Furthermore, in societies without writing, such a form can be thought of as used in instructing language learners on how a specific item is called (in case language teaching is practiced at all in the particular society). These contexts cannot in all cases be interpreted as instances of elliptic nominal predication of the type '(This is an) X' since the form of citation and predicate nominals need not coincide, as Creissels (2009: 450) points out (also compare the data in Chapter 3 on this issue).

The concept of a citation form was discussed prominently by Lyons, who defined it in the following way:

> By the citation-form of a lexeme is meant the form of the lexeme that is conventionally employed to refer to it in standard dictionaries and grammars of the language. [...] It is important to realize that the citation-form is indeed a form of the lexeme (being used for a particular reflexive or meta-linguistic purpose): it is not to be identified with the lexeme itself. (Lyons 1977: 19)

Lyons is careful to state that this meta-linguistic citation form may be different from the form speakers use in referring to a word. This distinction is probably more relevant for verbs than for nouns. While for verbs a variety of different traditions of choosing one form over the other in dictionaries and the like exist (e.g. infinitive; 1st person singular, present, indicative, active), for nouns most often the nominative case is chosen for this purpose (Aronoff 1994: 40). The citation form is set apart from another meta-linguistic form by Aronoff (1994: 41), the so-called 'lexical representation', which in contrast to the citation form is an abstract form never realized at the surface level (cf. the contrast between Semitic consonantal roots and the citation form of the corresponding lexeme).

The naming function is connected closely to the nominative case, as has already been discussed in the first chapter (Section 1.4). Though extra-syntactic functions do not play any role in modern grammatical theories, ancient grammarians put more emphasis on these uses when they chose to label the nominative as "*onomastikê ptôsis*, and to transpose this term into Latin as *casus nominativus* 'the case used to designate' " (Creissels 2009: 450). However, as has been discussed there, the nominative in marked-nominative languages most often does not fulfill this naming function, hence the suggestion by Mel'čuk (1997) and Creissels

(2009) to abandon the use of the term 'nominative' in these languages. Extra-syntactic functions, and especially the form I refer to as 'citation form' here, are one crucial aspect of Creissels's (2009) proposal of case-terminology. As in this study, he subsumes two functions under the label extra-syntactic use. The first one is the function of addressing someone ('function of call' in his terminology), which was discussed in the previous section as *form of address*. His other form of extra-syntactic use is the function of 'quotation and designation' (?)50]Creissels:2009, which corresponds to my *citation form*.

7.5 Research questions

In the subsequent sections I will investigate how the contexts just outlined are encoded in the languages of my sample. In short these contexts are:

- attributive possessors
- nouns used for addressing someone
- nouns in the citation form

Lander (2009: 590) notes that "languages often code the possessor in a similar way to the marked participant in a transitive construction." This would mean that marked-S languages should make strong use of the S-case (nominative or absolutive) for marking attributive possessors. While this pattern is for example found in Dinka (2) [3] the more common pattern in marked-S languages is to either use a different overtly-coded form as exemplified by Boraana Oromo (3) or the zero-coded case-form like in Cocopa (4). Furthermore, polyfunctionality of case-forms as attributive possessors and semantic cases such as local ablative or allative, another common pattern according to Lander (2009: 590), does not seem to be found in the marked-S languages.

(2) Dinka (Agar) (Nilotic; Sudan; Andersen 1991: 273)
 dhɔ́ɔŋ   ė̀   mə́riḁal   ạ̀-bɔ́
 boy.ANTGEN.ACC PART Marial.NOM DECL-come
 'Marial's boy is coming.'

---

[3] Andersen (1991) uses the following terminology: Genitive for the case that marks post-verbal (i.e. non-topical subjects) as well as attributive possessors, Antigenitive for the case that marks possessees.

7.5 Research questions

(3) Oromo (Boraana) (Eastern Cushitic; Ethiopia; Stroomer 1995: 35)
*mina ciif-**aa***
house chief-GEN
'the house of the chief'

(4) Cocopa (Yuman; California; Crawford 1966: 165)
***apá**   nʸawá*
man.ACC house.ACC
'the man's house'

Apart from the dependent-marking of attributive possessors, head-marking patterns are also found with some marked-S languages. Dinka, as demonstrated above (2), not only uses the overtly coded Nominative to mark the possessor in this context. There is also a special case-form labeled as the 'antigenitive' (gloss: ANTGEN) on the possessee. A case-form like this is found in Arbore as well (5).

(5) Arbore (Eastern Cushitic; Ethiopia; Hayward 1984: 151)
*gaydan-**ti**   géer*
hoe-ANTGEN old_man
'(the) old man's hoe'

Some languages of the Nilo-Saharan phylum have a more complex construction for attributive possession than the possessor and possessee in their respective case-forms. These complex constructions insert an additional marker between the two nouns as illustrated in (6). When the marker serves as a preposition in other contexts, it is usually glossed correspondingly. Otherwise it may simply be referred to as particle, or with more language-specific terminology like the 'associative marker' (glossed as AM) in Tennet (6). I will uniformly refer to such markers as possessive marker (POSS), even if information on other uses is provided in the grammar. If attributive possessors are in the zero-coded form of a noun, but combined with such a particle, one might argue that this particle serves as a kind of case-marking in a wider sense, and thus the noun is not zero-coded. However, these markers do appear with both zero-coded and case-marked forms of a noun. As such, the two systems (i.e. case-marking proper and particles) seem to be independent of one another, at least in the present sample (compare Section 7.6, Table 7.1). If a possessive marker (POSS) is used in the relevant construction, this information will be provided in addition to the case-form of the attributive possessor in the discussion of the data.

7 Non-clause-level case marking

(6) Tennet (Surmic; Sudan; Randal 1998: 230)
    mana cí ongol-o
    field AM elephant-GEN
    'elephant's field'

A distinction in encoding of alienable and inalienable possession is made by a few languages of the sample. As far as data are available, I will provide examples from both contexts.

For the next two roles, namely terms of address and citation form, far fewer different patterns are to be expected since these are basically one word (or at least one phrase) items. In addition, neither role is treated explicitly in most grammars, and when they are, just in passing. The basic distinction for terms of address is that between a dedicated form, often called Vocative, as in Gamo (7), or encoding via the basic zero-coded form of a noun, like in Nias (8). Other case-forms are rarely employed in this context. If other case-forms do occur in this context, they are usually restricted to a certain set of nouns. Free vocative particles are seldom found in the languages of my sample. If they do occur, these markers are optional and the noun can also be used without them to the same effect.

(7) Gamo (Omotic; Ethiopia; (Hompó 1990: 282, 283))
    danna-**wu**!
    judge-VOC
    'Oh, judge!'

(8) Nias (Sundic; Indonesia; Brown 2001: 59)
    Haiya ni-waö-u   ga, **amá**?
    what PASS-say-2SG.POSS here father
    'What is it you want here, Sir?'

With respect to the citation form of a noun, most grammars simply list this as one of the functions of the zero-coded case-form, without providing examples or discussing how this function was established in the research (e.g. whether it is a form actually used by the speakers, or something introduced by the linguist for some theoretical or practical reasons). This form seems to be most strongly correlated with the zero-coded case in the marked-S languages. The few cases in which alternative forms for this function exist are usually an even more reduced form, such as a nominal stem.

7.6 Nilo-Saharan

Most Nilo-Saharan languages do not have a special case-form to mark attributive possessors. Instead they usually use the accusative case-form in this context. The possessor is either just juxtaposed to the possessee, or additional material in form of a particle or preposition intervenes between the two nouns. Only in one language, Dinka, is the Nominative case used to encode attributive possessors (as seen in (2)). In the remaining languages, a special genitive case exists that is employed in this context. Most grammars do not provide any information on terms of address, which is probably due to the lack of a dedicated form or construction for this context. Only for Turkana is a special Vocative case mentioned. Finally, all Nilo-Saharan languages in my sample use the zero-coded accusative as the citation form of a noun.

In Datooga the possessed noun and the possessor are simply juxtaposed without any other overt marking of the possessive relationship. The possessor follows the possessee and is in the Accusative case (9), the possessee is marked for whichever grammatical relation it bears in the given sentence.

(9) Datooga (Nilotic; Tanzania; Kiessling 2007: 178, 179)

    a. *qá-bár màydá dêedạ*
       3SG-beat calf.ACC.CS cow.ACC
       'He beat the cow's calf.'

    b. *qá-bár máydá dêedạ*
       3SG.beat calf.NOM.CS cow.ACC
       'The cow's calf beat (him/her).'

Similarly in Maa (10) and Nandi (11), possessors are in the accusative case and preceded by the possessee. However, the possessive relation is additionally marked by some extra material, namely, the so-called Genitive particle *le/lo/loo* in Maa, which inflects for gender and number of the possessor (Tucker & Mpaayei 1955: 213), and a similar particle *a:p* in Nandi.

(10) Maa (Nilotic; Kenya; (Tucker & Mpaayei 1955: 213))

    a. *é-ípot olcoré ló layíònì*
       3SG-call friend.ACC POSS boy.ACC
       'He calls the friend of the boy.'

    b. *é-ípot olcóre ló layíònì*
       3SG-call friend.NOM POSS boy.ACC
       'The friend of the boy calls him.'

(11) Nandi (Nilotic; Kenya; Creider & Creider 1989: 69)
 ímpáreê:t a:p kipe:t
 field POSS Kibet
 'Kibet's field'

In Murle, attributive possessors are in a special case-form, dubbed as 'Genitive' in accordance with traditional Latinate case naming conventions. If a modifier follows the Genitive noun, the case-ending is dropped (Arensen 1982: 53–54). As in the other Nilo-Saharan languages, possessors are preceded by their possessee. And as in Maa and Nandi a particle (*ci* or *o*) intervenes between the two nouns (12). This particle is also used to introduce relative clauses. Tennet (13) exhibits a similar pattern. Attributive possessors are in the Genitive case and are preceded by possessees, and the so-called 'associative marker' intervenes between the two nouns. Note that in Tennet the Genitive case is identical to the Nominative for some nouns (Randal 1998: 225).

(12) Murle (Surmic; Sudan; Arensen 1982: 108)
 cirlil-i agam idiŋ ci ŋaa-**o**
 kite-NOM grab meat REL woman-GEN
 'The kite grabs the meat of the woman'

(13) Tennet (Surmic; Sudan; Randal 1998: 230)
 mana cí ongol-o̱
 field AM elephant-GEN
 'elephant's field'

Turkana (14) also has a special Genitive case-form to encode most attributive possessors. In this construction, as exemplified by Dimmendaal (1982: 266–268), the possessee precedes the possessor, and a particle/preposition glossed 'of' is inserted between the two nouns (14a). As exemplified below, the respective Accusative (14b) and Nominative (14c) case-forms differ in tone from the Genitive. With kinship terms, a slightly different construction is used (Dimmendaal 1982: 340). The basic structure is similar to the construction discussed above, but the possessor is in the Accusative case and obligatorily followed by a pronominal (15). Also, in this construction a different particle/preposition is used. [4]

---

[4] The noun ì-toò 'mother' is the only kinship term that uses the general possessive construction with the particle à and the possessor in the Genitive case. However, it is still followed by the obligatory pronominal found with other kinship terms (Dimmendaal 1982: 240).

(14) Turkana (Nilotic; Kenya; Dimmendaal 1982: 267, 384, 167)

    a. ɛ-muɲɛnˋà à-ɪtɛ̀   naˋ
       colour   of NC-cow.GEN this
       'the colour of this cow'

    b. è-lèpìˋ   ***a-ɪtɛˋ***   caaap, caaap
       3-milk-ASP NC-cow.ACC IDEOPH IDEOPH
       'She milked the cow.'

    c. è-ɔ̀ŋɔ̀rɪ-aa-n-à   ***a-ìtɛ̀***   naˋ
       3-brown-HAB-SG-VBLZ NC-cow.NOM this
       'This cow is brownish.'

(15) Turkana (Dimmendaal 1982: 340)

    a. è-yaˋ   kɛŋˋkà à-***pa***ˋ   kaŋˋ
       aunt.ACC his   with NC-father.ACC my
       'My father's aunt'

    b. a-mòtį̀ kà è-***ya***ˋ   kaŋˋ
       pot.ACC with NC-aunt.ACC my
       'my aunt's pot'

Dinka is exceptional compared with the other Nilo-Saharan languages in using the same case-form to encode (post-verbal) subjects and attributive possessors. In his (1991) paper, Andersen refers to this case-form as Genitive due to its property of marking adnominal possessors. However, the use to encode subjects (even though only if non-topical) sets this case apart from the Genitives of other Nilo-Saharan languages, which are not used to encode subjects at all. Another difference between Dinka and other Nilo-Saharan languages is the special case-marking of the possessee in attributive possessive constructions. The possessee in these contexts is marked in the so-called 'Antigenitive' (16a). If this possessed noun serves as a possessor itself (16d) or is a post-verbal subject the special tonal form of Antigenitive-Nominative (or Antigenitive-Genitive in Andersen's terms) is used.

(16) Dinka (Agar) (Nilotic; Sudan; Andersen 1991: 273)

    a. dhɔ́ɔŋ   è̦   ***má̦riǎ̦al***   à-bɔ́
       boy.ANTGEN.ACC PART Marial.NOM DECL-come
       'Marial's boy is coming.'

b. *mằriằal   ằ-bɔ́*
   Marial.ACC DECL-come
   'Marial is coming.'

c. *dhɔ̀ɔk   ằ-thɛ́ɛt   mā́riằal*
   boy.ACC DECL-beat.NTS Marial.NOM
   'Marial is beating the boy.'

d. *mòc   ằ-yêep   ḕ   yɛ́m   ḕ   dhɔ̀ɔŋ*
   man.ACC DECL-cut.ANTIP PREP axe.ANTGEN PART boy.ANTGEN.NOM
   ḕ   mā́riằal
   PART Marial.NOM
   'The man is cutting with Marial's boy's axe.'

Special forms of address are not common in Nilo-Saharan languages. However, the whole topic of address is treated only scantily in the grammars, if treated at all. This is not special about this language family but actually holds true for most grammars of the world's languages. For Datooga, an example using a form of address is provided. The Accusative is used in this context (17), like supposedly in most Nilo-Saharan marked-S languages, although at the present moment this remains unknown. In contrast, Turkana has a special Vocative case-form, which is discussed by Dimmendaal (1982: 67, 268–269). The tonal shape of nouns used in address (18) differs from other case-forms such as the Accusative for example, as exemplified in (19).

(17) Datooga (Kiessling 2007: 171)
    gwà-yéeʃà héew-ì   bálláandà qámnàa
    3SG-say bull.NOM-DEM.near.SG boy.ACC now
    gày-dá-lík-ɲì
    FUT-1SG-swallow-2SG.OBJ
    'This bull said: "Child, I'm going to swallow you now !"'

(18) Turkana (Dimmendaal 1982: 268, 269)
    a. *ŋì-dɛ`*
       'children!'
    b. *ḕ-kà-tuk-ò-nį*
       'chief!'

(19) Turkana (Dimmendaal 1982: 75)
ŋɪ-dɛ́   omwɔn´
NC-children.ACC four
'There are four children.'

Finally, all languages use the citation form as the Accusative case (or vice-versa). In languages that mark the distinction between nominative and accusative via a tonal contrast, the tonal shape of a noun in its citation form is taken as one criterion to determine the Accusative as the basic form and the Nominative as the derived form. This is discussed quite extensively for Dinka (Andersen 1991: 273) and Turkana (Dimmendaal 1982: 66).

Table 7.1 summarizes the data on non-clause-level case-marking in the Nilo-Saharan languages. Concerning the possessor, all possible combinations of zero-coded Accusative vs. overtly coded Genitive and the presence vs. absence of a possessive marker in the attributive possessive construction are attested. Any kind of particle- or preposition-like coding is abbreviated as 'POSS' in the tables in this chapter. Most languages use some type of overt marking, either case or possessive marker or both, in this context. Only Datooga has no possessive marker and no overt case-marking for this role. When considering only the actual case-marking, the data are split evenly between Accusative and Genitive forms, with a special use of the Nominative for this function in Dinka. On forms of address, little information can be found for the Nilo-Saharan languages. All that can be said is that there is some variation between the use of the Accusative (Datooga) and a special Vocative form (Turkana). The citation form is identical to the accusative for all languages.

language	Possessor	Address	Citation
Datooga	ACC	ACC	ACC
Dinka	POSS NOM	-	ACC
Maa	POSS ACC	-	ACC
Murle	GEN	-	ACC
Nandi	POSS ACC	-	ACC
Tennet	GEN	-	ACC
Turkana	POSS GEN/ POSS ACC	VOC	ACC

Table 7.1: Non-clause-level case-marking in Nilo-Saharan

7.7 Afro-Asiatic

Almost all Afro-Asiatic marked-nominative languages have a special, overtly marked, genitive case-form to encode attributive possessors. Apart from case-marking the possessive relation is expressed through juxtaposition of possessor and possessee without any additional marking through prepositions, particles or the like. Distinct vocative forms are found in quite a few languages of the sample. Moreover, the relation between citation form of a noun and the accusative is not as straightforward as in the Nilo-Saharan languages.

In both dialects of Oromo discussed in this study, attributive possessors are in the Genitive case-form. This is illustrated by examples from Harar (20) and Boraana (21a). Owens (1982: 50) provides additional data on focused possessors in Boraana Oromo, which like other focused constituents are in the Accusative case (21b).

(20) Oromo (Harar) (Eastern Cushitic; Ethiopia; Owens 1985: 103)
bif-níi **sárée** *fakkóotaa*
color-NOM dog.GEN ugly
'The dog's color is ugly.'

(21) Oromo (Boraana) (Eastern Cushitic; Ethiopia; Stroomer 1995: 35, Owens 1982: 50)

a. *mina ciif-**aa***
house chief-GEN
'the house of the chief'

b. ***nam*** *sùn mìni isa dansà*
man.ACC DEM house.ACC 3SG.M.POSS good
'As for the man, his house is good.'

In Gamo (22), K'abeena (23), Wolaytta (24), and Zayse (25), the genitive case is used to encode adnominal possessors as well. In all the languages, nominal possessors precede their possessees. Except for the second degree of definiteness, the Gamo Genitive is identical to the Accusative case (Hompó 1990: 380). [5] In Wolaytta, the Genitive case has two different forms according to Lamberti &

---

[5] Gamo distinguishes between four degrees of definiteness. The exact usage is not clear to Hompó (1990: 367), but the following description seem to hold more or less. Degree 1 and 2 are indefinite, degree 3 is specific to definite and degree 4 is definite. The forms used to encode degree 1–3 of definiteness are interwoven with the markers of subject- and object-case.

7.7 Afro-Asiatic

Sottile (1997: 217–218). Either the bare noun stem is used (24a, b) or it is derived from the Accusative by lengthening the final vowel of that case-form (24c, d).

(22) Gamo (Omotic; Ethiopia; Hompó 1990: 368, 375)

    a. *kaŝi   giggiso-i   mač'č'-á   oŝo-ko*
       food.ACC preparing-NOM woman-GEN work-COP

       'Preparing food is (a) woman's task.'

    b. *issi mač'č-**ai**   iz-a   goss-a-d-us*
       one woman-NOM 3SG.M-ACC madden-PM-TNS-COMPLX

       'A woman made him crazy.'

(23) K'abeena (Eastern Cushitic; Ethiopia; Crass 2005: 115)

    a. ***manci**-'i*   *bak'úlcutⁱ ba'o*
       husband.GEN-1SG.POSS mule.NOM disappear.PFV.3SG.F

       'My husband's mule has disappeared.'
       original translation: 'Das Maultier meines Ehemanns is verschwunden.'

    b. ***manco**-'i*   *maalda*   *mi*   *'aa'iyo?*
       wife.GEN-1SG.POSS silver_bracelet.ACC who.NOM take.PFV.3SG.M

       'Who took my wife's silver bracelet?'
       original translation: 'Wer/Was hat das Silberarmband meiner Ehefrau weggenommen?'

(24) Wolaytta (Omotic; Ethiopia; Lamberti & Sottile 1997: 217, 218)

    a. ***aliy**^a   keetta*
       Ali.GEN house

       'Ali's house'

    b. ***kaawuwa** keetta-ta*
       king.GEN   house-PL

       'some houses of the king'

    c. *kaawuw-**aa** keetta-ta*
       king-GEN   house-PL

       'some houses of the king'

    d. *aliy-**aa** kusshiy^a*
       Ali-GEN hand

       'Ali's hand'

7 Non-clause-level case marking

(25) Zayse (Omotic; Ethiopia; Hayward 1990: 251)
zikkólá paŋge
eagle.GEN wing
'(an) eagle's wing'

Arbore is the only Afro-Asiatic language in my sample that exhibits a different pattern in the attributive possessive construction. While the possessor is in the zero-coded Accusative case-form, the possessee is in the so-called Antigenitive form (26). In addition, the ordering of possessor and possessee is reversed in comparison to the other Afro-Asiatic languages. Instead of preceding the possessee, the possessor follows it.

(26) Arbore (Eastern Cushitic; Ethiopia; Hayward 1984: 151)
   a. *gaydan-ti   géer*
      hoe-ANTGEN old_man
      '(the) old man's hoe'
   b. *hikič-i   hóǧǧattu(-t)*
      axe-ANTGEN labourer
      '(the) labourer's axe
   c. *k'úb-a   neek'*
      forelimb-ANTGEN lion
      '(the) forelimb of a lion'

Gamo (27) and Wolaytta (28) have vocative case-affixes to mark terms of address. The endings vary with respect to number and gender of the addressee in Gamo; *-o/-wu* is used with masculine or neuter nouns, *-e* for feminine nouns and *-t-o* for the plural (Hompó 1990: 382–383). Wolaytta also has two different forms, namely *-ow* and *-ey*. Which factors influence the choice of one over the other is, however, not discussed by Lamberti & Sottile (1997: 66).

(27) Gamo (Hompó 1990: 282, 283)
   a. *danna-wu!*
      judge-VOC
      'Oh, judge!'
   b. *addez-o*
      man-VOC
      'Hey, man!'

(28) Wolaytta (Lamberti & Sottile 1997: 209)
aliy-ow, ta mat'aafa ekka!
Ali-voc my book take
'Ali, take my book.'

For K'abeena terms of address, a quite complex scenario is described by Crass (2005). The Vocative form is identical to the Accusative with personal names. With nouns referring to relatives, the Vocative is identical to the citation form, while with other nouns it is either identical to the Genitive, or else the Vocative is derived by affixation of the suffix -*o*, and for at least one noun the Vocative is identical to the root. It is possible to distinguish the Vocative from identical case-forms by means of the interjection *koo* (masculine) or *tee* (feminine) before the noun (Crass 2005: 95–96).

Gamo has a quite complex system of case-marking, which distinguishes between four degrees of definiteness/individuation. The citation form corresponds to the so-called 'first degree' Accusative, which is the least complex form of the paradigm. For this form, the Accusative and Genitive are the same (Hompó 1990: 370). The Arbore citation form is identical to the basic form (Accusative) for most nouns. For some nouns, however, the citation form is a reduced version of the Accusative. According to Hayward (1984: 133) these nouns drop the second of two final consonants or reduce it to a glottal stop when used in isolation. In K'abeena, different forms of a noun are used in citation as well. The Accusative is the form used as the most basic pattern (Crass 2005: 61). For proper names the citation form deviates from the Accusative in some cases. Lamberti & Sottile (1997: 67–68), in their grammar of Wolaytta, list an 'Absolutive' form and an 'Object' case of a noun (distinct from other case-forms such as the Nominative). In some of the noun classes those two forms differ. This difference consists of the following contrast: the so-called Absolutive form has an voiceless vowel as its last segment, while the Object form has the voiced counterpart. The Absolutive form seems to refer to nouns used in isolation, i.e. the citation form, while the Object form corresponds to the Accusative in the traditional sense. Lamberti & Sottile do not comment on this alternation, but in the phonology section they state that unstressed final vowels always seem to be devoiced (51–52), thus the variation between Absolutive and Object form might be due to its context (especially stress assignment, of which is only little understood so far).

A summary of all Afro-Asiatic marked-S languages is provided in Table 7.2. Most languages have an overtly coded genitive case to mark attributive possessors. The only exception is Arbore, which uses the zero-coded Accusative for this purpose. Three languages have a vocative case-form of the noun (Gamo,

K'abeena and Wolaytta), but in K'abeena this form can only be distinguished from other case-forms for a subset of nouns. All languages have a citation form that is identical to the accusative case at least for some nouns. In K'abeena and Arbore, sometimes the citation form is a reduced variety of the Accusative. The exact distribution of the different forms is, however, poorly understood. Thus the possibility cannot be ruled out that there is no actual paradigmatic contrast between the two forms, and the variation is rather triggered by other factors such as morphophonological processes or prosody.

language	Possessor	Address	Citation
Arbore	ACC	-	ACC/reduced form
Gamo	GEN	VOC	ACC
K'abeena	GEN	ACC/VOC/GEN	ACC/reduced form
Oromo (Boraana)	GEN	-	ACC
Oromo (Harar)	GEN	-	ACC
Wolaytta	GEN	VOC	ACC
Zayse	GEN	-	ACC

Table 7.2: Non-clause-level case-marking in Afro-Asiatic

7.8 Pacific

Attributive possessors are expressed by very different constructions in each of the marked-S languages of the Pacific region. Terms of address on the other hand are uniformly in the zero-coded form of a noun. This is also the form usually employed in citation. However, in Nias there is some variation between speakers as well as different nouns. Both forms of a noun, the Mutated and Unmutated form, occur as citation forms.

There are two constructions to express nominal possessors in Ajië; one for inalienable and one for alienable possession. Inalienable possession is expressed by mere juxtaposition of the possessor in the zero-coded form and the possessed item, with the possessor following the possessee (29a, b). In alienable possession, the possessor is preceded by the particle *i*, and also follows the possessee (29c). Since the morphological means of expression is identical to way the Nominative is encoded, this particle can actually be considered as part of a case paradigm, unlike similar markers in the Nilo-Saharan languages. I will therefore treat this particle, which is glossed as 'of' by Lichtenberk (1978), as a Genitive case-marker (and have altered the glossing respectively), just as the particle *na* is glossed as Nominative case.

(29) Ajië (Oceanic; New Caledonia; Lichtenberk 1978: 85, 86)
   a. *pwe **bwɛʔ***
      belly woman
      'the womans's belly'
   b. *karrɔ **kamɔʔ***
      body man
      'the man's body'
   c. *nevã i   wiʔ*
      land GEN man
      'the man's land'

In Nias attributive possessors are in the Mutated form of the noun (30) – cf. the Unmutated form of the noun *buaya* 'crocodile'. They immediately follow their possessee. Pronominal possessors are expressed via person agreement suffixes. This construction is used for alienable and inalienable possession alike (Brown 2001: 374).

(30) Nias (Sundic; Indonesia; Brown 2001: 374)
   telau mbuaya
   head crocodile.MUT
   'the head of the crocodile'

Savosavo has a special case-form to express attributive possessors (among other functions): the Genitive. The attributive possessive construction is illustrated in (31).

(31) Savosavo (Solomons East Papuan; Solomon Islands; Wegener 2008: 132)
   ko   tada lo-**va**   ti=gho   te
   3SG.F.GEN man 3.SG.M-GEN.M tea=3SG.F.NOM EMPH
   pala-tu,   *bo kokoa*
   make.3SG.M.OBJ-PRS.IPFV or 3SG.F.POSS.M
   'Is she making her husband's tea or hers?'

All Pacific marked-S languages use the zero-coded form of a noun in addressing someone (i.e. Accusative or Unmutated form). This is illustrated by the following examples from Ajië (32), Nias (33) and Savosavo (34).

7 Non-clause-level case marking

(32) Ajië (Kasarhérou (née de la Fontinelle) 1961: 199)
 ngɛ:ʔ pɛ-ßi para e-'kona ...
 grandmother take-go PL product-fish
 'Grandmother, take the fish.'
 original translation: 'Grand-mère, emporte les poissons.'

(33) Nias (Brown 2001: 59)
 Haiya ni-waö-u ga, **amá**?
 what PASS-say-2SG.POSS here father
 'What is it you want here, Sir?'

(34) Savosavo (Wegener 2008: 127)
 minister, secretary, dulo bo-tu me=me kati ka zui
 minister secretary all go-REL 2PL=EMPH.2PL CERT already end
 so=gha=e me=na
 ATT=PL=EMPH 2PL=NOM
 'Minister, Secretary, you all who went, you will all be fired.'

Usually, the zero-coded case-form (accusative or ergative) is considered to be the citation form of a noun in the marked-S languages of the Pacific. For Nias Brown (2001: 69) states that the "unmutated form of a noun is usually its citation form", but apparently some speakers also employ the Mutated form (Absolutive) for citation (Lea Brown, p.c.). This behavior, which might be viewed as a reinterpretation of the different forms of the nouns, is especially frequent with a limited set of nouns.

A summary of the Pacific date is given in Table 7.3. Only Ajië makes a distinction between alienable and inalienable possession. This distinction is in accordance with the prediction by Chappell & McGregor (1996: 4–5), according to which inalienable possession tends to be expressed by mere juxtaposition of the (zero-coded form of the) noun, while alienable possession is expressed via overt coding through genitive case. Nias uses the overtly coded Absolutive case (the so-called Mutated form) to code nominal possessors. This is one of the few examples supporting Lander's (2009: 590) claim that this relation is encoded by the overtly marked transitive case-form. Terms of address are uniformly in the zero-coded accusative/ergative case in all marked-S languages of this region. Also the citation form tends to be identical to the zero-coded form, but in Nias some reorganization of the paradigm can possibly be observed.

language	Possessor	Address	Citation
Ajië	GEN/ACC	ACC	ACC
Nias	ABS	ERG	ERG/ABS
Savosavo	GEN	ACC	ACC

Table 7.3: Non-clause-level case-marking in the Pacific region

7.9 North America

The Yuman languages of North America use the zero-coded accusative case-form for encoding attributive possessors. Wappo and Maidu, the other marked-S languages of this region, have a special genitive case for this purpose. In Wappo, however, the Genitive is only used for alienable possession, while inalienable possessors are encoded in the Accusative. Furthermore, the possessive relation is marked via juxtaposition of the two nouns (i.e. possessor and possessee) rather than by means of adpositions or particles. Possessor agreement marking is found on the possessee, which is optional in most languages if the possessor is expressed as a full noun. Terms of address are encoded in either the accusative form or via special vocative affixes. In Maidu, the Nominative is sometimes employed in this context. Usually, the citation form coincides with the accusative case of a noun, but for two languages there is a minor variation of this pattern.

Mojave expresses attributive possession by preposing the noun referring to the possessor in its zero-coded form to the possessee (35). For alienable possession, the prefix n^y- is inserted between person marker and noun stem. This marker may also appear with nouns which have a full-noun possessor (Munro 1976: 16–18).

(35) Mojave (Munro 1976: 50, 18)

    a. *vidan^y john*   *n^y-ava:-č*
        this   John.ACC   POSS-house-NOM
        'This is John's house'

    b. *k^{w}aθəʔide: n^y-ava:*
        doctor.ACC   POSS-house
        'the doctor's house'

The other Yuman languages behave in a parallel fashion: in Cocopa (36), Mesa Grande Diegueño (37), Jamul Tiipay (38)[6], and Maricopa (39), the zero-coded possessor precedes the possessee.

---

[6] The exact morphological structure of the last word in the Jamul Tiipay example, especially the function of the segments <ta>, is unclear. This is marked via the asterisk by Miller (2001).

7 *Non-clause-level case marking*

(36) Cocopa (Crawford 1966: 165)
    apá   *nʸawá*
    man.ACC house.ACC
    'the man's house'

(37) Diegueño (Mesa Grande) (Gorbet 1976: 17)
    kʷsya:y   *nʸ-kuci:*
    doctor.ACC POSS-knife
    'the doctor's knife'

(38) Jamul Tiipay (Miller 2001: 152)
    Evelyn   *nye-armewil uutak-x*   *ta*paa-ch*   ...
    Evelyn.ACC ALI-car   make_open-IRR ta*be_present-SSBJ
    'He was trying to break into Evelyn's car ...'

(39) Maricopa (Gordon 1986: 31, 40)
  a. ***Bonnie***   *s'aw*
     Bonnie.ACC offspring.ACC
     'Bonnie's baby'
  b. ***Bonnie***   *s'aw*   *ime*
     Bonnie.ACC offspring.ACC leg.ACC
     'Bonnie's baby's leg'
  c. *'iipaa-ny-a*   *ny-va-ny-sh*   *vtay-m*
     man-DEM-AUGV POSS-house-DEM-NOM big-RLS
     'That man's house is big.'

The same pattern is found in Havasupai (40), Walapai (41), and Yavapai (42), which form a distinct subgroup within the Yuman languages. For Yavapai, this context is discussed in some more detail. The pattern of a zero-coded possessor is used for both inalienable possession (42a) and alienable possession (42b).

(40) Havasupai (Kozlowski 1972: 57)
  a. *jan*   *lwa*
     John.ACC wife
     'John's wife'
  b. *pa*   *ñu-hu*
     man.ACC DEM-head
     'the man's/his head'

(41) Walapai (Watahomigie et al. 2001: 76)
 Joe búd-a-ch ya:d-i-k-yu
 Joe.ACC 3.hat-DEF-NOM 3.fly-suddenly-SSBJ-AUX
 'Joe's hat flew away.'

(42) Yavapai (Kendall 1976: 60)
   a. kiθar-c **hamsi ktyo:ca** mpar ckʸo:-kñ
      dog-NOM hamsi_ktyocha.ACC leg bite-COMPL
      'A dog bit Hamsi-ketyocha's leg.'
   b. **lupi** hanaq
      Lupe.ACC necklace
      'Lupe's necklace'

In Wappo, two different constructions are used to encode alienable and inalienable possession. Genitive marking is only used for alienable possession (43a), while in inalienable possession, the attributive possessor is zero-coded (43b).

(43) Wappo (Thompson et al. 2006: 14, 15)
   a. ah ce met'e ce k'ew-**meʔ** k'ešu paʔ-is-taʔ
      1SG.NOM DEM woman DEM man-GEN meat eat-CAUS-PST
      'I made the woman eat the man's meat'
   b. **c'ic'a** khap-i keʔte-khiʔ
      bird.ACC wing-NOM broken-STAT
      'The bird's wing is broken.'

In Maidu, attributive possessors are marked with Genitive case (44). No distinction between alienable and inalienable possession is mentioned in the grammar. Only nouns which serve as subject, object, or location can be modified with a Genitive NP (Shipley 1964: 30–31).

(44) Maidu (Shipley 1964: 31)
 wélkʼetʼi-m kylókbe-m ʔas wépa-**k** kylé-m
 frog-NOM old_woman-NOM EMPH coyote-GEN woman-NOM
 macʼój-ʔam
 say-PSTPUNC.3
 'They say that Frog Old Woman was Coyote's wife'

7 Non-clause-level case marking

Many Yuman languages use the zero-coded Accusative case-form of a noun as a term of address. Among these languages are Cocopa (45), Mesa Grande Diegueño (46), and Jamul Tiipay (47).

(45) Cocopa (Crawford 1966: 179)

a. *nʸcá*
 mother.ACC
 'Mother!'

b. *xmík*
 young_man.ACC
 'Young man!'

(46) Diegueño (Mesa Grande) (Langdon 1970: 158)

a. xawka **margarit** təmuwa=a
 hello Margaret.ACC you_are_sitting=Q
 'Hello, Margaret, how are you?'

b. **mayʔpay** kəyəwip!
 you_people.ACC you_all_listen
 'Listen, all you people!'

(47) Jamul Tiipay (Miller 1990: 128)
perxaaw maayich m-rar m-wa-ch-m-yu
fox.ACC what 2-do 2-be_sitting-SSBJ-2-be
'What are you doing here, Fox?'

In some other Yuman languages, special forms are used in this context. Walapai has two Vocative affixes, -*é* for addressees near the speaker (proximal), and -*ó*/-*wo* for addressees who are out of sight (48). As for the citation form, Munro (1976: 129, footnote 3) notes that some Mojave speakers add a final schwa to nouns used for addressing.

(48) Walapai (Watahomigie et al. 2001: 56)
*nya misi:-**ye**! Gwe ma-ma:-j-a!*
1SG.POSS girl-PL.VOC thing 2>3-eat-PL-IMP
'My daughters! Eat!'

Information on terms of address in Wappo is provided by the earlier grammar by Radin (1929). It is unclear whether this system was still used in the moribund stage of the language described by Thompson et al. (2006). Usually the zero-coded Accusative form is used for address. However, there is a tendency to use a different form, either by shortening stems with terminal vowels or by using the Nominative (Radin 1929: 130). For a specific set of nouns, which Radin (1929: 130, 133) calls 'relationship terms', a special Vocative form is used when the addressee is invisible or far away (-sta). Maidu employs the Nominative as a form of address for all nouns except for a certain class of kinship terms. For these nouns the Accusative form is used instead (Shipley 1964: 30).

All Yuman languages use the Accusative form of a noun as the citation form. However, in Mojave another pattern is described, in which many speakers show a tendency to add -a or -ə to any noun in isolation including the citation form (Munro 1976: 129, footnote 3). In Wappo too, the Accusative form is used in citation (Li et al. 1977). Maidu uses the noun stem as a citation form, and this form is identical to the Accusative of a noun for all vowel final stems. Some speakers always use the object form as citation form, according to Shipley (1964: 30).

language	Possessor	Address	Citation
Cocopa	ACC	ACC	ACC
Diegueño (Mesa Grande)	ACC	ACC	ACC
Havasupai	ACC	-	ACC
Jamul Tiipay	ACC	ACC	ACC
Maidu	GEN	NOM/ACC	ACC/stem
Mojave	ACC	ACC/-ə	ACC/-ə
Walapai	ACC	VOC	ACC
Wappo	GEN/ACC	ACC(/VOC)	ACC
Yavapai	ACC	-	ACC

Table 7.4: Non-clause-level case-marking in North America

Table 7.4 summarizes the data from the North American languages. Except for Maidu, all languages use the accusative for attributive possessors. In Wappo, this construction is limited to inalienable possession, while alienable possession is expressed via Genitive case. This pattern nicely fits the prediction by Chappell & McGregor (1996: 4–5), according to which constructions that mark alienable possession are prone to use more overt material than constructions that mark inalienable possession. As a term of address, the accusative (most Yuman languages, some Maidu and Wappo nouns), special vocative forms (Walapai, and Wappo, with some restrictions), and the Nominative (Maidu, with some restrictions), are used. All languages make use of the accusative form in citation to some extent. In Mojave and Maidu, there is some variation in the form used in citation between different speakers.

7.10 Summary

The final overview of the encoding of attributive possessors and extra-syntactic functions in marked-S languages is given in Table 7.5 on the next page. About half the languages use the zero-coded form of a noun to encode attributive possessors; most of these languages can be found in North America. Roughly the other half has a dedicated genitive case for attributive possessors, which is distinct from the marking of the overtly coded transitive argument. Only two languages (Dinka and Nias) use the form corresponding to the transitive argument (A or P) which receives overt coding. This pattern was predicted to be quite common by Lander (2009: 590), but this prediction has not been borne out by the marked-S languages in my sample. As for terms of address, the zero-coded form of a noun is also frequently used. In a number of languages of Africa (especially in Afro-Asiatic), and in Wappo at an earlier stage, special vocative forms exist(ed). In Maidu (Nominative) and K'abeena (Genitive), some other case-forms are employed in this context, but this is always limited to a specific set of nouns. No case-form other than the zero-coded one is used as a citation form of a noun in any of the languages, except for a reinterpretation of the relation between Mutated and Unmutated nouns in Nias. Otherwise, if the form used in citation differs from the zero-coded case-form, it is a reduced form of the noun (Arbore, K'abeena, Maidu). In sum, the correlation between zero-coded transitive case-form and citation form appears to be very strong. This finding indicates that there is no direct correlation between the nominative case and the citation form of a noun by itself. Rather the relation is between the zero-coded form of a noun and the citation form. The zero-coded form, however, corresponds to the nominative in the majority of languages.

7.10 Summary

language	Possessor	Address	Citation
Ajië	GEN/ACC	ACC	ACC
Arbore	ACC	-	ACC/reduced form
Cocopa	ACC	ACC	ACC
Datooga	ACC	ACC	ACC
Diegueño (Mesa Grande)	ACC	ACC	ACC
Dinka	NOM	-	ACC
Gamo	GEN	VOC	ACC
Havasupai	ACC	-	ACC
Jamul Tiipay	ACC	ACC	ACC
K'abeena	GEN	ACC/GEN	ACC/reduced form
Maa	ACC	-	ACC
Maidu	GEN	NOM/ACC	ACC/stem
Mojave	ACC	ACC/-ə	ACC/-ə
Murle	GEN	-	ACC
Nandi	ACC	-	ACC
Nias	ABS	ERG	ERG/ABS
Oromo (Boraana)	GEN	-	ACC
Oromo (Harar)	GEN	-	ACC
Savosavo	GEN	ACC	ACC
Tennet	GEN	-	ACC
Turkana	GEN	VOC	ACC
Walapai	ACC	VOC	ACC
Wappo	GEN/ACC	ACC(/VOC)	ACC
Wolaytta	GEN	VOC	ACC
Yavapai	ACC	-	ACC
Zayse	GEN	-	ACC

Table 7.5: Overview on the non-clause-level case-marking

Part III

Analysis of the data

8 Typological comparison of marked-S languages

8.1 Introduction

In the previous chapters I have presented an in-depth investigation of the coding patters of a number of S-like roles (and other roles commonly associated with the nominative case in standard nominative-accusative languages) in marked-S languages. Nominal case-marking, and more precisely the contrast between overtly coded forms and zero-coded forms, has been the central aspect of what I have called the 'micro-alignment' system of these languages. In this chapter, I will employ the data collected in the individual chapters in order to produce two typologies. First, I will compare the data based on the different roles that I have investigated. For each of these roles the extent to which they behave like regular S arguments will be investigated. The other base of comparison is the language (and genus) level. In this typology of marked-S languages I will compare how similar the languages of this type behave with respect to one another. It will also be investigated whether distinct subtypes of marked-S languages can be identified. Based on this data, the difference between the weak and strong form (cf. Section 1.5.3) of the functional marked-S hypothesis by König (2006) will be put to a test.

In Section 8.2 I give a brief discussion on the nature of typological comparisons with focus on the statistical validity of the results. Also, information is provided on how the data has been organized for the typological interpretation in the following sections. Afterwards, the data collected in this study will be compared on the basis of the roles that were studies (Section 8.3). Following this, the data will be presented from point of view of the individual languages (Section 8.4). At least the marked-S languages of North America appear to form a distinct subtype, which behaves differently from the well-known marked-S languages of East Africa. While the first two data analysis sections present the data in the form of numbers and percentages in the form of ranked tables, Section 8.5 uses phylogenetic networks produced with the NeighborNet algorithm (Bryant & Moulton 2004) for visualization. Section 8.6 provides a discussion of the geog-

8 Typological comparison of marked-S languages

raphy of the marked-S type of coding. The languages of my sample are located in three macro-areas: North-East Africa, the North American West Coast, and the Pacific. For each of these macro-areas, the influence that genealogy and areal proximity could have had on the development of the rare marked-S type of language are discussed. Finally, the findings are summarized in Section 8.7.

8.2 Making generalizations

Traditional large scale typologies attempt to make statements about the worldwide distribution of certain linguistic features. These distributions can then be used to arrive at cross-linguistic generalizations and to describe general tendencies of linguistic behavior. The nature of this study does not allow for a classical typological sample that is balanced for areal and genealogical affiliation. The phenomenon studied is known to be extremely rare on a world-wide basis and geographically highly skewed. Given the rarity of the phenomenon of marked-S coding, the primary goal of this study has instead been to collect data from as many languages exhibiting this pattern as possible. In the previous chapters (3–7) all marked-S languages for which data on one of the roles was available have been included into the discussion. For a number of languages, only very few of the roles studied were represented in the available data. This has not been a problem, given the more descriptive nature of these chapters. However, large sets of missing data are problematic for making typological generalizations and for statistical analysis of the data. Therefore not all languages mentioned before will be included in the following analysis.

Figure 8.1 shows the distribution of all languages that have been discussed at some stage in Chapters 3 to 7.[1] Out of these 33 languages, ten languages have data for less than half of the roles on which data has been collected (the number of roles studied is 17 in total, including the transitive roles of A and P). These languages are not included in the following.[2] The remaining 23 languages are visualized on the map in Figure 8.2.

The data collected in this study provides information on the encoding of individual roles in individual languages. Both types of entities, i.e. roles and langu-

---

[1] The maps shown in this chapter were generated with the interactive tool of the *World Atlas of Language Structures* (Haspelmath et al. 2005), which was developed by Hans-Jörg Bibiko.

[2] The languages which have been excluded from the analysis in the present chapter are all of the Pacific languages with the marked-S pattern only for emphatic subjects discussed in Chapter 5, namely Eipo, Kaki Ae, Nabak, Waskia and Yawuru. In addition, the Yuman languages Cocopa, Maricopa and Walapai have been excluded due to lack of data, as well as the Nilotic languages Päri, which has the marked-S pattern only in some non-basic clauses, and Dinka.

8.2 Making generalizations

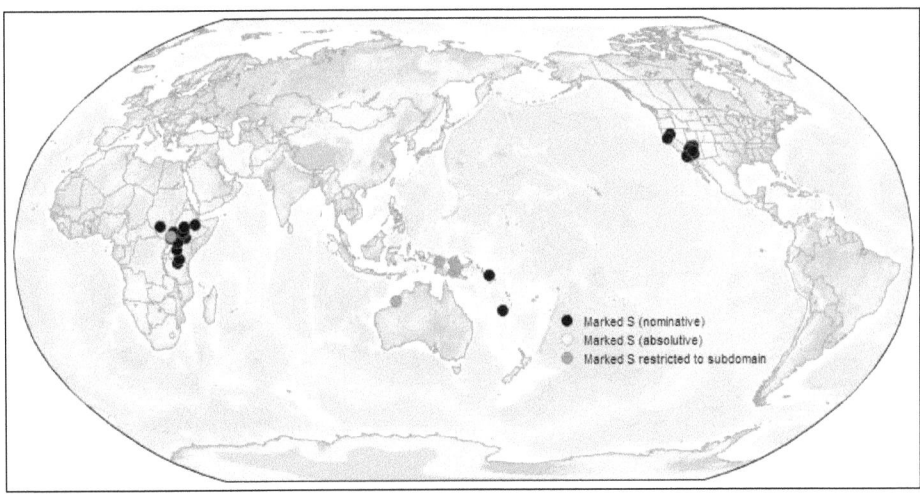

Figure 8.1: Distribution of the languages studied in Chapters 3–7

ages, can be used as the means of comparison, and indeed both will be used in the next sections. In the remainder of this section I will discuss the two means of comparison. The language level will be discussed first, followed by the role level.

When making typological generalizations over a number of languages, one runs into a problem when trying to arrive at meaningful results. Statistical analysis of the data demands independence of the data. This criterion is, however, not necessarily met by language data that comes from related languages; and, as Dryer (1989) remarks, all languages in the world might well be related to one another. If a sample of languages contains a large number of related languages sharing a linguistic feature (potentially due to their common origin), this feature might wrongly be shown to be a significantly preferred across the world's languages, though in fact this preference only holds for the respective genealogical grouping. This and related problems are discussed in Dryer (1989) and Bickel (2008b); these two papers also propose solutions on how to avoid misinterpretation of typological preferences. In short, the suggested solutions propose genealogical (and also areal) control of samples, even though if taken to the extreme, this procedure can lead to very small sample sizes, leading to other statistical difficulties.

Two questions arise when attempting to balance data sets according to genealogy (and areal distribution). First, between which groupings of languages can relative independence of the data be expected, and second, how does one then proceed to balance the data between those groupings in the analysis. Dryer (1989: 267) proposes the genus as the level of relatedness above which one can assume

8 Typological comparison of marked-S languages

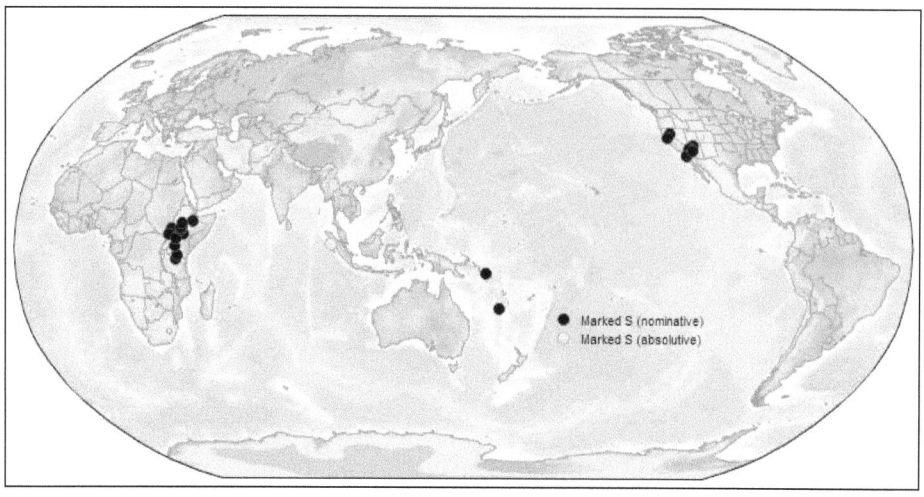

Figure 8.2: Distribution of the languages used for comparison

relative independence of data points, though he notes that different linguistic features have different levels of stability and therefore some features might be considered independent on a smaller or larger time scale. Accordingly, with this the data will be analyzed on the genus level in addition to the analysis based on individual languages. The genera used in this study are taken from the classification used in Haspelmath et al. (2005). Different methods are available to balance the data with respect to the groups one has established for the analysis. The first possibility is to pick a representative language for each of the defined groups and use the data of this language. However, based on the language choice, the data representing a group of languages might not be representative for the group as a whole. Another possibility is to include more languages for each group in order to take into account in-group variation but to weight the data of the individual groups with respect to each other in the later analysis. This procedure provides 'controlled genealogical sampling' (Bickel 2008b). I have chosen a similar method for analyzing marked-S languages on a genealogically controlled level (though the details differ from Bickel's proposal). For each role that is investigated, an average figure of the encoding-pattern has been calculated based on the languages of the respective genealogical grouping. The same has also been done to determine the coding-pattern of the individual languages in case they allow for alternative constructions to encode a certain role. Both types of data, based on individual language data and grouped genealogically, are presented in the following, and the results are compared.

In addition to the distinction between the level of individual languages and genus, another contrast is made in my analysis of marked-S languages. For each dataset, I provide two types of coding. In Section 1.5, I have distinguished between the weak and strong version of the functional explanation of marked-S. In general, the functional hypothesis proposed by König (2006) lessens the impact of the marking of the S, A and P roles. It takes other roles into consideration and states that the overall distribution of the less-coded form (the zero-case in my terminology) should have a wider distribution as the form it corresponds to with respect to the S, A and P encoding would have in non-marked-S languages. What exactly is meant by wider distribution is, however, left a bit vague. Two possible interpretations are, first, that the zero-case is used in more contexts than the S-case (weak version) or, second, that the zero-case is used in more contexts than all other (overt) case-forms together (strong version). In accordance with these two versions of the hypothesis, I have compared two different encodings of the role-encoding data in marked-S languages. In the first variant, I code whether a role is encoded by the same case-form as the prototypical P or A role (dubbed the zero-case in this study), or as the S+A/P role. In addition, roles that are coded by neither of the two case-forms are listed in a separate column as 'other'. The second coding used for the data strictly distinguishes whether a role is encoded by zero-coding or by overt material. For many roles, the second coding can be derived from the first coding by adding up the S-case and other case columns. However, the zero- versus overt-coding data-representation also includes forms of overt coding other than case-marking. For example, the genitive particles found in the attributive possessive construction in many languages (cf. Chapter 7) are represented as overt material.

8.3 Comparison across roles

The roles studied in the previous chapters show varying tendencies of behavior similar or dissimilar to that of S arguments in terms or their overt coding. While all of the roles are found to be encoded with the S-case in at least one language of my sample, the proportions of S-like and non-S-like encoding exhibit wide variation between the individual roles. While subjects of locational clauses are almost always encoded like standard intransitive subjects of a language, the form used in citation is only encoded in this way as an alternative strategy in one language, namely Nias (a behavior that most likely is a very recent innovation). Further, for the roles investigated, if a case-form other than the S-case is chosen, then the zero-case is the most likely alternative, although this varies between the

8 Typological comparison of marked-S languages

roles, too. For attributive possessors, the tendency to choose the zero-coded case is equally strong as the tendency to employ a special overtly coded case-form, a genitive. These findings apply to the total set of individual languages as well as to a genealogically controlled sample. In this section I will discuss these results in more detail.

role	∅-case		S-case		other		total
	No.	%	No.	%	No.	%	languages
S argument	0	0%	23	100%	0	0%	23
Locational S	0.5	2%	21.5	98%	0	0%	22
S VDC	3.5	23%	11.5	77%	0	0%	15
Positive existentials	4.5	23%	14.5	73%	1	5%	20
Adverbial clauses	2	22%	6.5	72%	0.5	6%	9
Nominal predication	7	33%	14	67%	0	0%	21
Negative existentials	4	40%	6	60%	0	0%	10
Relative clauses	6	35%	10	59%	1	6%	17
Emphatic S	7	41%	8	47%	2	12%	17
Complement clause	3	60%	2	40%	0	0%	5
Predicate nominal	17	77%	4	18%	1	5%	22
Term of address	8.5	65%	0.5	4%	4	31%	13
Attributive possessor	10	43.5%	1	4%	12	52%	23
Citation form	22.5	98%	0.5	2%	0	0%	23

Table 8.1: Overview on percentage of zero-case and S-case-marking for different roles

Table 8.1 lists the roles studied. For each role, it is indicated which percentage of the languages uses a certain case-form. Three different case values are distinguished, namely the zero-case, the S-case and other, if a different case-form altogether is used for the respective role. If a language uses more than one strategy for a role, both patterns are included and a mean score from all different constructions is listed for the encoding of the role. If, for example, a language has two constructions that encode a context and the relevant role is encoded using the S-case in the first construction and the zero-case in the second construction, this role is represented with the value 0.5 in both columns. The roles are listed in decreasing order according to the percentage the S-case is used for encoding.[3]

---

[3] The percentages have been rounded to full integers in the following. Therefore, the values in

8.3 Comparison across roles

The data in table 8.1 show that the role that behaves most like intransitive S arguments in terms of overt coding is the subject of locational clauses. This role is marked with the S case in 98 % of the languages, while it is encoded with the zero case in only 2 %. On the other end of the scale is the citation form of a noun. Figures for this role are the reverse of those of the locational subject, with 2 % being encoded with the S-case and 98 % with the zero-case. In between these two extremes, the other roles line up. The non-clause-level roles all have percentages below five for the S-case encoding, but they still differ in their encoding behavior. While the citation form, as mentioned above, almost exclusively makes use of the zero-case, half of the attributive possessors are encoded by a different case-form altogether, and roughly the other half is encoded by the zero-case. Terms of address are located in between these to patterns with roughly a third of the languages using a different case-form altogether, and about two thirds using the zero-case.

There are a number of roles that behave more like intransitive S arguments in terms of their encoding. In addition to subjects of locational clauses, most roles that will be subsumed under the subject category in most grammars are encoded like intransitive S arguments quite regularly. Subjects of valency-decreasing constructions (77 %), positive existential constructions (73 %), adverbial clauses (72 %) and nominal predications (67 %) are regularly marked with the same case as prototypical S arguments in two thirds of the languages in the sample or more. Negative existential constructions (60 %) and relative clauses (59 %) still use the S-case in more than half of the cases. Emphatic subjects (47 %) and complement clauses (40 %) are encoded like typical S arguments in just below fifty percent of the languages. Finally, predicate nominals (18 %) are seldom encoded in the S-case in marked-S languages. This role is similar to the non-clause-level roles since it does not represent a type of subject.

Table 8.2 distinguishes whether a role is coded through overt marking or without any overt material. As noted above (Section 8.2), other overt material such as particles has been included here, so that the figures for the zero-case in Table 8.1 and the zero-coded in this table do not always coincide. The two extremes are the same as in the previous table, with subjects of locational clauses being overtly coded in 98 % of the cases and the citation form being overtly coded in only 2 %. The roles that make frequent use of case-forms other than the S-case or zero-case end up in different positions than in the previous table. Attributive possessors (57 % of overt coding versus 4 % of S-case-marking) and terms of address (35 % vs. 4 %) are found in a higher position of the table accordingly.

---

one row of the table add up to 101 % instead of 100 % for some rows.

8 *Typological comparison of marked-S languages*

role	zero-coding		overt coding		total
	No.	%	No.	%	languages
S argument	0	0 %	23	100 %	23
Locational S	0.5	2 %	21.5	98 %	22
S VDC	2.5	17 %	12.5	83 %	15
Adverbial clauses	2	2 %	7	78 %	9
Positive existentials	4.5	23 %	15.5	78 %	20
Emphatic S	5	29 %	12	71 %	17
Nominal predication	7	33 %	14	67 %	21
Relative clauses	6	35 %	11	65 %	17
Negative existentials	4	40 %	6	60 %	10
Attributive possessor	10	43 %	13	57 %	23
Complement clause	3	60 %	2	40 %	5
Term of address	8.5	65 %	4.5	35 %	13
Predicate nominal	17	77 %	5	23 %	22
Citation form	22.5	98 %	0.5	2 %	23

Table 8.2: Overview on percentage of zero versus overt coding for different roles

Also, roles that are encoded via constructions that include additional overt (but non-case) morphology on the respective roles have been affected. Again, the attributive possessor is subject to this (due to encoding with genitive particles) and also the emphatic S role, which has a figure of 71 % overt coding as compared to 47 % of S-case-marking. In some other cases, the addition of the roles marked by other cases have led to minor changes in positioning since Table 8.1 is ordered according to the percentage of S-case-marking. Apart from these deviations, the ranking of roles remains stable between the two tables. This indicates that there is only a slight difference in the results, depending on whether one tests the weak of strong version of the functional marked-S hypothesis. Moreover, the results differ only for a subset of roles.

In the two following tables, the same data is presented, but now the level of comparison is not the number of languages that encode a particular role in a given way, but the genus level. The languages of my sample belong to 10 different genera. The data represents the Nilotic and Surmic languages (both of the Nilo-Saharan family), Eastern Cushitic and Omotic (both Afro-Asiatic) and the Yuman languages. Furthermore, there are five languages that do not have any closely-related languages within the sample and thus are the only representatives of their family. These languages are Nias (Sundic), Ajië (Oceanic), both of the Austronesian family, Savosavo (Solomons East Papuan), Maidu (Maiduan) and Wappo (Wappo). For the languages that are the single representative of their genus, their data has been used to represent the respective genus. For genera with more than one representative, an average figure has been calculated for each role.

role	∅-case		S-case		other		total
	No.	%	No.	%	No.	%	genera
S argument	0	0 %	10	100 %	0	0 %	10
Locational S	0.5	5 %	9.5	95 %	0	0 %	10
Positive existentials	1.9	19 %	7.8	78 %	0.3	3 %	10
S VDC	1.8	23 %	6.2	77 %	0	0 %	8
Adverbial clauses	1	20 %	3.5	70 %	0.5	10 %	5
Nominal predication	3	33 %	6	66 %	0	0 %	9
Negative existentials	3.3	42%	4.7	58%	0	0%	8
Relative clauses	3	38 %	4	50 %	1	13 %	8
Emphatic S	4.6	46 %	4.9	49 %	0.5	5 %	10
Complement clause	3	60 %	2	40 %	0	0 %	5
Predicate nominal	8	80 %	1.8	18 %	0.3	3 %	10
Attributive possessor	3	30 %	1	10 %	6	60 %	10
Term of address	6	67 %	0.5	6 %	2.5	28 %	9
Citation form	9.5	95 %	0.5	5 %	0	0 %	10

Table 8.3: Overview on percentage of zero-case and S-case-marking for different roles by genus

The data in Table 8.3 is divided into zero-case, S-case and other case. It basically shows the same picture as Table 8.1. There are only two instances in which the two tables deviate from each other in the absolute rankings of the roles. Both attributive possessors and terms of address, as well as subjects of valency-decreasing constructions and positive existential predication have switched positions. Otherwise, the rankings are identical. Apart from these minor variations in ordering, there are some differences between the language and genus level in terms of the individual percentages. This is due to the fact that the total number of genera is only 10, which increases the overall percentage of rarely attested patterns that are found in genera with only a few or a single member within the sample. These data have been organized into zero and overt coding in Table 8.4.

8 Typological comparison of marked-S languages

role	zero-coding		overt coding		total
	No.	%	No.	%	genera
S argument	0	0 %	10	100 %	10
Locational S	0.5	5 %	9.5	95 %	10
S VDC	1.5	19 %	6.5	81 %	8
Positive existentials	1.9	19%	8.1	81%	10
Adverbial clauses	1.25	25 %	3.75	75 %	5
Attributive possessor	3	30 %	7	70 %	10
Nominal predication	3	33 %	6	67 %	9
Emphatic S	3.3	33 %	6.7	67 %	10
Relative clauses	3	38 %	5	63 %	8
Negative existentials	3.3	42 %	4.7	58 %	8
Complement clause	3	60 %	2	40 %	5
Term of address	6	67 %	3	33 %	9
Predicate nominal	8	80 %	2	20 %	10
Citation form	9.5	95 %	0.5	5 %	10

Table 8.4: Overview on percentage of zero versus overt coding for different roles by genus

The relation between Table 8.4 and Table 8.2 is not as straightforward as between the two tables that have just been compared. The majority of roles have kept an identical or almost identical position between the two tables. However, there is one notable difference. The attributive possessor scores four positions higher on the genus level than on the language level. This indicates that languages that use the zero-case for this role are somewhat overrepresented in the sample. All other roles have the same rank between the two levels of comparison or deviate only by one position. Roles that show this minimal variation between the two tables are adverbial clauses and positive existential predications as well as subjects of nominal predications and emphatic subjects; both pairs have switched positions between the two tables. As in the previous table, though, the ranking is rather stable for the language and genus level as with respect to overt versus zero-coding, the individual percentages differ occasionally.

Finally, comparing the data on genus level for the encoding as zero-case, S-case and other with the encoding as overt versus zero-coding a number of deviations between the rankings can be found. The attributive possessor is six positions lower in Table 8.3 than in Table 8.4. This has also been the biggest difference on language level between the two encodings. Subjects of negative existentials, meanwhile, score two positions higher in the first table if one takes into account the intervening attributive possessor (otherwise the difference is three positions). Again, taking into account, the already mentioned differences, three more minor deviations in terms of pairwise switching of positions exist between the two tables. These pairs of roles are: subjects of valency-decreasing constructions and positive existential predications; emphatic subjects and subjects of relative clauses; as well as terms of address and predicate nominals.

8.4 Comparison across languages

While the previous section analyzed the data from the perspective of the different roles investigated in this study, this section takes a closer look at the different marked-S languages. More precisely, the similarities and differences in encoding of the respective roles are investigated. Again, both types of encoding have been taken into account. The first type distinguishes between coding in terms of zero-case (i.e. P/A coding) versus S(+A/P)-case versus other case-form. The second type strictly differentiates between overt and zero-coding. Even though in the last section the data on individual versus genus level has proved to be almost identical, this section analyzes the data from both the language and the genus level. In addition, for each language its genus is listed in the language level tables and the overall similarity within the individual genera is discussed.

I have ranked the languages in Table 8.5 on the following page with respect to the percentage of roles covered by the zero-case from high to low. The scores range from 67 % of roles being coverd by the zero-case to a 23 % coverage. These data show that languages of the marked-S type do not behave in a uniform way. Furthermore, while some languages indeed have a wide range of contexts in which the zero-case is used, some marked-S languages do so only rarely. The languages which make use of the zero-case to a lesser degree, however, often employ other overtly coded case-forms than the S-case for the roles studied here. Remember that in some of the languages both case-forms, the zero-case and the S-case, are overtly coded. The 'unmarked' status of the zero-case is justified by its use in extra-syntactic contexts in these languages. The Omotic languages are of this type of marked-S language. Interestingly, these languages appear to make little use of the zero-case in comparison with other marked-S languages and thus are found near the bottom end of Table 8.5. This is especially obvious for Gamo, which is the Omotic language with the best data coverage in the sample. Since the total number of contexts that employ the zero-case in the related languages

8 Typological comparison of marked-S languages

language	∅-case		S-case		other		total
	No.	%	No.	%	No.	%	roles
Diegueño (Mesa Grande), Yuman	8	67 %	4	33 %	0	0 %	12
Ajië, Oceanic	7	58 %	4.5	38 %	0.5	4 %	12
Datooga, Nilotic	7	58 %	5	42 %	0	0 %	12
Maa, Nilotic	6	50 %	6	50 %	0	0 %	12
Jamul Tiipay, Yuman	7.5	58 %	5.5	42 %	0	0 %	13
Wappo, Wappo	8	50 %	7	44 %	1	6 %	16
Nias, Sundic	7.5	54 %	6.5	46 %	0	0 %	14
Oromo (Boraana), Eastern Cushitic	5	45 %	5	45 %	1	9 %	11
Mojave, Yuman	7	44 %	9	56 %	0	0 %	16
Havasupai, Yuman	4.5	45 %	5.5	55 %	0	0 %	10
Savosavo, Solomons East Papuan	6.5	43 %	6	40 %	2.5	17 %	15
Tennet, Surmic	5.5	42 %	6.5	50 %	1	8 %	13
Turkana, Nilotic	6	40 %	7	47 %	2	13 %	15
Yavapai, Yuman	5	39 %	8	62 %	0	0 %	13
Nandi, Nilotic	4.5	38 %	7.5	63 %	0	0 %	12
Zayse, Omotic	3	33 %	5	56 %	1	11 %	9
Murle, Surmic	4	33 %	7	58 %	1	8 %	12
Arbore, Eastern Cushitic	3	30 %	5	50 %	2	20 %	10
Wolaytta, Omotic	2.5	28 %	4.5	50 %	2	22 %	9
Oromo (Harar), Eastern Cushitic	3	23 %	7	54 %	3	23 %	13
Gamo, Omotic	3	23 %	8	62 %	2	15 %	13
K'abeena, Eastern Cushitic	3.5	23 %	10	67 %	1.5	10 %	15
Maidu, Maiduan	2.5	23 %	7.5	68 %	1	9 %	11

Table 8.5: Overview on percentage of zero-case and S-case-marking for different languages

is equally low, the higher percentage of use of the zero-case given for Zayse and Wolaytta are probably a result of their small number of contexts attested. Most languages of a genus tend to be scattered over roughly the same region of the table. While the Omotic languages are found in the lower half of the table, the Yuman languages are located in the upper half. The Eastern Cushitic languages, except for Boraana Oromo, are found in the lower ranks as well. The Surmic languages (Tennet and Murle) score in the lower mid region of the table. Only the Nilotic languages are mixed with two languages (Datooga and Maa) located close to the top of the table and two other languages (Turkana and Nandi) in the lower middle of the ranking. Notably, these groupings do not reflect the

8.4 Comparison across languages

genealogical grouping within the Nilotic languages but rather appear to be a reflex of the languages' geographical location.[4] Of the languages in the sample that are the single representative of their genus, the two Austronesian languages Nias (Sundic) and Ajië (Oceanic) are among the highest ranked, together with North-American Wappo; all these languages use the zero-case for half of the roles studied or more. Non-Austronesian Savosavo scores just above the middle of the ranking. Finally, Maidu is located near the bottom end among the Omotic and Eastern Cushitic languages of the Afro-Asiatic family.

genus	∅-case		S-case		other		total
	No.	%	No.	%	No.	%	roles
Oceanic	7	58 %	4.5	38 %	0.5	4 %	12
Sundic	7.5	54 %	6.5	46 %	0	0 %	14
Wappo	8	50 %	7	44 %	1	6 %	16
Nilotic	7.2	48 %	7	47 %	0.8	5 %	15
Yuman	7	44 %	9	56 %	0	0 %	16
Solomons East Papuan	6.5	43 %	6	40 %	2.5	17 %	15
Surmic	6	43 %	7	50 %	1	7 %	14
Eastern Cushitic	4.1	27 %	8.6	57 %	2.3	16 %	15
Maiduan	2.5	23 %	7.5	68 %	1	9 %	11
Omotic	2.8	20 %	9.2	66 %	2	14 %	14

Table 8.6: Overview on percentage of zero-case and S-case-marking for different genera

Table 8.6 summarizes the data organized by genus. For genera that are represented by more than one language the data of the individual languages from the genus has been averaged like in the previous section. Again the ordering is according to the percentage of roles covered by the zero-case beginning with the highest percentage. This table repeats the general picture lined out in the previous discussion of the languages. Oceanic, Sundic and Wappo, which are all represented through a single language in the sample, mark the top of the ranking by genus. Afterwards, Nilotic, Yuman, Solomons East Papuan, and Surmic follow in the mid-field. And as was to be expected from the data of the individual languages, the ranking is concluded by Eastern Cushitic, Maiduan, and Omotic.

---

[4] Genealogically, Maa and Turkana group together as East Nilotic and Datooga and Nandi as South Nilotic. The geographical distribution of the languages will be discussed later in Section 8.6. The curious reader may skip ahead to Figure 8.7 for a map of the East African marked-S languages.

8 Typological comparison of marked-S languages

The relatively low ranking of Yuman might be surprising at first glance, since the last table has been topped by a language of this genus. However, since the overall number of Yuman languages is the sample is the largest of all genera, its overall impact on the ranking of the whole genus has not been large in the end.

language, genus	zero-coding		overt coding		total
	No.	%	No.	%	roles
Diegueño Mesa Grande, Yuman	8	67 %	4	33 %	12
Ajië, Oceanic	7	58 %	5	42 %	12
Datooga, Nilotic	7	58 %	5	42 %	12
Jamul Tiipay, Yuman	7.5	58 %	5.5	42 %	13
Nias, Sundic	7.5	54 %	6.5	46 %	14
Maa, Nilotic	6	50 %	6	50 %	12
Wappo, Wappo	8	50 %	8	50 %	16
Havasupai, Yuman	4.5	45 %	5.5	55 %	10
Mojave, Yuman	7	44 %	9	56 %	16
Tennet, Surmic	5.5	42 %	7.5	58 %	13
Turkana, Nilotic	6	40 %	9	60 %	15
Yavapai, Yuman	5	38 %	8	62 %	13
Nandi, Nilotic	4.5	38 %	7.5	63 %	12
Savosavo, Solomons East Papuan	5.5	37 %	9.5	63 %	15
Zayse, Omotic	3	33 %	6	67 %	9
Murle, Surmic	4	33 %	8	67 %	12
Arbore, Eastern Cushitic	3	30 %	7	70 %	10
Wolaytta, Omotic	2.5	28 %	6.5	72 %	9
Oromo (Boraana), Eastern Cushitic	3	27 %	8	73 %	11
K'abeena, Eastern Cushitic	3.5	23 %	11.5	77 %	15
Oromo (Harar), Eastern Cushitic	3	23 %	10	77 %	13
Gamo, Omotic	3	23 %	10	77 %	13
Maidu, Maiduan	2.5	23 %	8.5	77 %	11

Table 8.7: Overview on percentage of zero-case and overt coding for different languages

The languages are also ranked for the data organized by zero-coding versus overt coding, like has been done with the roles. The picture for the individual languages, as represented in Table 8.7 has not changed in most cases. The most remarkable difference is the ranking of Boraana Oromo, which has fallen 11 positions from rank 8 to 19. This is the one language in which the re-coding to overt versus zero-coding has the strongest effect, since Boraana Oromo uses overt non-case morphology combined with the zero-case-form for a number of roles. A smaller re-ranking can be found with Savosavo which falls 4 positions as compared to the previous table. Like Boraana Oromo, Savosavo encodes some roles with overt non-case morphology. The other languages occupy identical positions in the two rankings.

language family	∅-coding		overt coding		total
	No.	%	No.	%	roles
Oceanic	7	58 %	5	42 %	12
Sundic	7.5	54 %	6.5	46 %	14
Wappo	8	50 %	8	50 %	16
Nilotic	7.2	48 %	7.8	52 %	15
Yuman	7.2	45 %	8.8	55 %	16
Surmic	6	43 %	8	57 %	14
Solomons East Papuan	5.5	37 %	9.5	63 %	15
Eastern Cushitic	3.5	23 %	11.5	77 %	15
Maiduan	2.5	23 %	8.5	77 %	11
Omotic	2.8	20 %	11.2	80 %	14

Table 8.8: Overview on percentage of zero-coding and overt coding for different genera

Despite the major difference in ranking seen for Boraana Oromo on the language level, on genus level no large rearrangements happen. Table 8.8 presents the ranking of genera in the zero- versus overt-encoding. Compared with the ranking of genera based on S-case, zero-case or other case-form represented in Table 8.6 above, there are almost no changes. Only Surmic and Solomons East Papuan have switched positions between the two tables. This corresponds to the drop in position by Savosavo, which is the only language of this family in the sample, on the language level. The rankings of the other genera remain stable between the two genus level tables.

8.5 Similarity networks

The two previous sections have compared the micro-alignment data from languages of the marked-S type as defined in Chapter 2. Two different perspectives

8 *Typological comparison of marked-S languages*

have been chosen, the similarity/difference between the pre-defined contexts and between the individual languages. For each of the scenarios, I have established a ranking from the most S-like context to the least S-like contexts or the language which makes the widest/narrowest use of the zero-case-form respectively. These ranking are very easy to interpret, but they reduce a complex and potentially multi-dimensional data set to a linear order. A more sophisticated and mathematically more complex way to analyze the data are (phylogenetic) networks. The algorithms used to calculate these networks were originally developed to analyze and compare gene sequences of biological species, however, the basic mechanisms can also be used for comparison of linguistic data. Phylogenetic networks are generalized versions of tree-structures that allow the inclusion of conflicting information into tree-structures. In comparison with the linear ordering of the tables presented in the previous sections, these tree-like manifestations allow the addition of another dimension to the data analysis. If, for instance, half of the languages of the sample use the zero-case for role A and the other half of the sample uses the zero-case for role B, a linear ranking based on percentages would show these contexts next to each other in the ranking. This might be interpreted as a relation between roles A in B given only the linear ranking. However, in the scenario described above, there is no similarity between the two roles.[5] A similarity network can visualize this difference between the two roles that would appear to behave identical in a table ranked by percentages. In the following, I will give a brief introduction to interpreting similarity networks. However, it should be kept in mind that although they can be a visual aid to discover interesting relationships within data sets, a lot of complexity has to be reduced for the visual representation and thus they are not devoid of artifacts. Afterwards, I will present and discuss the networks generated from the data on marked-S languages. It has been demonstrated in the two proceeding sections that there is no big difference in the results between the encoding of the roles as either zero-case, S-case and other case-form, or zero versus overt encoding. In this section, I have therefore chosen to only analyze one kind of data encoding. The data sets which have been chosen are the ones that distinguish between zero-case, S-case and other case-forms. This data represents the weak form of the functional marked-S hypothesis (marked-S languages should encode more roles with the zero-case than with the S-case-form). If the weak hypothesis does not

---

[5] In this made up example, there is in fact a negative correlation between the two roles. However, as the statistically inclined reader will be well aware of, correlations, be they positive or negative, do not imply causation. Also, such clear-cut distributions as described in the scenario above, are unlikely to occur in naturalistic data.

arrive at any meaningful results, the stronger version will likely fail to do so as well.

The graphs in this section have been produced by NeighborNet, a neighbor joining algorithm that produces phylogenetic networks.[6] The algorithm is described in Bryant & Moulton (2004); a more detailed discussion on the analysis of genealogical data through split networks is given in Huson & Bryant (2006). The traditional method of representing phylogenetic relationships, be they for species or human languages, is the (phylogenetic) tree. However, due to vertical transfer, missing data, and other factors, it is not always possible to construct a perfect treelike structure from data sets. Network structures can include conflicting data and thus are a good choice to represent linguistic data. For this study, the reconstruction of prehistory is not much of an issue. The mechanisms used for constructing genealogical trees can, however, equally well be used to analyze data sets with respect to how similar/diverse the individual taxa are. Traditional tree-building methods join two neighboring nodes and amalgamate them to a single node. Instead, NeighborNet joins three neighboring nodes and combines them to form two superior nodes. While points of divergence between the taxa are represented through the bifurcations at the respective mother node in a tree, in the network a split is represented through a set of parallel edges. In general it can be said that the more treelike a part of the network looks, i.e. by clearly branching of from the rest of the network, the clearer the split is.

Figure 8.3 on the next page shows the network produced by the data on roles coded through S-case, zero-case or other case-form ordered by genus (the equivalent of Table 8.3). Similarly to the representation in the table, the network shows an almost scalar gradient from roles that behave very alike to the S role to roles that behave unlike it. The transitive A and P roles have been included in the graphic as well, since all but one language of the sample is of the marked-nominative type A is almost lined up with S and P is at the other end of the graph (together with the citation form). Apart from the gradual shift from S-like to non-S-like role, which is visualized through the long vertical extension of the network as compared to the horizontal dimension, the graph is almost separated into two distinct halves through a kind of waistline in the middle. This waistline nicely separates the roles which are some type of subject from the other roles such as attributive possessors, citation form and so on. Emphatic subjects are located at the border of these two parts of the network, just on the non-S-like side. This corresponds to their status as not being the grammatical subject of the

---

[6] I am very grateful to Michael Cysouw, who helped me with producing the NeighborNet networks.

8 *Typological comparison of marked-S languages*

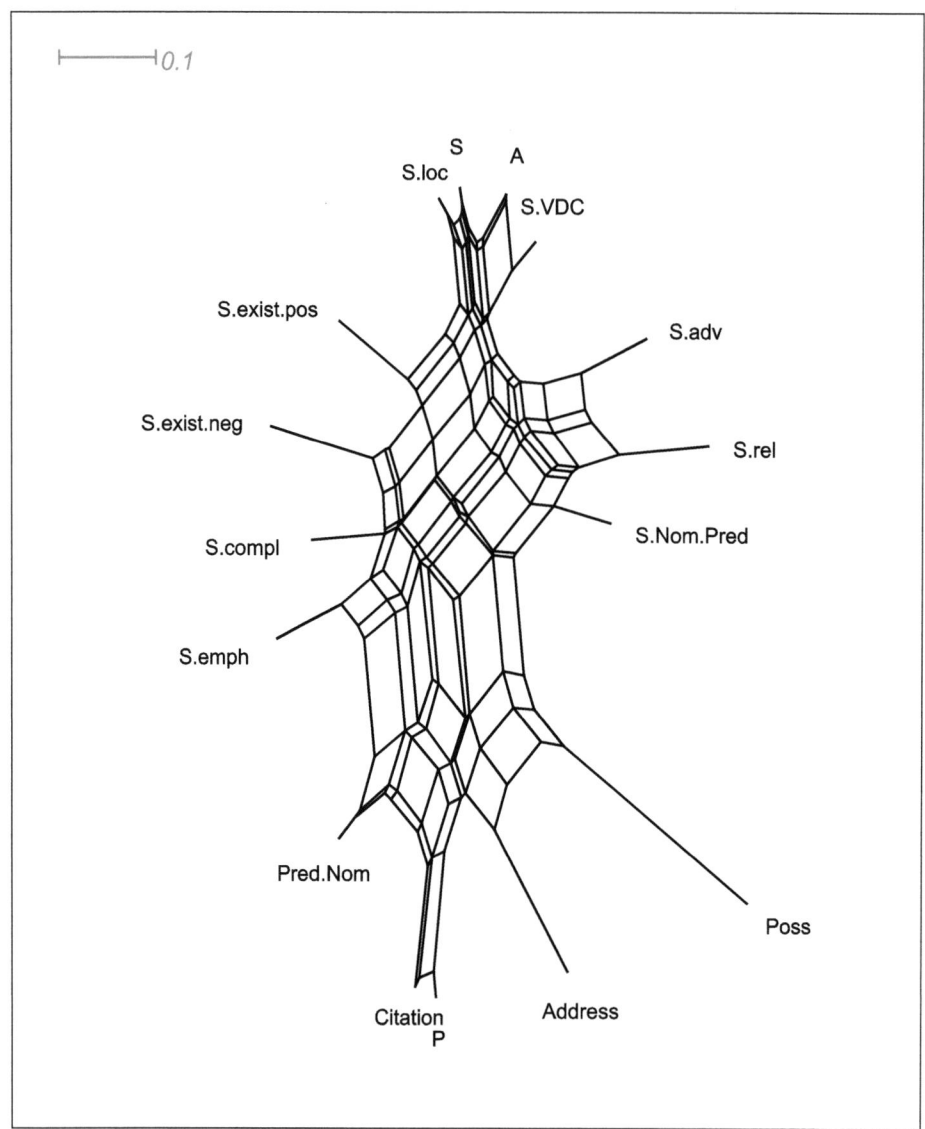

Figure 8.3: Network of zero-case and S-case-marking for different roles by genus

clause in at least some marked-S languages. In these languages they are rather analyzed as predicate nominals (cf. Chapter 3), next to which they are found in figure 8.3. Furthermore, there is a small separation between relative clauses and adverbial clauses and the rest of the network. Complement clauses, on the other hand, do not form a sub-branch with these two other types of dependent clauses, but are found on the other side of the network. This might suggest that relative and adverbial clauses do behave more like each other while complement clauses show different behavior for the languages of the sample. One should be cautious, however, since data on one or more types of dependent clause is lacking for most languages, and this affiliation between relative and adverbial clauses might be an artifact created because of these missing data. Locational and existential predictions have been analyzed as making frequent use of the same constructions (Chapter 4). This tendency, however, is not visually manifested in the network as the subjects of these predications do not constitute a separate branch. Locational subjects rather seem to go together with regular S arguments and subjects of valency-decreasing constructions. The fact that locational clauses use constructions similar to standard intransitive clauses, while existentials occasionally use other constructions, has also been noted in Chapter 4. Meanwhile, subjects of positive and negative existentials are found in adjacent positions of the network. However, since the data on negative existentials is rather scarce and the two roles do not form a branch structure together, this fact should not be overrated.

The next network groups the data by languages (see Figure 8.4 on the following page). The most salient subdivision of the language network is the one between the Yuman languages and Wappo, which form a North-West American subtype of marked-S, and the rest of the network. The other American language of this sample, i.e. Maidu, does not belong to this typological subgrouping. The Nilotic language Datooga also appears to be more similar in type to the American languages than to any other language in the sample. Also, the groupings within the Yuman genus are quite accurately mirrored by the network. Mesa Gande Diegueño and Jamul Tiipay both belong to the Delta-California branch of Yuman, while Yavapai, Walapai and Havasupai form the Arizona Pai branch. Mojave, which is located between these two groups in the network, belongs to the River Yuman branch. Other genealogical groupings that are represented in the network are the Afro-Asiatic languages from the Omotic and Eastern Cushitic branch (except Arbore, which is separated from its related languages). Even though these languages are found in an continuous segment of the network (with intervening Maidu, which exhibits the most areally atypical pattern of the sample), they do

8 Typological comparison of marked-S languages

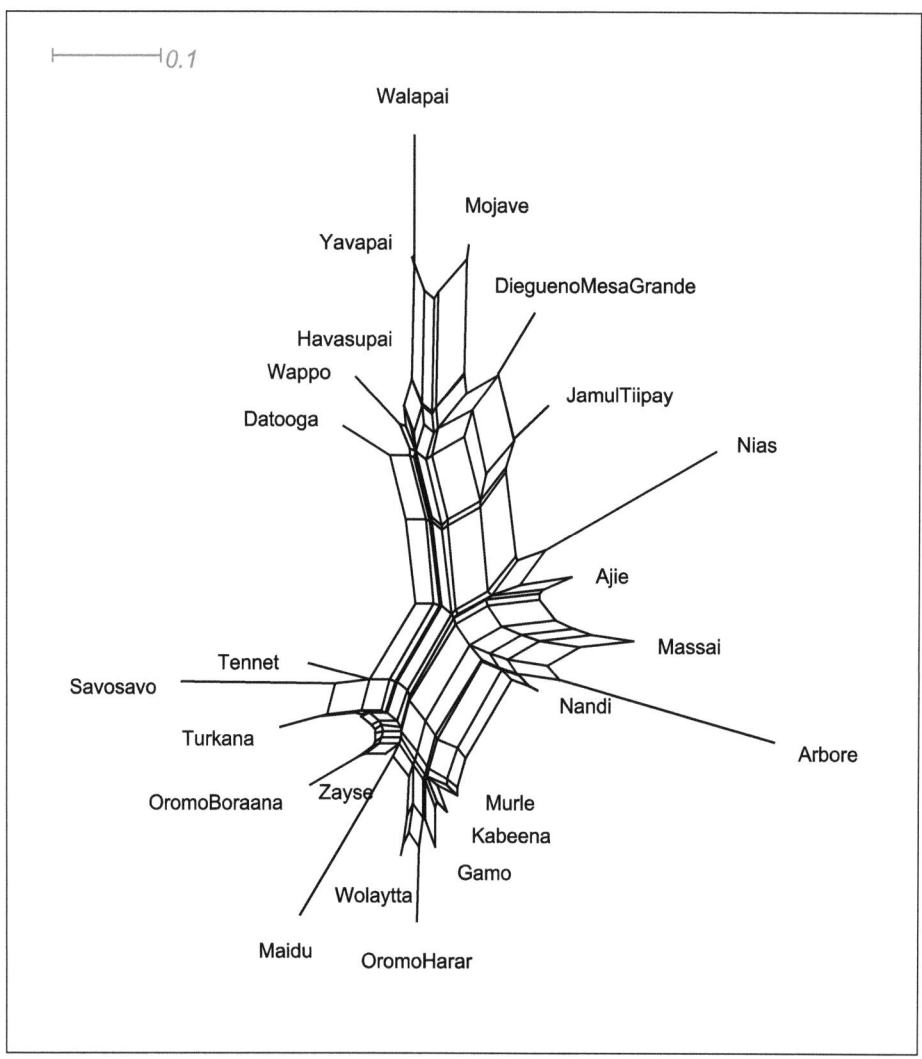

Figure 8.4: Similarity network of the languages studied

8.5 Similarity networks

not form a clear branch structure that would set them off from other languages. However, there is a distinct African subgroup, although it is not limited to the languages of the Afro-Asiatic family. If one adds the non-related Surmic languages (Murle and Tennet) and the Nilotic language Turkana of the Nilo-Saharan family as well as Maidu and Savosavo, a distinct group separated from the remaining languages by a branch-like structure can be identified.

The Austronesian languages Ajië and Nias are located in adjacent position at the border between the North American and African languages, but like the Afro-Asiatic language, they do not form an individual branch structure. The Nilotic languages, on the other hand, are scattered all over the network and so do not form any continuous subsection of the network. This genus has already been shown to be the most divergent at the tabular ranking in the previous section.

Finally the data is grouped by genus (Figure 8.5). For this network, Maidu

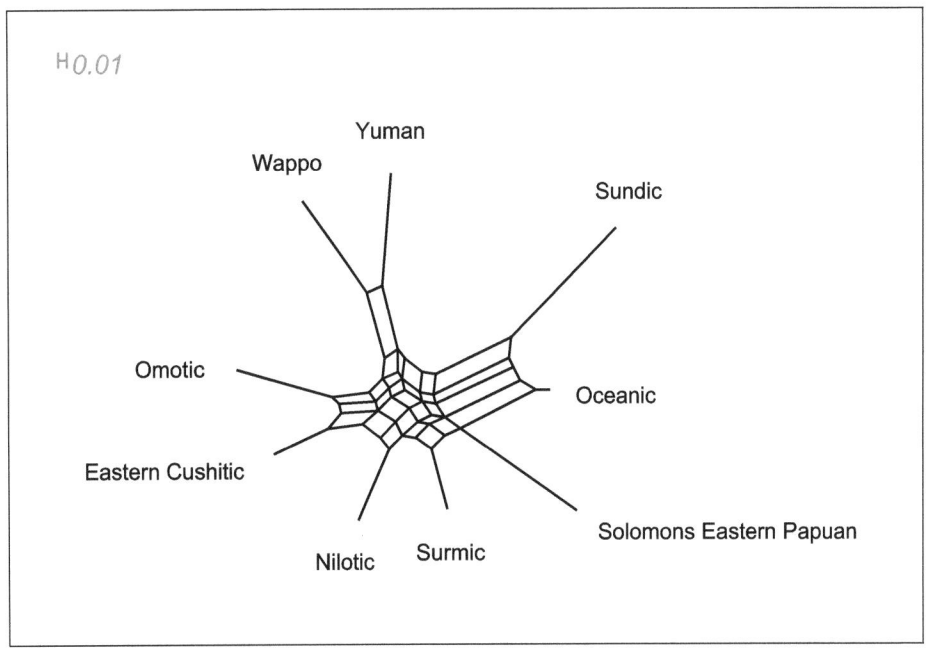

Figure 8.5: Similarity network of the genera studied

(Maiduan) has been eliminated. It has already been noted that Maidu behaves quite unusual compared with the marked-S languages in its macro-area. Also compared with the total set of marked-S languages, it stands out by employing the S-case almost like would be expected from a regular nominative-accusative

8 Typological comparison of marked-S languages

language. Other than the Omotic marked-S languages, which also make wide use of the S-case, and which have overtly coded forms for both S-case and zero-case, on the formal level Maidu is a typical marked-S language.

Also when analyzing the language-internal grouping of uses in the Maidu data, the picture is confusing. The semantic map in Figure 8.6 visualizes the use of S-case (red/subj), zero-case (blue/zero) and other case-forms (black/other) in Maidu.[7] The arrangement of the roles is derived from the usage of these case-

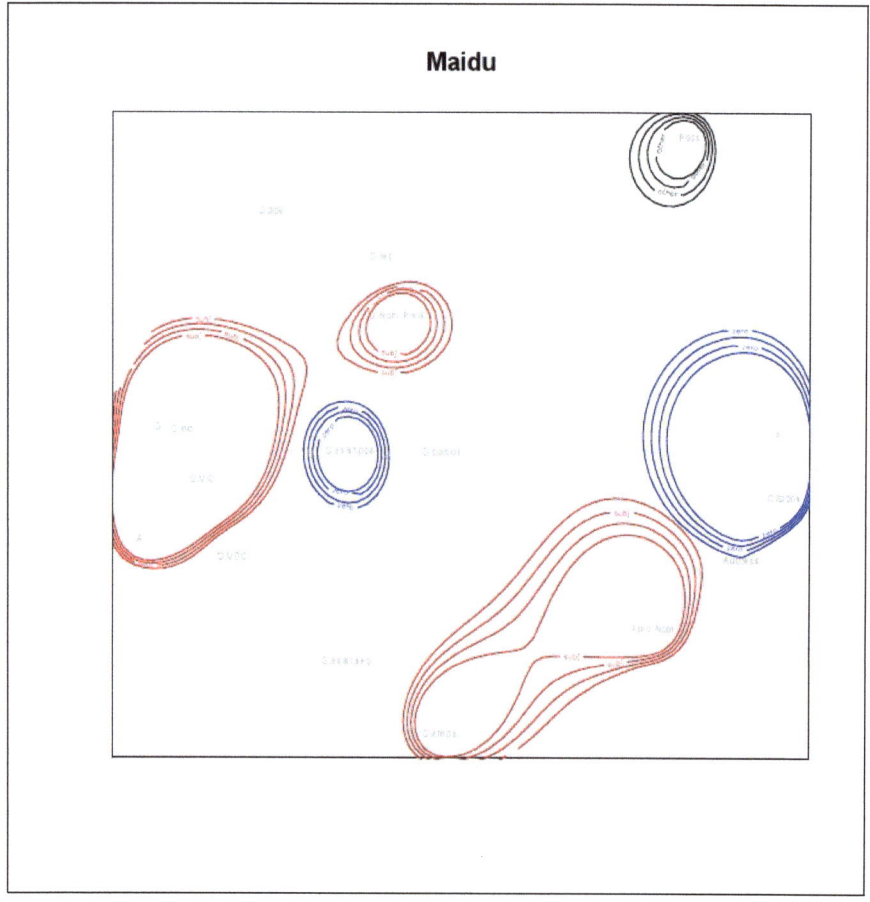

Figure 8.6: Maidu semantic map (MDS)

forms for the individual roles across all languages of the sample via multidimensional scaling (MDS). Semantic maps derived through MDS and how they can be

---
[7] Again, I have to thank Michael Cysouw. This time for producing and sharing this semantic map.

used to analyze and understand the nature of linguistic meanings are discussed by Cysouw (2010). While the other languages use the individual case-forms for continuous parts of the semantic map (or at least only one case-form shows discontinuous usage), Maidu rather constitutes a semantic patchwork.

Furthermore, including Maidu into the genus level network gives no clear picture. If one excludes this data, the genealogical and areal groupings come out quite nicely, as demonstrated in Figure 8.5. The North American languages have already formed a distinct subgroup on the language level. Not surprisingly, Yuman and Wappo also form the most clear subgrouping in this graph. They branch off almost tree-like from the other genera. The African genera also form a distinct area of the network, and especially the Afro-Asiatic genera Omotic and Eastern Cushitic even form a small separate branch. The two Nilo-Saharan genera, Nilotic and Surmic, are adjacent to one another, though they form no branch-like structure. The Austronesian genera, Sundic and Oceanic, also from a separate branch of the network (though the branching is not particularly strong) with Solomons East Papuan, the other Pacific genus, in adjacent position.

8.6 Geographical patterns

It has been noted several times in this study that the distribution of marked-S languages is highly skewed in terms of geography. North-East Africa, where the pattern is found in both the Afro-Asiatic and Nilo-Saharan family, appears to be a breeding ground for languages of this type. Another area in which marked-S languages appear frequently (as compared with the overall distribution over the world) is the lower North American Pacific coast. The majority of marked-S languages found in this region are closely-related with one another as they belong to one genus (i.e. Yuman). However, two unrelated marked-S languages, namely Wappo and Maidu, do occur in the same macro-area. Finally the Pacific macro-area is home to some languages of the marked-S type. The three Pacific languages with the most prominent marked-S pattern are stretched out over a quite large area. However, if additionally to Nias, Ajië and Savosavo the less prototypical marked-S languages of the same region are included, such as the ones discussed in Chapter 5.3, the Pacific exhibits an above-average concentration of marked-S languages as well. In this section, I will take a closer look at the areal patterings of marked-S languages.

The largest number of languages in my sample is found in North-East Africa. In addition to the large number for the African marked-S languages, they also exhibit genealogical diversity as they are represented by four distinct genera belonging to the Afro-Asiatic (Omotic and Cushitic) and Nilo-Saharan (Surmic and

8 *Typological comparison of marked-S languages*

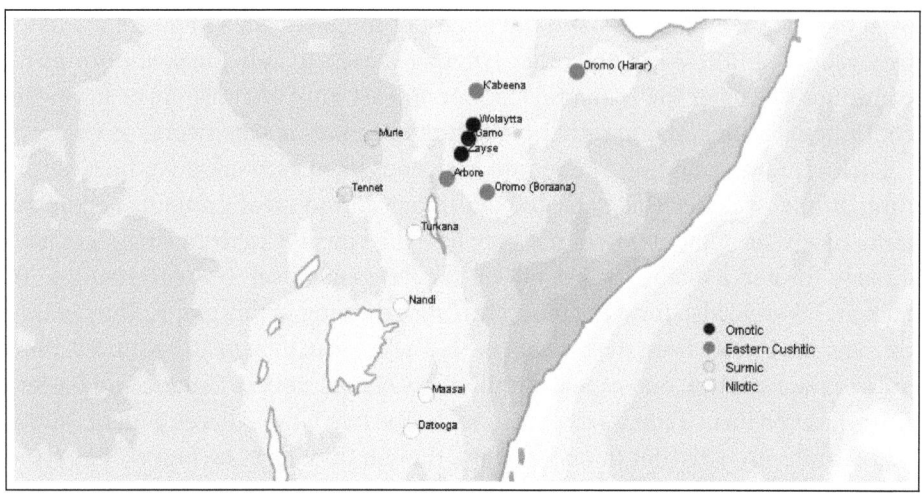

Figure 8.7: Marked-S languages of East Africa by genus

Nilotic) families (cf. Figure 8.7).[8] Marked-S patterns have been reported from other genera of this area, but the data available for them was not suitable to include in this study. Areal influence is often proposed as an explanation if a certain linguistic pattern is found in a group of geographically adjacent but non-related languages, even more so if the respective pattern is rare on a world-wide basis. The locus of the African marked-S languages has been suggested as a linguistic area on several occasions. Güldemann (2005) describes a pattern of forming complex predicates through a special type of auxiliary that is uniquely found in the region referred to as Chad-Ethiopia macro-area. This region has been described as a linguistic area in earlier work by Greenberg (1983), Ferguson (1976) and Heine (1976), though the name and exact boundaries of the supposed area differ between the authors. However, the existence of an 'Ethiopian language area' is disputed by Tosco (2000). Yet, his main argument is not that there has not been linguistic contact between unrelated languages in this area, but that the influence has been unidirectional. He lists multi-directional influence and divergence towards a common model as defining criteria for linguistic areas. The network in Figure 8.4 has shown that the African languages do not group according to their genealogical affiliations in most cases with respect to the roles studied here. Only the Omotic languages in combination with most Cushitic languages do occur in adjacent position. However, they do not exhibit any clear

---

[8] The language Maa is represented with its alternative name Maasai in the map.

8.6 Geographical patterns

tree-like branching from the other African languages (and also the Pacific languages plus Maidu). Instead they all are of the same general type, with the exclusion of Datooga, which is more similar to the North American languages in its behavior. Notably Datooga, which is the least typical African marked-S language, is spoken at the periphery of the geographical region these languages cover. In addition, Datooga and Maa are the two African languages that make the widest use of the zero-case and thus have been shown to behave quite differently than the two other Nilotic languages in the sample in Table 8.1. Indeed, Maa is the language that is spoken closest to Datooga, though it is not the language which is related most closely in terms of genealogy.

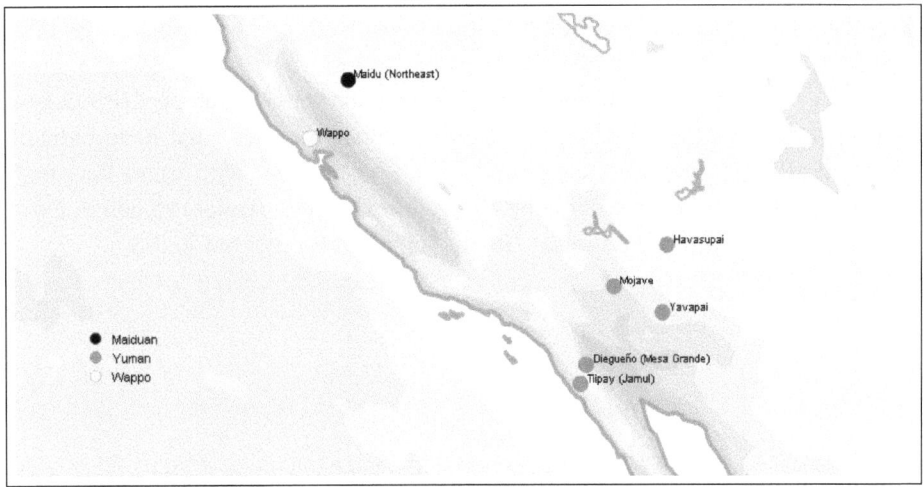

Figure 8.8: Marked-S languages of North-West America by genus

The second larger grouping of marked-S languages is found in North-West America. These languages are far less genealogically diverse than their African counterparts. The majority of languages belongs to the Yuman genus, which is completely of the marked-S type, except for only one language, namely Kiliwa (Mixco 1965), which is also seen as the language that first branched of within the genus (Joël 1998). Apart from the Yuman languages, two other marked-S languages of this region are studied here. Wappo and Maidu are both located quite a stretch to the North from the Yuman languages (cf. Figure 8.8), so that the American languages do not form a contiguous area. Apart from the close geographical distance between Maidu and Wappo, these two languages do not show a similar linguistic behavior. Wappo rather conforms to the most frequent type of American marked-S languages with the Yuman languages. Maidu does

8 Typological comparison of marked-S languages

not show any similarities to this type. In the network in Figure 8.4, it is located somewhere between Omotic and some Cushitic languages, the main similarity to which is Maidu's equally high percentage of S-case use. For the Yuman languages of North America, genealogy is probably the main factor behind their common typological profile with respect to their marked-S case-system. Wappo is a language of the same greater area which is not related to this genus. However, it has a typological profile similar to the Yuman languages. No contact history between the Yuman languages and Wappo is known and the geographical distance between the languages (in addition to the large number of intervening languages) makes this scenario not very likely. However, one should not rule out that in prehistoric times both Wappo and the Yuman languages were part of a larger linguistic area in which marked-S languages were more abundant. If one takes this scenario seriously, Maidu, which is located more closely to Wappo, could also have been a part of this area. Still, Maidu's marked-S system is distinct from the other North American languages. So the system either must have radically changed after the hypothetical period of intense contact with other languages of the marked-S type, or it could be a development independent of contact with languages that exhibit the typical North American type of marked-S.

Figure 8.9: Marked-S languages of the Pacific by genus

Finally, the sample included three marked-S languages from the larger Pacific region. Comparing their distribution (cf. Figure 8.9), it becomes clear that arguing for contact between these languages as source for the marked-S pattern would be rather difficult given that these three languages are stretched out from the West Coast of Sumatra to the Solomon Islands and down to New Caledonia. In addition, the genealogical relation between these languages is very distant (Nias and Ajië belong to different genera of the Austronesian family) or non-existent (as between Savosavo and the other two languages). In between the three languages studied in detail lies the entire Indonesian Archipelago including all of Papua as well as large stretches of the Pacific Ocean. However, within this area there are a number of languages exhibiting a pattern that resembles the marked-S languages in some respect. I have discussed this pattern, which consists of overt subject-marking only in certain, mostly emphatic, contexts, in Chapter 5. Adding these languages to the map, as done in Figure 8.10, at least the Eastern half of the region pictured here gets closer resemblance to an geographically contiguous area, which includes Savosavo and Ajië at its periphery.

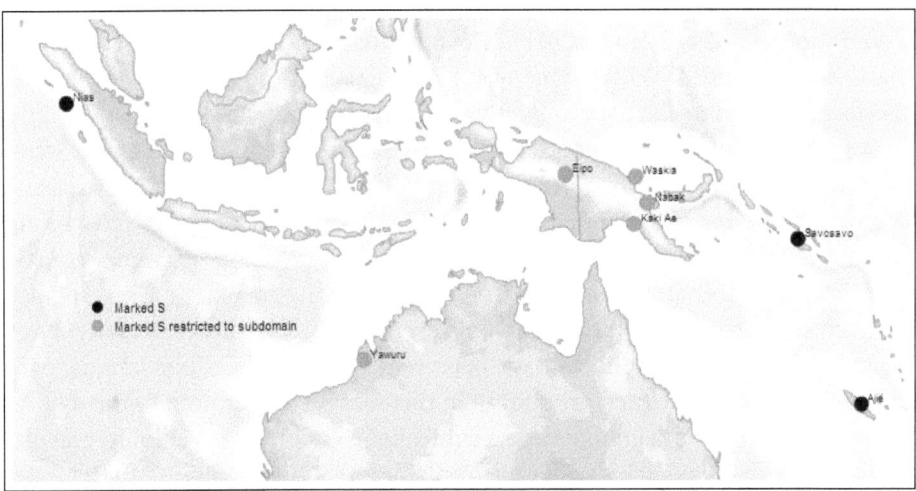

Figure 8.10: Marked-S languages of the Pacific including full and restricted patterns

8.7 Summary

In this chapter, I have presented a summary of the data gathered through Chapters 3–7. The micro-alignment approach I have chosen for the investigation of marked-S languages consists of collecting data on the case-marking patterns for a number of roles. These roles were selected from several contexts that include a subject-like role (such as nominal predications or existentials), or roles that are

8 Typological comparison of marked-S languages

commonly associated with the so-called 'unmarked case' of standard nominative-accusative and ergative-absolutive languages (i.e. the nominative or absolutive respectively). The data collected on the case-marking of these roles have been analyzed from two perspectives: from the point of view of these roles and the point of view of the languages studied.

I have demonstrated that the encoding of the roles chosen for this micro-typology of the marked-S coding-system range from (almost) exclusive encoding with the S-case to zero-coding in almost all instances. Roles that do not constitute any type of subject, though they have been associated with the nominative case in previous work, are especially likely to be zero-coded. These roles are the citation form and predicate nominals, as well as attributive possessors and terms of address. The latter two are, however, also frequently encoded through other overt non-S-case case-forms.

Variation is not only found between the different roles but also between the marked-S languages. While some make strong use of the zero-case, others use this form more sparsely. Especially the Omotic languages and Maidu do not differ strongly from standard nominative-accusative languages in the use of the S-case. On the other end of the hierarchy, there are the distantly related Austronesian languages Ajië and Nias, a number of the North American Yuman languages and Wappo as well as the Nilotic languages Datooga and Maa. These languages make especially wide use of the zero-case and also employ it for some types of subjects.

Given the rarity of the phenomenon, this study has included as many languages as possible and no quotas have been set in advance, e.g. one language per genus (or other pre-defined grouping). In this section, in addition to the data set including the individual languages, a controlled version in which only one data point per genus was included for each role has also been presented. The differences between the two sets of data, the language and genus level, have been very small.

Also, two different encodings for the case-marking have been employed for the data. These two codings roughly correspond to the weak and strong interpretation of König's (2006) functional marked-S hypothesis. The weak version states that the zero-case should be employed in more contexts in marked-S languages than the overtly coded S-case. To analyze this version of the hypothesis the data has been coded according to whether a role is marked with the zero-case, S-case or another case-form. The strong version of the hypothesis states that the zero-case should be more frequent than any other type of encoding, respectively the data has been coded as zero-coding and overt coding to test this claim. The differences between the two types of coding have been minor and are mostly restricted to non-subject roles such as attributive possessors. Most languages either choose the zero-case or the S-case for the majority of roles investigated in this study.

In addition, the data have been analyzed in form of phylogenetic networks produced through the NeighborNet algorithm. The networks in general confirm the picture gained from the depiction in the form of tables ranked by percentage of use of the individual case-forms. The roles appear to show a clear separation between those that constitute some kind of subject and those that have different, mostly non-clause level, functions. The data on the languages do not show any neat subtypes of marked-S languages apart from the grouping of the Yuman languages and Wappo. The data on the genus level, meanwhile, produced an accurate picture of the genealogical and areal groupings of languages. However, one language, namely Maidu, had to be excluded in order to arrive at this neat depiction.

Geographically, the languages of the sample can bee grouped as belonging to three marco-areas: North-Eastern Africa, the North American West Coast, and the Pacific. The languages of North America, to the exclusion of Maidu, do form the most distinct subtype in all analyses of the data. These languages mostly belong to the Yuman genus. However, non-related Wappo also behaves quite similarly to the Yuman languages. The other type of marked-S languages against which the American type can be set off consists mostly of the African languages. The Afro-Asiatic languages, especially of the Omotic genus, are another potential subtype of marked-S languages. However, these languages do not form as distinct a subtype branching off from other languages as does the American type. Nilo-Saharan, the other African language family, generally tends to cluster around the Afro-Asiatic languages. These languages do not provide a legitimate grouping with each other, especially the languages of the Nilotic genus do not exhibit a uniform behavior according to the methods of comparison employed. Languages of the Pacific are too few within the sample to make any strong claims about a distinct type. Yet, the two Austronesian languages Ajië and Nias behave quite similarly to one another in the different modes of analysis used in this chapter.

9 Conclusion

9.1 Summary of the findings

In this study, I have analyzed the micro-alignment of a number of marked-S languages. Marked-S languages exhibit a peculiar pattern of encoding the basic (in-)transitive roles S, A and P in that they overtly mark the S relation of intransitive verbs while using a non-overtly coded form of a noun for one of the arguments of transitive verbs (for more details cf. the definition and examples of marked-S languages in Section 1.2). In addition to the S, A and P roles, this study has investigated the coding of a number of additional S-like roles. The additional roles have been selected from the contexts defined in Chapter 2. While some of these roles behaved like regular overtly-marked intransitive S arguments in most languages, others were almost exclusively encoded by the zero-coded case-form. Figure 9.1 summarizes the results of the previous chapter, in which the different contexts have been compared with one another. The roles have been ordered with respect to their likeliness to be encoded in the same way as intransitive S arguments in the languages of the sample. The further to the top a role is located, the more often it is encoded with the S-case. Roles that are represented next to each other in Figure 9.1 exhibit almost identical behavior in this respect. These preferences are quite stable between different calculations, both when including all individual languages on which enough data was available (without employing any mechanisms of genealogical and/or areal control) and when the data were normalized to include only one data point per genus.

Two different methods of analysis, first through a ranking by percentage and second through the more sophisticated NeighborNet algorithm, have revealed a similar pattern for the different roles, namely, a gradual shift from coding via S-case to coding via zero-case. The subject-like roles, especially subjects of locational clauses, being the one extreme and extra-syntactic roles, especially the citation form of a noun, being the other.

Apart from distinguishing which roles behave most or least like intransitive S arguments in their encoding, the similarities and differences between the individual languages have also been evaluated. There is a clear subtype of marked-S

9 Conclusion

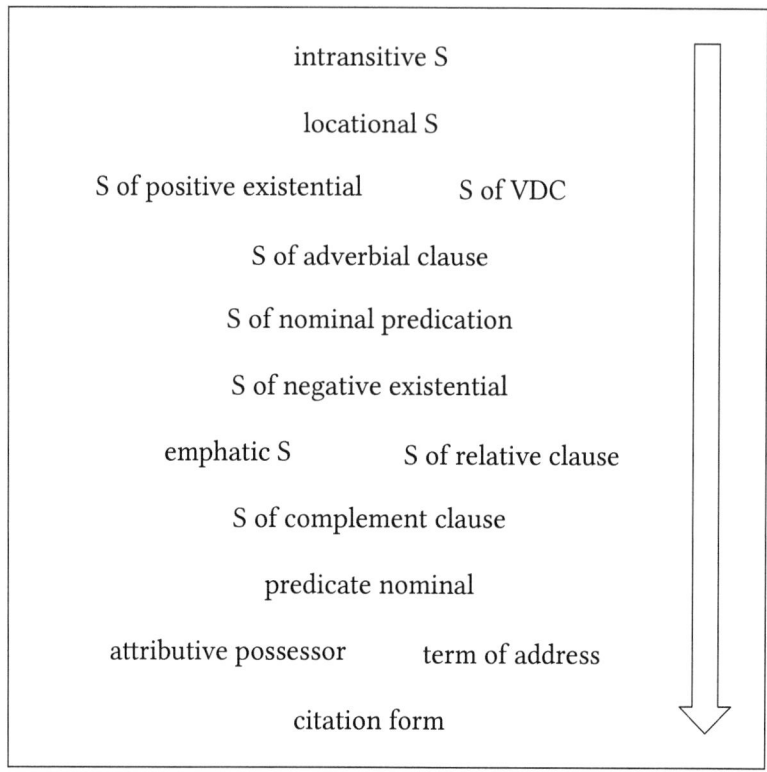

Figure 9.1: Coding of S-like roles in marked-S languages (ordered from most S-like to least S-like)

languages to which most marked-S languages of North America belong (excluding only Maidu). Further, there is an African type of marked-S comprising the Afro-Asiatic languages of the Omotic and East Cushitic genera as well as Surmic. The Nilotic languages do not behave in a consistent pattern that would allow to classify them as following one or the other pattern. Languages of the Pacific exhibit some similarities, but the data does not justify proposing a distinct subtype of marked-S for them.

After this brief summary of the results, I will now discuss the implications of these findings for the understanding of marked-S languages. The central motivation of this study has been to test whether the unexpectedness of the marked-S coding-pattern based on the purely formal aspects of the system can be adequately explained in terms of functional motivations, as it has been proposed in König (2006). This major question will be addressed in Section 9.2. While an important factor in understanding marked-S languages, the range of functions a case-form has cannot be the sole explanation for their existence. Furthermore, to allow for meaningful generalizations over the functions of marked and unmarked case-forms, one needs to apply a consistent definition of markedness that is independent of functional considerations. Further, I will review the micro-alignment approach that I have used for this investigation and comment on its usefulness and limitations in Section 9.3. I also pointed out in the introductory chapter (Section 1.6) that marked-S languages are a serious challenge for some of the more formalistic approaches to alignment and case-assignment in particular. I will take up this discussion in Section 9.4 and comment on the possibilities of integrating the finding on marked-S languages into these formal approaches. Finally, I will address some questions that remain open or have been raised by the findings of this study, and which should be targeted in future research (Section 9.5).

9.2 Generalizations about the functional motivations for marked-S languages

Marked-S languages have caught the attention of linguists based on a strictly formal criterion, namely the overt marking of the S argument found with these languages. The unexpectedness of the marked-S system is for example expressed as Universal 38 in Greenberg (1963: 75). The two points of view from which the existence of this unusual case-systems have been considered are the historical development of these systems and their functionally-based motivations. Of course, these two points of view do not have to be mutually exclusive. Historical changes in the grammar of a language can certainly have a functional motivation; some linguists will even argue that they must have one. In contrast to the formal definition, a functional definition of marked-S languages has also been proposed (König 2006). In this definition, the functional range of individual case-forms is the central criterion for the 'markedness' or 'unmarkedness' ascribed to each case-form. The functional aspect, i.e. the number of functions covered by the case-forms, is an important aspect in the study of marked-S languages. However, the number of roles covered by either zero-case or S-case does vary considerably between the languages studied here.[1]

---

[1] As defined in Section 1.4 the term S-case is employed for the case-form that covers the function of encoding transitive S arguments (i.e. the nominative in nominative-accusative languages and the absolutive in ergative-absolutive languages). The term zero-case refers to the case-form that is used for the non-S-case-marked argument of transitive verbs, and that is zero-coded in marked-S languages (i.e. the accusative in nominative-accusative languages and the ergative in ergative-absolutive languages).

9 Conclusion

For some languages the existence of marked-S coding cannot be plausibly argued for based on functional motivations of this type. From the point of view of the formal encoding of case-forms, the Californian language Maidu is a regular marked-S language with an overt Nominative case-marker and a zero-coded Accusative. Yet, the range of functions that the zero-coded Accusative covers does not extend far beyond the encoding of transitive P arguments. Maidu is, however, not the only problematic case for the functional account of marked-S languages. The languages that are identified as being of the marked-S type by a functional rather than purely formal definition, i.e. the languages referred to as Type 2 marked-nominative languages by König (2006: 658), do not use the 'zero-coded' form for as many of the roles as the languages meeting the strict form-based definition do. For the Type 2 marked-nominative languages, the function of the accusative case as citation form (and in other extra-syntactic contexts) is taken as the main argument to consider this form as being the more basic form. Based on the data collected in this study, the use as a citation form is also the main function of the zero-coded form after its use as the case-form of transitive P arguments, while the Type 2 languages do not extend its use to more subject-like roles.

Taking a radically economical approach to case-marking, one could propose the following explanation. If two case-forms of a noun do differ in the number of segments they consist of, the form that has the smaller number of segments will be preferred because of its lower production effort. If the two case-forms consist of the same amount of segments, no such pressure exists to choose one form over the other. Linguistic explanations that propose such radically economy-based argumentations can be criticized on various grounds. One argument against this approach would be that actual ease of articulation rather than the bare number of segments is a stronger factor. Extra segments added to a form, such as final vowels, can lead to a less complex syllable structure and thus increase the ease of articulation. Consequently this entire discussion returns to the initial question of how one defines the concept of linguistic markedness, which I discussed in Section 1.3. Since different definitions of markedness can result in different identification of marked versus unmarked forms in individual languages, there is always the possibility of choosing the definition that best fits one's analysis of any language (e.g. defining the 'marked' form as the one with the more marked syllable structure even though this might be the morphologically zero-coded form). While this approach improves the consistency of an analysis on a per-language level, comparability between languages and consequently cross-linguistic generalizations over marked-S coding are rendered meaningless, since this leads to a circular definition of the marked-S system. If one chooses the definition of marked versus unmarked case-form which best fits the prediction that the unmarked form is used in more contexts, then it necessarily follows that the unmarked form is made a wider use of in marked-S languages.

9.3 Concluding remarks on the micro-alignment approach

As Chapter 8 has shown, languages belonging to the marked-S coding type behave quite differently in terms of micro-alignment structures. While the pattern of marking the S, A and P functions of prototypical verbs employs the same pattern of case-marking in these languages, the marking of other types of clauses differs strongly between the languages. Differences in encoding between different clause-types or based on other factors, like the ones discussed in Section 2.2 are also known from languages with other coding-systems. Still, coarse classifications of language as being of the nominative-accusative or ergative-absolutive type are made frequent use of in linguistic studies. Since much of the debate on marked-S languages focuses on overt coding properties (and the unexpectedness of this pattern), an in-depth investigation of the coding-patterns of more than just the most basic clauses is necessary to fully understand this unusual pattern.

The contexts and roles chosen in this study have been defined based on the variation that the languages studied here exhibited. Data for all languages was basically gathered in a parallel fashion and not one language after the other, since the study of one language potentially revealed a new pattern of variation that could profitably be included in the study. On the other hand, based on an initial list of possibly interesting domains of grammar, data have been collected on roles that did not show any interesting patterns in any or almost any languages of the sample and have thus not been presented in the final study.

A small drawback of this approach is the frequent omission of parts of the grammar in the description of languages that do not exhibit any variation in the respective domain.[2] Negative evidence, especially when dealing with a very limited set of examples as data base, cannot be taken as evidence of the absence of a certain pattern in a given languages. This has led to a considerable number of missing data points. Consequently, the respective percentage of languages that deviate from the pattern conceived as the norm, i.e. S-case-marking on subject-like roles, might be a little too high in the figures presented in Chapter 8. This

---

[2] The same is, however, true for most comparative work that is carried out through available descriptions of languages.

9 Conclusion

is based on the assumption that if a grammar does not discuss a given context, there will more likely be no variation from the standard pattern in this domain. In addition, the larger the number of languages studied, the larger the number of contexts of interest will become with this approach. Consequently, when relying largely on secondary data, the larger the number of missing data points will become.

Given these limitations, the micro-alignment approach – however, this is true for any approach that aims at including very fine-grained distinctions on any domain of grammar – is best employed in more detailed studies operating samples of a smaller size. Preferably, primary data on the languages studied should be available, which is, however, difficult and tedious to obtain for the majority of the world's languages. The approach is less applicable in large scale typological studies aiming at a large number of languages included.

9.4 Consequences for formal theories

For the languages of the marked-S type one can identify a case-form that can be analyzed as a default case, a notion that many formal theories employ. However, this case-form is not necessarily linked to the form that is used to encode the subject function in a clause. For most marked-S languages, the case-form that should be considered the default case by factors such as which form is the most basic one in terms of morphological structure (derived forms versus underived forms). The form which is used in extra-syntactic contexts does coincide with the form used to encode the non-subject argument in basic transitive clauses.

In Chapter 1, I briefly introduced the feature system of Lexical Decomposition Grammar (LDG, Wunderlich 1997; Stiebels 2002). In this approach, the default status, which is ascribed to the nominative or absolutive case, is mirrored through the feature representation of the default case, which is an empty set. Other cases have non-empty sets of features, and thus are more restricted in their use.

As argued above for marked-S languages, one has to assume that the accusative case (or respectively the ergative case) functions as the default case. If one wants to keep the generalization that the default case-form should have a feature representation consisting of an empty set of features, and thus being potentially employable in all contexts, one would have to assume that the cases used in marked-S languages have a different set of features than the standard feature representations proposed in LDG (cf. Section 1.6). The following feature representations could be employed:

9.4 Consequences for formal theories

- marked-nominative: [-hr]
- default accusative: [ ]
- marked-absolutive: [-lr]
- default Ergative: [ ]

(1) and (2) demonstrate the linking of a basic transitive verb using these feature specifications. As in in the standard LDG approach, feature specifications for the arguments of a verb are derived from the semantic form and the theta-structure of a verb. The cases that are available from the lexicon of the language are then matched to the argument positions based on their feature specification, choosing the most concrete case available for each position (2). In marked-nominative languages, the overtly coded nominative and default accusative are available. Both argument positions could be filled with the default accusative. However, the nominative is a better match for the x argument since it is the more concrete case (i.e. it has more features specified) and its feature specification as [-hr] ('there is no higher role') is compatible with the feature specification of this argument position. Conversely, in marked-absolutive languages the two available case-forms, the overtly coded absolutive and default ergative, are matched to the x and y argument position by the same mechanism.

(1) $\underbrace{\lambda x \; \lambda y \; \lambda s}_{\text{theta-structure}}$ $\underbrace{\{see\,(x,y)\}(s)}_{\text{semantic form}}$

(2)
	λy	λx
	+hr	-hr
	-lr	+lr
marked-nominative	ACC	NOM
marked-absolutive	ABS	ERG

The standard case-representations of LDG only make use of features that have a positive specification. In contrast, for the specifications I proposed for the cases of marked-S languages, negative feature specifications are used. This procedure goes against most considerations relevant to the setup of feature systems, in which negative feature specifications are often equated with underspecification with respect to the given feature. Without doubt, the introduction of the additional cases and their proposed feature specifications would deprive the LDG approach of some of its elegance. Yet one could argue that this dispreferred feature specification employed to model case-assignment in marked-S languages is reflected through their cross-linguistic rarity. Another possibility, which would not make it necessary to include negative feature specification for the representation of cases would be to introduce a new set of features for languages of the marked-S type. Since this section is not meant as a proposal to reformulate LDG, but rather a sketch of how marked-S languages could be integrated into that theory, I have restricted myself to employing the features that are already provided by the theory.

However, there is another issue that makes the inclusion of marked-S languages into the LDG theory problematic. While the proposed feature values lead to the right case-assignment for prototypical transitive and intransitive clauses (2), some minor clause-types can not easily be analyzed by the modified feature system. The previous chapters illustrated that marked-S languages make common use of the zero-case in subject like roles, e.g. the subject of existential clauses (cf. Chapter 4). While there is, in principle, no conflict in assigning the default accusative to existential subjects, the Elsewhere Principle would predict that nominative case is assigned to these arguments. Lexical case-assignment is possible within the LDG framework, but it is counter-intuitive to the whole notion of a default case if the default case would have to be lexically assigned.

At the present moment, marked-S languages pose a challenge to LDG and other formal theories that employ similar mechanisms for case-assignment. The issues raised here should be resolved by the proponents of such theories if they want to make general claims about the nature of case-assignment in human language. At present it appears that one has at least to abandon one central assumption in order to include marked-S languages. If one keeps the standard LDG case features for marked-S languages, that will assign the nominative (or absolutive) case to all subjects automatically, while clause-types that take zero-coded accusative (or ergative) subject could be handled through lexical case-assignment. In this case, the notion of default case becomes somewhat arbitrary, since many properties typically associated with default case-forms (e.g. use in citation) are not fulfilled by the case-form that has the default feature representation. If one accepts the default accusative and default ergative as legitimate cases in the theory, one has to resolve the problem of lexical assignment of default case (or possibly find other mechanisms to block the assignment of the marked-nominative/marked-absolutive in some contexts).

While the existence of marked-S languages results in abandoning at least one of the major generalizations for the LDG approach, other formal approaches to case-marking have no such principled difficulties in integrating languages of this type. Yet these other approaches would still benefit from considering marked-S

9.4 Consequences for formal theories

languages. De Hoop & Malchukov (2008), Malchukov (2008) and Malchukov & de Hoop (2011) provide an optimality-theoretic approach that can account for a number of splits in alignment systems found in different languages of the world.[3] These analyses draw on the two prominent functions of case-marking, the discriminating function and the identifying function (Mallinson & Blake 1981: 91–939). Constraints motivated by the two functions and their respective rankings are employed to account for splits based on factors such as the animacy and definiteness of the nouns involved. The approach has also been extended to alignment splits that are conditioned by the tense or aspect of the clause (Malchukov & de Hoop 2011; Malchukov 2014). All languages modeled in these papers are of the standard, i.e. non-marked, types of nominative-accusative or ergative-absolutive alignment. A modeling of languages of the marked-S type in this approach would definitely be useful in order to expand the explanatory power of the approach. I will not attempt to give a fully-fledged optimality-theoretic analysis of marked-S coding at this point, but rather limit myself to a few general reflections on the integration of marked-S languages into an optimality-theoretic approach. In order to model the general pattern of marked-S languages in this approach, constraints that penalize overt morphology cannot be ranked very highly, since overt marking of intransitive S arguments would not be possible when these constraints were undominated. However, these markedness constraints do apparently have some effect in these languages, since the case-form with less or no overt coding is preferred for a number of different roles. Furthermore, the approach of de Hoop & Malchukov (2008) and Malchukov & de Hoop (2011) does not included data with the same level of granularity as I have discussed in this study, but rather have focused on prototypical transitive clauses, somewhat neglecting more specialized clause-types such as nominal predication, existential predication, and the like. More fine-grained information on the alignment system of a language could very probably be included in this approach. However, they might increase the complexity of the analysis considerably. Also, most optimality-theoretic analyses do not aim at depicting the entire complexity of a single language but highlight more fundamental differences between a number of languages which can

---

[3] Optimality Theory (mostly abbreviated as OT) is a formal mechanism that describes languages and more particularly linguistic variation though a set of supposedly universal and violable constraints. The ranking of these constraints, which differs between languages, leads to different outputs in the surface grammar of individual languages. The more highly a constraint is ranked in a language, the more important it is in that language and the more likely the effects of that constraint will be visible in the surface structure of that language. For a more detailed discussion of Optimality Theory, the reader is referred to the literature (Prince & Smolensky 2004; Kager 1999; Legendre et al. 2001).

9 Conclusion

be accounted for by the rearrangement of a small number of selected constraints. However, in order to plausibly model the grammar of an individual language (or even all possible grammars of the world's languages), optimality-theoretic approaches should eventually be able to account for these variations between different types of constructions.

9.5 Future research

This study has demonstrated that the usage of the zero-case and S-case differ greatly between individual languages. As pointed out already in Section 2.6, another interesting factor to investigate would be actual usage-frequencies of the two forms. Especially for the languages that do not use the zero-case to encode a large number of roles, it would be a worthwhile research question to gather data on the usage frequency of the two case-forms. Factors such as the frequent omission of overt subject NPs could lead to the situation that the form used to encode the non-subject argument of transitive clauses is indeed used more often in discourse.

Another point that could not be addressed in sufficient detail here is the intriguing marked-S pattern found in a number of languages spoken in the Pacific area. These languages exhibit the marked-S coding properties only in certain discourse contexts, mostly associated with constituent focus. To reach a better understanding of this type of marked-S structure, original fieldwork on a number of these languages would doubtless be necessary.

For all areas which I have studied, some kind of contact scenario that can explain the existence of the marked-S pattern appears to be plausible. In East-Africa, the common assumption appears to be that the pattern originated within the languages of the Afro-Asiatic family and spread to surrounding languages such a the Surmic languages of the Nilo-Saharan family and the Nilotic language Turkana, which pattern along with the Afro-Asiatic marked-S languages. Also the similarity of the coding-pattern of the Yuman languages and the unrelated language Wappo could hypothetically be the traces of a prior, and supposedly larger, areal marked-S pattern in North America, including intervening languages that abandoned the marked-S system or became extinct before they could be documented. As I have pointed out, in order to study the marked-S languages of the Pacific region and its geographical distribution and possible contact scenarios, first the majority pattern of this region, i.e. discourse-based overt S-marking, has to be studied in more depth.

In all three cases, a historical study of the contact-situation between the rele-

9.5 Future research

vant languages would contribute much to the understanding of the phenomenon of marked-S. Historical data might also give a better understanding of the origin of the marked-S pattern altogether. Different explanations for the origin of this coding-system have been discussed in Section 1.5. While for some areas, an origin within the discourse structure of a language appears to be plausible, this source appears to be especially likely for the languages of the Pacific. In other areas, namely North America, discourse structure does not seem to have any impact on the marked-S systems of the languages. This observation hints at the possibility that the phenomenon of marked-S coding has a number of different pathways that lead to this pattern. Ultimately, the different types of marked-S languages my study identified might well be a residue of these distinct pathways leading to the marked-S structure. Thus the functions covered by the overtly coded S-case (and respectively, the functions not covered by it) will likely prove to be explainable by the diachrony of the case-marker.

Bibliography

Adger, David & Gillian Ramchand. 2003. Predication and equation. *Linguistic Inquiry* 34(3). 325–359.

Aissen, Judith. 1999. Markedness and subject choice in Optimality Theory. *Natural Language & Linguistic Theory* 17. 673–711.

Aissen, Judith. 2003. Differential object marking: Iconicity vs. economy. *Natural Language & Linguistic Theory* 21. 435–483.

Andersen, Torben. 1988. Ergativity in Pari, a Nilotic OVS language. *Lingua* 75. 289–324.

Andersen, Torben. 1991. Subject and topic in Dinka. *Studies in Language* 15(2). 265–294.

Anderson, Stephen R. 1976. On the notion of subject in ergative languages. In Charles N. Li (ed.), *Subject and topic*, 1–23. New York: Academic Press.

Anderson, Stephen R. 1977. On mechanisms by which languages become ergative. In Charles N. Li (ed.), *Mechanisms of syntactic change*, 317–363. Austin, London: University of Texas Press.

Andrzejewski, B. W. 1962. Warfare in Borana Galla stories and fables. *African Language Studies* 3. 116–136.

Arensen, Jon. 1982. *Murle grammar*, vol. 2 Occasional Papers in the Study of Sudanese Languages. Juba: Summer Institute of Linguistics.

Aronoff, Mark. 1994. *Morphology by itself. Stems and inflectional classes.* Cambridge, MA: MIT Press.

Battistella, Edwin. 1996. *The logic of markedness.* New York: Oxford University Press.

Biber, Douglas. 1990. Methodological issues regarding corpus-based analyses of linguistic variation. *Literary and Linguistic Computing* 5. 257–69.

Biber, Douglas. 1993. Representativeness in corpus design. *Literary and Linguistic Computing* 8. 243–57.

Biber, Douglas, Susan Conrad & Randi Reppen. 1998. *Corpus linguistics: Investigating language structure and use.* Cambridge: Cambridge University Press.

Bickel, Balthasar. 2007. Typology in the 21st century: Major current developments. *Linguistic Typology* 11. 239–251.

9 Bibliography

Bickel, Balthasar. 2008a. On the scope of the referential hierarchy in the typology of grammatical relations. In Greville Corbett & Michael Noonan (eds.), *Case and grammatical relations. Studies in honor of Bernard Comrie*, 191–210. Amsterdam: John Benjamins.

Bickel, Balthasar. 2008b. A refined sampling procedure for genealogical control. *Sprachtypologie und Universalienforschung* 61. 221–233.

Bickel, Balthasar. 2011. Grammatical relations typology. In Jae Jung Song (ed.), *The Oxford handbook of language typology*, 399–444. Oxford: Oxford University Press.

Bickel, Balthasar & Johanna Nichols. 2009. Case marking and alignment. In Andrej Malchukov & Andrew Spencer (eds.), *The Oxford handbook of case*, 304–321. Oxford, New York: Oxford University Press.

Birk, D. B. 1976. *The Malakmalak language, Daly river (Western Arnhem Land)*. Canberra: Pacific Linguistics.

Brown, Lea. 2001. *A grammar of Nias Selatan*. Sydney: University of Sydney dissertation.

Bruil, Martine. 2014. *Clause-typing and evidentiality in Ecuadorian Siona*. Leiden: University of Leiden dissertation.

Bryant, David & Vincent Moulton. 2004. Neighbor-Net: An agglomerative method for the construction of phylogenetic networks. *Molecular Biology and Evolution* 21(2). 255–265.

Buth, Randall J. 1981. Ergative word order – Luwo is OVS. *Occasional Papers in the Study of Sudanese Languages* 1. 74–90.

Butt, Miriam & Tracy Holloway King. 2004. The status of case. In Veneeta Dayal & Anoop Mahajan (eds.), *Clause structure in South East Asian languages*, 153–198. Dordrecht: Kluwer Academic Publishers.

Chappell, Hilary & William McGregor. 1996. Prolegomena to a theory of inalienability. In Hilary Chappell & William McGregor (eds.), *The grammar of inalianability*, 3–30. Berlin: Mouton de Gruyter.

Chomsky, Noam. 1993. A minimalist program for linguistic theory. In Kenneth Hale & Samuel J. Keyser (eds.), *The view from Building 20: Essays in linguistics in honor of Sylvain Bromberger*, 1–52. Cambridge, MA: MIT Press.

Clark, Eve V. 1978. Locationals: Existential, locative, and possessive constructions. In Joseph H. Greenberg (ed.), *Universals of human language, Vol. 4: Syntax*, 85–126. Stanford: Stanford University Press.

Clifton, John M. 1997. The Kaki Ae language. In Stephen A. Wurm (ed.), *Some endangeres languages of Papua New Guinea: Kaki Ae, Musom, and Aribwatsa*, 3–65. Canberra: Pacific Linguistics.

Comrie, Bernard. 1978. Ergativity. In Winfred P. Lehmann (ed.), *Syntactic typology*, 329–394. Hassocks (Sussex): The Harvester Press.

Comrie, Bernard. 1997. The typology of predicate case marking. In Joan Bybee, John Haiman & Sandra A. Thompson (eds.), *Essays on language function and language type: Dedicated to T. Givón*, 39–50. Amsterdam, Philadelphia: John Benjamins.

Crass, Joachim. 2005. *Das K'abeena. Deskriptive Grammatik einer hochlandkuschitischen Sprache*, vol. 23 Cushitic Language Studies. Köln: Köppe.

Crawford, James. 1966. *The Cocopa language*. Berkeley: University of California dissertation.

Creider, Chet A. & Jane Tapsubei Creider. 1989. *A grammar of Nandi*. Hamburg: Buske.

Creissels, Denis. 2009. Uncommon patterns of core term marking and case terminology. *Lingua* 119(3). 445–459.

Croft, William. 2000. *Explaining language change: An evolutionary perspective*. Harlow: Longman.

Croft, William. 2003. *Typology and universals*. Cambridge: Cambridge University Press.

Crysmann, Berthold. 2009. Deriving superficial ergativity in Nias. In Stefan Müller (ed.), *Proceedings of the 16th international conference on head-driven phrase structure grammar*, Stanford, CA: CSLI Publications.

Cysouw, Michael. 2010. Semantic maps as metrics on meaning. *Linguistic Discovery* 8(1). 70–95.

Daniel, Michael & Andrew Spencer. 2009. The vocative – an outlier case. In Andrej Malchukov & Andrew Spencer (eds.), *The Oxford handbook of case*, 626–634. Oxford, New York: Oxford University Press.

de Hoop, Helen & Andrej L. Malchukov. 2008. Case-marking strategies. *Linguistic Inquiry* 39(4). 565–587.

de Hoop, Helen & Bhuvana Narasimhan. 2005. Differential case-marking in Hindi. In Mengistu Amberber & Helen de Hoop (eds.), *Competition and variation in natural languages: The case for case*, 321–345. Amsterdam: Elsevier.

de la Fontinelle, Jacqueline. 1976. *La langue de Houailou (Nouvelle-Calédonie): Description phonologique et description syntaxique*. Paris: SELAF.

Detges, Ulrich. 2009. How useful is case morphology? The loss of the Old French two-case system within a theory of Preferred Argument Structure. In Jóhanna Barðdal & Shobhana L. Chelliah (eds.), *The role of semantic, pragmatic, and discourse factors in the development of case*, 93–120. Amsterdam: John Benjamins.

Dimmendaal, Gerrit Jan. 1982. *The Turkana language*. Leiden: Rijksuniversiteit te Leiden.

Dixon, R. M. W. 1972. *The Dyirbal language of North Queensland.* Cambridge: Cambridge University Press.

Dixon, R. M. W. 1979. Ergativity. *Language* 55(1). 59–138.

Dixon, R. M. W. 1994. *Ergativity.* London: Cambridge University Press.

Dixon, R. M. W. 2010a. *Basic linguistic theory, Volume 1. Methodology.* Oxford, New York: Oxford University Press.

Dixon, R. M. W. 2010b. *Basic linguistic theory, Volume 2. Grammatical topics.* Oxford, New York: Oxford University Press.

Dixon, Roland B. 1911. Maidu. In Franz Boas (ed.), *Handbook of the American Indian languages*, 679–734. Washington: Government Printing Office.

Dixon, Roland B. 1912. *Maidu texts*, vol. 5 Publications of the American Ethnological Society. Leyden: Late E. J. Brill.

Donohue, Mark & Lea Brown. 1999. Ergativity: Some additions from Indonesia. *Australian Journal of Linguistics* 19(1). 57–76.

Doron, Edit. 1988. The semantics of predicate nominals. *Linguistics* 26. 281–301.

Dowty, David. 1991. Thematic proto-roles and argument selection. *Language* 67(3). 547–619.

Dryer, Matthew S. 1982. In defense of a universal passive. *Linguistic Analysis* 10(7). 53–60.

Dryer, Matthew S. 1989. Large linguistic areas and language sampling. *Studies in Language* 13. 257–292.

Dryer, Matthew S. 2005a. Order of relative clause and noun. In Haspelmath et al. (2005) chap. 90, 366–369.

Dryer, Matthew S. 2005b. Order of subject, object and verb. In Haspelmath et al. (2005) chap. 81, 330–333.

Du Bois, John W. 1987. The discourse basis of ergativity. *Language* 63. 805–855.

Fabian, Grace, Edmund Fabian & Bruce Waters. 1998. *Morphology, syntax and cohesion in Nabak, Papua New Guinea.* Canberra: Pacific Linguistics.

Fenk-Oczlon, Gertraud. 2001. Familiarity, information flow, and linguistic form. In Joan Bybee & Paul Hopper (eds.), *Frequency and the emergence of linguistic structure*, 431–448. Amsterdam: John Benjamins.

Ferguson, Charles A. 1976. The Ethiopian language area. In M. Lionel Bender, J. Donald Bowen, Robert L. Cooper & Charles A. Ferguson (eds.), *Language in Ethiopia*, 63–76. London: Oxford University Press.

Fillmore, Charles J. 1968. The case for case. In Emmon Bach & Robert T. Harms (eds.), *Universals in linguistic theory*, 1–88. New York and others: Holt, Rinehart and Winston Inc.

Frajzyngier, Zygmunt & Erin Shay. 2003. *Explaining language structure through systems interaction.* Amsterdam: John Benjamins.

Freeze, Ray. 1992. Existentials and other locatives. *Language* 68(3). 553–595.

Gilligan, Gary Martin. 1987. *A cross-linguistic approach to the pro-drop parameter.* Los Angeles: University of Southern California dissertation.

Goldberg, Adele E. 2006. *Constructions at work: The nature of generalization in language.* Oxford: Oxford University Press.

Gorbet, Larry Paul. 1976. *A grammar of Diegueño nominals.* New York, London: Garland.

Gordon, Lynn. 1986. *Maricopa morphology and syntax.* Berkeley, Los Angeles, London: University of California Press.

Greenberg, Joseph H. 1963. Some universals of grammar with particular reference to the order of meaningful elements. In Joseph H. Greenberg (ed.), *Universals of human language*, 58–90. Cambridge, MA: MIT Press.

Greenberg, Joseph H. 1983. Some areal characteristics of African languages. In Ivan R. Dihoff (ed.), *Current approaches to African linguistics 1*, 3–22. Dordrecht/Cinnaminson: Foris.

Güldemann, Tom. 2005. Complex predicates based on generic auxiliaries as an areal feature in Northeast Africa. In F. K. Erhard Voeltz (ed.), *Studies in African linguistic typology*, 131–154. Amsterdam: John Benjamins.

Haig, Geoffrey, Stefan Schnell & Claudia Wegener. 2011. Comparing corpora from endangered language projects: Explorations in language typology based on original texts. In Geoffrey Haig, Nicole Nau, Stefan Schnell & Claudia Wegener (eds.), *Documenting endangered languages: Achievements and perspectives*, 55–86. Berlin: Mouton de Gruyter.

Halliday, M. A. K. 1967. Notes on transitivity and theme in English: Part 2. *Journal of Linguistics* 3(2). 199–244.

Halpern, Abraham M. 1946. Yuma III: Grammatical processes and the noun. *International Journal of American Linguistics* 12(4). 204–212.

Handschuh, Corinna. 2008. Split marked-S case systems. In Marc Richards & Andrej Malchukov (eds.), *Scales*, vol. 86 Linguistische Arbeitsberichte, Institut für Linguistik, Universität Leipzig.

Handschuh, Corinna. 2014. Scalar and non-scalar alignment-splits in marked-S languages. In Ina Bornkessel-Schlesewsky, Andrej Malchukov & Marc Richards (eds.), *Scales: A cross-disciplinary perspective on referential hierarchies*, Berlin: Mouton. In press.

Haspelmath, Martin. 1990. The grammaticization of passive morphology. *Studies in Language* 14(1). 25–72.

Haspelmath, Martin. 2006. Against markedness (and what to replace it with). *Journal of Linguistics* 42. 25–70.

9 Bibliography

Haspelmath, Martin. 2009. Terminology of case. In Andrej Malchukov & Andrew Spencer (eds.), *The Oxford handbook of case*, 505–517. Oxford, New York: Oxford University Press.

Haspelmath, Martin. 2010. Comparative concepts and descriptive categories in cross-linguistic studies. *Language* 86(3). 663–687.

Haspelmath, Martin, Matthew Dryer, David Gil & Bernard Comrie (eds.). 2005. *The world atlas of language structures*. Oxford: Oxford University Press.

Hayward, Dick. 1984. *The Arbore language. A first investigation*, vol. 2 Cushitic Language Studies. Köln: Köppe.

Hayward, Richard J. 1990. Notes on the Zayse language. In Richard J. Hayward (ed.), *Omotic language studies*, 210–355. London: School of Oriental and African Studies, University of London.

Hayward, Richard J. 1998. Qafar (East Cushitic). In Andrew Spencer & Arnold M. Zwicky (eds.), *The handbook of morphology*, 624–647. Oxford, Malden: Blackwell.

Heeschen, Volker. 1998. *An ethnographic grammar of the Eipo language. Spoken in the central mountains of Irian Jaya (West New Guinea), Indonesia*. Berlin: Reimer.

Heger, Klaus. 1990/91. Noeme als Tertia Comparationis im Sprachvergleich. *Vox Romanica* 49–50. 6–30.

Heine, Bernd. 1976. *A typology of African languages: Based on the order of meaningful elements*. Berlin: Reimer.

Heine, Bernd. 1997. *Possession. Cognitive sources, forces, and grammaticalization*. Cambridge: Cambridge University Press.

Hengeveld, Kees. 1992. *Non-verbal predication. Theory, typology, diachrony*, vol. 15 Functional Grammar Series. Berlin, New York: Mouton de Gruyter.

Hompó, Éva. 1990. Grammatical relations in Gamo: A pilot sketch. In Richard J. Hayward (ed.), *Omotic language studies*, 356–405. London: School of Oriental and African Studies, University of London.

Hosokawa, Komei. 1991. *The Yawuru language of West Kimberley. A meaning-based description*. Canberra: Australian National University dissertation.

Huson, Daniel H. & David Bryant. 2006. Application of phylogenetic networks in evolutionary studies. *Molecular Biology and Evolution* 23(2). 254–267.

Jespersen, Otto. 1992 [1924]. *The philosophy of grammar. With a new introduction and index by James D. McCawley*. Chicago: University of Chicago Press.

Joël, Judith. 1998. Another look at the Paipai-Arizona Pai divergence. In Leanne Hinton & Pamela Munro (eds.), *Studies in American Indian languages. Description and theory*, 32–40. Berkeley, Los Angeles: University of California Press.

Kager, René. 1999. *Optimality theory*. Cambridge: Cambridge University Press.

Kasarhérou (née de la Fontinelle), Jacqueline. 1961. Prosodèmes de la langue mélanésienne de Houaïlou (Nouvelle-Calédonie). *Bulletin de la Société de Linguistique* 56(1). 181–201.

Keenan, Edward L. & Bernard Comrie. 1977. Noun phrase accessibility and universal grammar. *Linguistic Inquiry* 8(1). 63–99.

Keenan, Edward L. & Matthew S. Dryer. 2007. Passives in the world's languages. In Timothy Shopen (ed.), *Language typology and syntactic description. Vol. I: Clause structure*, 325–361. Cambridge: Cambridge University Press.

Keller, Rudi. 1994. *Sprachwandel*. Tübingen, Basel: Francke.

Kendall, Martha B. 1976. *Selected problems in Yavapai syntax. The Verde Valley dialect*. New York, London: Garland Publishing Inc.

Kiessling, Roland. 2007. The "marked nominative" in Datooga. *Journal of African Languages and Linguistics* 28(2). 149–191.

Kiparsky, Paul. 1973. "Elsewhere" in phonology. In Stephen Anderson & Paul Kiparsky (eds.), *A festschrift for Morris Halle*, 93–106. New York: Holt.

Klaiman, M.H. 1991. *Grammatical voice*. Cambridge: Cambridge University Press.

König, Christa. 2006. Marked nominative in Africa. *Studies in Language* 30(4). 705–782.

König, Christa. 2008. *Case in Africa*. Oxford: Oxford University Press.

Kozlowski, Edwin Louis. 1972. *Havasupai simple sentences*. Bloomington: Indiana University dissertation.

Lamberti, Marcello & Roberto Sottile. 1997. *The Wolaytta language*, vol. 6 Studia Linguarum Africae Orientalis. Köln: Köppe.

Lambrecht, Knud. 1996. *Information structure and sentence form. Topic, focus and the mental representations of discourse referents*. Cambridge: Cambridge University Press.

Lander, Yury. 2009. Varieties of genitive. In Andrej Malchukov & Andrew Spencer (eds.), *The Oxford handbook of case*, 581–592. Oxford, New York: Oxford University Press.

Langdon, Margaret. 1970. *A grammar of Diegueño: The Mesa Grande dialect*, vol. 66 University of California Publications in Linguistics. Berkeley, Los Angeles, London: University of California Press.

Langdon, Margaret & Pamela Munro. 1979. Subject and (switch-)reference in Yuman. *Folia Linguistica* 13. 321–344.

Legendre, Géraldine, Jane Grimshaw & Stan Vikner (eds.). 2001. *Optimality theoretic syntax*. Stanford, CA: MIT Press.

Lehmann, Winfred P. 1974. *Proto-Indo-European syntax*. Austin, TX: University of Texas Press.

9 Bibliography

Levin, Beth. 1993. *English verb classes and alternations*. Chicago: University of Chicago Press.

Li, Charles N., Sandra A. Thompson & Jesse O. Sawyer. 1977. Subject and word order in Wappo. *International Journal of American Linguistics* 43. 85–100.

Lichtenberk, Frantisek. 1978. A sketch of Houailou grammar. In *Working papers in linguistics 10*, 76–116. Manoa, HI: Department of Linguistics, University of Hawaii.

Lynch, John. 1998. *Pacific languages: An introduction*. Honolulu, HI: University of Hawaii Press.

Lyons, John. 1967. A note on possessive, existential and locative sentences. *Foundations of Language* 3(4). 390–396.

Lyons, John. 1968. Existence, location, possession and transitivity. In B. Van Rootselaar & J. F. Staal (eds.), *Logic, methodology and philosophy of science iii*, 495–504. Amsterdam: North-Holland.

Lyons, John. 1977. *Semantics*. Cambridge: Cambridge University Press.

Malchukov, Andrej L. 2008. Animacy and asymmetries in differential case marking. *Lingua* 118. 203–221.

Malchukov, Andrej L. 2014. Towards a typology of split ergativity: A TAM-hierarchy for alignment splits. In Ina Bornkessel-Schlesewsky, Andrej Malchukov & Marc Richards (eds.), *Scales: A cross-disciplinary perspective on referential hierarchies*, Berlin: Mouton. In press.

Malchukov, Andrej L. & Helen de Hoop. 2011. Tense, aspect, and mood based differential case marking. *Lingua* 121. 35–47.

Mallinson, Graham & Barry J. Blake. 1981. *Language typology. Cross-linguistic studies in syntax*. Amsterdam, New York, Oxford: North-Holland.

Maslova, Elena. 2000. A dynamic approach to the verification of distributional universals. *Linguistic Typology* 4(3). 307–333.

McEnery, Anthony, Richard Xiao & Yukio Tono. 2006. *Corpus-based language studies: An advanced resource book*. London, New York: Routledge.

McGregor, William B. & Jean-Christophe Verstraete. 2010. Optional ergative marking and its implications for linguistic theory. *Lingua* 120(7). 1607–1609.

Mel'čuk, Igor. 1997. Grammatical cases, basis verbal constructions, and voice in Maasai: Towards a better analysis of the concepts. In Wolfgang U. Dressler, Martin Prinzhorn & John R. Rennison (eds.), *Advances is morphology*, vol. 97 Trends in Linguistics, 131–170. Berlin: de Gruyter.

Merlan, Francesca. 1989. *Mangarayi*. London, New York: Routledge.

Miestamo, Matti. 2009. Implicational hierarchies and grammatical complexity. In David Gil, Geoffrey Sampson & Peter Trudgill (eds.), *Language complexity as an evolving variable*, 80–97. Oxford: Oxford University Press.

Miller, Amy. 2001. *A grammar of Jamul Tiipay*. Berlin, New York: Mouton de Gruyter.

Miller, Amy Whitmore. 1990. *A grammar of Jamul Diegueño*. San Diego: University of California dissertation.

Mixco, Mauricio Jesús. 1965. *Kiliwa grammar*. Berkeley: University of California dissertation.

Munro, Pamela. 1976. *Mojave syntax*. New York, London: Garland Publishing Inc.

Munro, Pamela. 1977. From existential to copula: The history of Yuman BE. In Charles N. Li (ed.), *Mechanisms of syntactic change*, 445–490. Austin, London: University of Texas Press.

Munro, Pamela. 1980. On the syntactic status of switch-reference clauses: The special case of Mojave comitatives. In Pamela Munro (ed.), *Studies of switch-reference*, vol. 8 UCLA Papers in Syntax, 144–166. Los Angeles, CA: UCLA, Department of Linguistics.

Myhill, John. 2001. Typology and discourse analysis. In Deborah Schiffrin, Deborah Tannen & Heidi E. Hamilton (eds.), *The handbook of discourse analysis*, 161–174. Malden, MA/Oxford: Blackwell.

Newman, John (ed.). 2009. *The linguistics of eating and drinking*. Amsterdam: John Benjamins.

Nichols, Johanna. 2008. Why are stative-active languages rarer in Eurasia? Typological perspectives on split subject marking. In Mark Donohue & Søren Wichmann (eds.), *The typology of semantic alignment*, 121–140. Oxford: Oxford University Press.

Noonan, Michael. 2007. Complementation. In Timothy Shopen (ed.), *Language typology and syntactic description. Vol. II: Complex constructions*, 52–150. Cambridge: Cambridge University Press.

Owens, Jonathan. 1982. Case in the Booran dialect of Oromo. *Afrika und Übersee* 65. 43–74.

Owens, Jonathan. 1985. *A grammar of Harar Oromo*, vol. 4 Cushitic Language Studies. Köln: Köppe.

Payne, Doris L. 2007. The existential toe-hold of a split-S system? Paper given at the conference of the Association of Linguistic Typology 7, Paris, France.

Payne, Thomas E. 1997. *Describing morphosyntax. A guide for field linguists*. Cambridge: Cambridge University Press.

Pensalfini, Rob. 1999. The rise of case suffixes as discourse markers in Jingulu— a case study of innovation in an obsolescent language. *Australian Journal of Linguistics* 19(2). 225–240.

Plank, Frans. 1985. The extended accusative/restricted nominative in perspective. In Frans Plank (ed.), *Relational typology*, vol. 28 Trends in Linguistics, Studies and Monographs, 269–310. Berlin: Mouton.

Prince, Alan & Paul Smolensky. 2004. *Optimality theory: Constraint interaction in generative grammar.* Malden, MA: Blackwell.

Pustet, Regina. 2003. *Copulas. Universals in the categorization of the lexicon.* Oxford Studies in Typology and Linguistic Theory. Oxford: Oxford University Press.

Radin, Paul. 1929. *A grammar of the Wappo language.* Berkeley, CA: University of California Press.

Randal, Scott. 1998. A grammatical sketch of Tennet. In Gerrit J. Dimmendaal & Marco Last (eds.), *Surmic languages and cultures*, 219–272. Köln: Köppe.

Redden, James E. 1966. Walapai II: Morphology. *International Journal of American Linguistics* 32. 209–236.

Reh, Mechthild. 1996. *Anywa language. Description and internal reconstruction.* Köln: Köppe.

Rizzi, Luigi. 1986. Null objects in Italian and the theory of pro. *Linguistic Inquiry* 17(3). 501–557.

Ross, Malcolm. 1978. *A Waskia grammar sketch and vocabulary.* Canberra: Pacific Linguistics.

Sasse, Hans-Jürgen. 1984. Case in Cushitic, Semitic and Berber. In James Bynon (ed.), *Current progress in Afro-Asiatic linguistics*, 111–126. Amsterdam: John Benjamins.

Sasse, Hans-Jürgen. 1987. The thetic/categorial distinction revisited. *Linguistics* 25(1). 511–580.

Sawyer, Jesse O. 1980. The non-genetic relationship of Wappo and Yuki. In Kathryn Klar, Margaret Langdon & Shirley Silver (eds.), *American Indian and Indoeuropean studies. Papers in honor of Madison S. Beeler*, The Hague, Paris, New York: Mouton.

Seiler, Hansjakob. 2000. *Language universals research: A synthesis.* Tübingen: Gunter Narr Verlag.

Shibatani, Masayoshi. 1991. Grammaticalization of topic into subject. In Elizabeth Closs Traugott & Bernd Heine (eds.), *Approaches to grammaticalization. volume ii: Focus on types of grammatical markers*, 94–133. Amsterdam, Philadelphia: John Benjamins.

Shipley, William F. 1964. *Maidu grammar.* Berkeley, Los Angeles: University of California Press.

Siewierska, Anna. 2005a. Alignment of verbal person marking. In Haspelmath et al. (2005) chap. 100, 406–409.

Siewierska, Anna. 2005b. Passive constructions. In Haspelmath et al. (2005) chap. 107, 434–437.

Siewierska, Anna. 2005c. Verbal person marking. In Haspelmath et al. (2005) chap. 102, 414–417.

Silverstein, Michael. 1976. Hierarchy of features and ergativity. In R. M. W. Dixon (ed.), *Grammatical categories in Australian Languages*, 112–171. Canberra: Australian Institute of Aboriginal Studies.

Stassen, Leon. 1997. *Intransitive predication* Oxford Studies in Typology and Linguistic Theory. Oxford: Clarendon Press.

Stassen, Leon. 2009. *Predicative possession*. Oxford, New York: Oxford University Press.

Stiebels, Barbara. 2002. *Typologie des Argumentlinkings: Ökonomie und Expressivität* Studia Grammatica. Berlin: Akademie Verlag.

Stroomer, Harry. 1995. *A grammar of Boraana Oromao (Kenya)*, vol. 11 Cushitic Language Studies. Köln: Köppe.

Sweet, Henry. 1876. *Words, logic and grammar*. London: Asher.

Taylor, Nicholas. 1994. *Gamo syntax*. London: University of London dissertation.

Thompson, Sandra A., Robert E. Longacre & Shin Ja J. Hwang. 2007. Adverbial clauses. In Timothy Shopen (ed.), *Language typology and syntactic description. Vol. II: Complex constructions*, 237–300. Cambridge: Cambridge University Press.

Thompson, Sandra A., Joseph Sung-Jul Park & Charles N. Li. 2006. *A reference grammar of Wappo*, vol. 138 University of California Publications in Linguistics. Berkeley, Los Angeles, London: University of California Press.

Tosco, Mauro. 1994. On case marking in the Ethiopian language area (with special reference to subject marking in East Cushitic). In *Atti della 7a giornata di studi camito-semitici e indoeuropei*, 225–244. Milano: Centro studi camito-semitici.

Tosco, Mauro. 2000. Is there an "Ethiopian Language Area"? *Anthropological Linguistics* 42(3). 329–365.

Trask, R. L. 1979. On the origins of ergativity. In Frans Plank (ed.), *Ergativity. Towards a theory of grammatical relations*, 385–404. London: Academic Press.

Tucker, Archibald N. & John Tompo ole Mpaayei. 1955. *A Maasai grammar with vocabulary*, vol. 2 Publications of the African Institute, Leiden. London, New York, Toronto: Longmans, Green and Co.

Urban, Greg. 1985. Ergativity and accusativity in Shokleng (Gê). *International Journal of American Linguistics* 51(2). 164–187.

Vennemann, Theo. 1975. An explanation of drift. In Charles N. Li (ed.), *Word order and word order change*, 264–306. Austin, TX: University of Texas Press.

Ward, Gregory & Betty Birner. 2001. Discourse and information structure. In Deborah Schiffrin, Deborah Tannen & Heidi E. Hamilton (eds.), *The handbook of discourse analysis*, 119–137. Malden, MA/Oxford: Blackwell.

Watahomigie, Lucille J., Jorigine Bender, Sr. Philbert Watagomigie & Akira Y. Yamamoto. 2001. *Hualapai reference grammar. Revised and expanded edition* Endangered Languages of the Pacific Rim Publications Series, A2-003. Osaka: ELPR.

Wegener, Claudia. 2008. *A grammar of Savosavo, a Papuan language of the Solomon Islands.* Nijmegen: Radboud Universiteit Nijmegen dissertation.

Whitehead, Carl R. 1981. Subject, object, and indirect object: Towards a typology of Papuan languages. *Language and Linguistics in Melanesia* 13. 32–63.

Wierzbicka, Anna. 1995. A semantic basis for grammatical typology. In Werner Abraham, T. Givón & Sandra A. Thompson (eds.), *Discourse grammar and typology. Papers in honor of John W.M. Verhaar*, 179–209. Amsterdam: John Benjamins.

Witzlack-Makarevich, Alena. 2011. *Typological variation in grammatical relations.* Leipzig: Universität Leipzig dissertation.

Wunderlich, Dieter. 1997. Cause and the structure of verbs. *Linguistic Inquiry* 28(1). 27–68.

Wunderlich, Dieter & Renate Lakämper. 2001. On the interaction of structural and semantic case. *Lingua* 111. 277–418.

Yip, Moira, Joan Maling & Ray Jackendoff. 1987. Case in tiers. *Language* 63(2). 217–250.

Zipf, George Kingsley. 1935. *The psycho-biology of language.* Cambridge, MA: The Riverside Press.

Name index

Adger, David, 57
Aissen, Judith, 21
Andersen, Torben, 24, 26, 113, 115, 155, 171, 174, 179, 181
Anderson, Stephen R., 16, 26
Andrzejewski, B. W., 161
Arensen, Jon, 10, 67, 81, 140, 157, 158, 178
Aronoff, Mark, 173

Battistella, Edwin, 8
Bender, Jorigine, 10, 61, 191, 192
Biber, Douglas, 45, 135
Bickel, Balthasar, x, 7, 19, 24, 28, 29, 33, 201, 202
Birk, D. B., 47
Birner, Betty, 102
Blake, Barry J., 20, 237
Brown, Lea, x, 7, 13, 40, 43, 44, 70, 79, 93, 103, 106, 120, 150–154, 176, 187, 188
Bruil, Martine, 111
Bryant, David, 199, 215
Buth, Randall J., 24, 26
Butt, Miriam, 16

Chappell, Hilary, 171, 188, 193
Chomsky, Noam, 8, 20, 24
Clark, Eve V., 77, 86
Clifton, John M., 108, 109, 124
Comrie, Bernard, x, 3, 28, 32, 55
Conrad, Susan, 135

Crass, Joachim, 10, 40, 65, 86, 87, 112, 118, 162–164, 183, 185
Crawford, James, 6, 10, 44, 147, 175, 190, 192
Creider, Chet A., 68, 81, 103, 114, 156, 159, 178
Creider, Jane Tapsubei, 68, 81, 103, 114, 156, 159, 178
Creissels, Denis, 11, 173, 174
Croft, William, 14, 34, 171
Crysmann, Berthold, 7
Cysouw, Michael, ix, 221

Daniel, Michael, 172
de Hoop, Helen, ix, 21, 237
de la Fontinelle, Jacqueline, 71, 120, 152
Detges, Ulrich, 17
Dimmendaal, Gerrit, x
Dimmendaal, Gerrit Jan, 11, 68, 82, 83, 99, 103, 113, 157, 158, 178–181
Dixon, R. M. W., 3, 10, 14–16, 26, 29, 32, 33, 42, 55, 76, 107, 133, 144, 156, 170–172
Dixon, Roland B., 91, 126
Donohue, Mark, 40, 106, 120
Doron, Edit, 57
Dowty, David, 36
Dryer, Matthew S., 27, 133, 137, 138, 201
Du Bois, John W., 14

Name index

Fabian, Edmund, 124
Fabian, Grace, 124
Fenk-Oczlon, Gertraud, 45
Ferguson, Charles A., 222
Fillmore, Charles J., 36, 56
Frajzyngier, Zygmunt, 36
Freeze, Ray, 77

Gilligan, Gary Martin, 46
Goldberg, Adele E., 35
Gorbet, Larry Paul, 55, 59, 90, 147, 148, 190
Gordon, Lynn, 61, 63, 190
Greenberg, Joseph H., 3, 4, 20, 27, 128, 222, 231
Güldemann, Tom, x, 222

Haig, Geoffrey, 49
Halliday, M. A. K., 100
Halpern, Abraham M., 11
Handschuh, Corinna, 29, 40
Haspelmath, Martin, ix, 3, 8, 9, 34, 137
Hayward, Dick, 66, 87, 105, 106, 117, 161, 162, 175, 184, 185
Hayward, Richard J., 41, 65, 88, 184
Heeschen, Volker, 125
Heger, Klaus, 34
Heine, Bernd, 76, 170, 222
Hengeveld, Kees, 53
Hompó, Éva, 10, 18, 65, 87, 117, 163, 164, 176, 182–185
Hosokawa, Komei, 124
Huson, Daniel H., 215
Hwang, Shin Ja J., 133, 134, 139, 143

Jackendoff, Ray, 56
Jakobson, Roman, 8
Jespersen, Otto, 17, 172

Joël, Judith, 223

Kager, René, 237
Kasarhérou (née de la Fontinelle), Jacqueline, 152, 188
Keenan, Edward L., 28, 138
Keller, Rudi, 14
Kendall, Martha B., 10, 61, 90, 127, 146, 147, 149, 191
Kiessling, Roland, 11, 40, 68, 81, 113, 177, 180
King, Tracy Holloway, 16
Kiparsky, Paul, 22
Klaiman, M.H., 138
König, Christa, 8–11, 13, 16, 18, 19, 31, 33, 63, 99, 104, 113, 114, 199, 203, 226, 230–232
Kozlowski, Edwin Louis, 62, 91, 149, 190

Lakämper, Renate, 22
Lamberti, Marcello, 18, 66, 88, 183–185
Lambrecht, Knud, 101, 102
Lander, Yury, 174, 188, 194
Langdon, Margaret, 10, 90, 145, 147, 192
Lehmann, Winfred P, 15
Levin, Beth, 138
Li, Charles N., 10, 12, 15, 53, 59, 63, 91, 112, 126, 139, 142, 143, 149, 191–193
Lichtenberk, Frantisek, 71, 93, 94, 120, 152, 186, 187
Longacre, Robert E., 133, 134, 139, 143
Lynch, John, 123
Lyons, John, 76, 77, 170, 173

Malchukov, Andrej L., x, 21, 33, 237

Maling, Joan, 56
Mallinson, Graham, 20, 237
Maslova, Elena, 17
McEnery, Anthony, 45
McGregor, William, 171, 188, 193
McGregor, William B., 48, 100, 107
Mel'čuk, Igor, 11, 173
Merlan, Francesca, 41, 42
Miestamo, Matti, 24, 76
Miller, Amy, 48, 62, 90, 146, 189, 190
Miller, Amy Whitmore, 90, 127, 192
Mixco, Mauricio Jesús, 223
Moulton, Vincent, 199, 215
Moyse-Faurie, Claire, 120
Munro, Pamela, 10, 48, 61, 63, 79, 89, 126, 137, 140, 143–145, 147, 148, 189, 192, 193
Myhill, John, 101

Narasimhan, Bhuvana, 21
Nichols, Johanna, 29, 42
Noonan, Michael, 135

Owens, Jonathan, 11, 65, 86, 87, 117, 141, 161, 164, 182

Park, Joseph Sung-Jul, 10, 12, 53, 59, 63, 91, 112, 126, 139, 142, 143, 149, 191, 192
Payne, Doris L., 83, 84, 141, 160
Payne, Thomas E., 55, 60, 75, 78, 89, 97, 101, 104, 109, 117, 132, 133, 136, 166, 171
Pensalfini, Rob, 110
Plank, Frans, 10
Prince, Alan, 237
Pustet, Regina, 25, 54

Radin, Paul, 15, 192, 193
Ramchand, Gillian, 57

Randal, Scott, 58, 67, 80, 84, 85, 105, 106, 115, 137, 141, 156, 159, 176, 178
Redden, James E., 61
Reh, Mechthild, 16
Reppen, Randi, 135
Rizzi, Luigi, 46
Ross, Malcolm, 108, 111, 122, 123

Sasse, Hans-Jürgen, 102
Sawyer, Jesse O, 16
Schnell, Stefan, 49
Seiler, Hansjakob, 34
Shay, Erin, 36
Shibatani, Masayoshi, 109
Shipley, William F., 18, 59, 63, 92, 148, 149, 191, 193
Siewierska, Anna, 25, 136, 137, 149
Silverstein, Michael, 29, 32, 33, 40
Smolensky, Paul, 237
Sottile, Roberto, 18, 66, 88, 183–185
Spencer, Andrew, 172
Stassen, Leon, 25, 53, 54, 57, 58, 75, 170
Stiebels, Barbara, 22, 234
Stroomer, Harry, 10, 48, 65, 111, 117, 161, 164, 165, 175, 182
Sweet, Henry, 21

Taylor, Nicholas, 118
Thompson, Sandra A., 10, 12, 15, 53, 59, 63, 91, 112, 126, 133, 134, 139, 142, 143, 149, 191–193
Tompo ole Mpaayei, John, 10, 67, 160, 177
Tono, Yukio, 45
Tosco, Mauro, 16, 222
Trask, R. L., 33
Tucker, Archibald N., 10, 67, 160, 177

Name index

Urban, Greg, 43

Vennemann, Theo, 15
Verstraete, Jean-Christophe, 48, 100, 107

Ward, Gregory, 102
Watagomigie, Sr. Philbert, 10, 61, 191, 192
Watahomigie, Lucille J., 10, 61, 191, 192
Waters, Bruce, 124
Wegener, Claudia, x, 10, 49, 59, 69, 70, 95, 107, 120–122, 133, 152–154, 187, 188
Whitehead, Carl R., 108
Wierzbicka, Anna, 34
Witzlack-Makarevich, Alena, 34
Witzlack-Makarevich, Alene, x
Wunderlich, Dieter, 22, 234

Xiao, Richard, 45

Yamamoto, Akira Y., 10, 61, 191, 192
Yip, Moira, 56

Zipf, George Kingsley, 44

Language index

ǁAni, 25*

Ajië, 69, 71, 73, 93, 94, 96, 97, 119, 120, 125, 128, 129, 152, 155, 167, 186–189, 195, 207, 210–212, 219, 221, 225–227
Anejom, 25*
Arbore, 59*, 66, 67, 72, 73, 87, 88, 97, 105, 106, 116, 117, 119, 128, 129, 161, 162, 166, 167, 175, 184–186, 194, 195, 210, 212, 217
Asuriní, 28*
Atayal, 25*

Batak, 25*

Chamorro, 25*
Chechen, 6, 7
Cocopa, 6, 10, 44, 147, 150, 167, 174, 175, 189, 190, 192, 193, 195, 200*
Cubeo, 28*

Datooga, 11, 40, 68, 69, 73, 80, 81, 85, 97, 113, 116, 128, 129, 177, 180, 181, 195
Diegueño (Jamul), *see* Jamul Tiipay
Diegueño (Mesa Grande), 10, 55, 58, 61, 64, 73, 89, 90, 92, 96, 147, 148, 150, 167, 189, 190, 192, 193, 195, 210, 212, 217
Dinka (Agar Dialect), 115

Dinka (Agar), 113–116, 129, 174, 175, 177, 179, 181, 194, 195, 200*

Ecuadorian Siona, 111*
Eipo, 108, 125, 126, 129, 200*
English, 35–37, 57, 75, 77*, 77, 78, 101, 104, 134*, 135, 138, 171, 172

Finnish, 37*, 76
French, 17, 57
French (Old), 17

Gamo, 10, 18, 65, 67, 73, 87, 88, 97, 117–119, 129, 163, 164, 166, 167, 176, 182*, 182–186, 195, 209, 210, 212
German, 21, 36, 37*, 37, 41, 131, 138
Gyarong, 19*

Havasupai, 61, 62, 64, 66, 72, 73, 90–92, 97, 148–150, 167, 190, 193, 195, 210, 212, 217
Hixkarayana, 28*
Houailou, *see* Ajië
Hualapai, *see* Walapai

Ijo, 25*
Indonesian, 25*

Jamul Tiipay, 48, 62, 64, 72, 73, 89*, 89, 90, 92, 96, 97, 127–129, 146, 150, 167, 189, 190, 192, 193, 195, 210, 212, 217

Language index

Japanese, 37*

K'abeena, 10, 40, 65, 67, 73, 86–88, 97, 112, 117–119, 129, 162–164, 166, 167, 182, 183, 185, 186, 194, 195, 210, 212
Kaki Ae, 108, 109, 123–126, 129, 200*
Kanuri, 37*
Kera, 25*
Khoekhoe, 25*
Kisi„ 25*
Kunimaipa, 108

Luwo, 26

Maa, 10, 11, 16, 67*, 67, 69, 73, 83*, 83–85, 97, 113, 114, 141, 156, 160, 167, 177, 178, 181, 195, 210, 211*, 212, 222*, 223, 226
Maasai, *see* Maa
Maidu, 18, 58, 59, 63, 64, 73, 91, 92, 97, 126–129, 148, 149, 167, 189, 191, 193–195, 207, 210–213, 217, 219–221, 223, 224, 226, 227, 230, 232
Malakmalak, 47
Mangarayi, 28, 41, 42
Maori, 37*
Maricopa, 61, 63, 64, 73, 189, 190, 200*
Mesa Grande Diegueño, 55, 59
Mojave, 10, 48, 61, 64, 73, 79, 89, 92, 97, 126–129, 137, 140, 142–146, 148, 150, 167, 189, 192–195, 210, 212, 217
Mupun, 25*
Murle, 10, 67, 69, 73, 80, 81, 85, 97, 140, 157, 158, 160, 166, 167, 178, 181, 195, 210, 212, 219, 258

Murle, 157, 158

Nabak, 108, 124–126, 129, 200*
Nadëb, 25*
Nakanai, 25*
Nandi, 67–69, 73, 80, 81, 85, 97, 102, 103, 113, 114, 116, 128, 129, 156, 159, 160, 167, 177, 178, 181, 195, 210, 211*, 212
Nias, x, 7*, 7, 13, 42–44, 47, 69, 70*, 70, 71, 73, 79, 93*, 93, 96*, 96, 97, 103, 106, 119, 120, 125, 128, 129, 150–155, 166, 167, 176, 186–189, 194, 195, 203, 207, 210–212, 219, 221, 225–227
Noon, 25*

Oirata, 40
Old French, 17
Oromo (Boraana), 48, 64, 65, 67, 73, 87, 88, 97, 110, 111, 116, 117, 119, 128, 129, 161, 164, 165*, 165–167, 174, 175, 182, 186, 195, 210, 212, 213
Oromo (Harar), 11, 64, 65, 67, 73, 86, 88, 97, 116, 117, 119, 128, 129, 140, 141, 161, 163, 164, 166, 167, 182, 186, 195, 210, 212

Päri, 16, 26, 28*, 28, 155, 160, 167, 200*
Palikur, 25*
Panyjima, 25*

Qafar, 41

Russian, 41, 76

Savosavo, x, 10, 49*, 58, 59, 69–71, 73, 94–97, 107, 119–122, 125,

129, 133, 152–155, 166, 167, 187–189, 195, 207, 210–213, 219, 221, 225
Selknam, 25*, 28*
Sema, 25*
Siroi, 108

Tennet, 54, 58, 67–69, 73, 80, 84, 85, 97, 105, 106, 113, 115, 116, 128, 129, 137, 141, 156, 158–160, 167, 175, 176, 178, 181, 195, 219
Tiguk, 25*
Tiriyo, 28*
Turkana, x, 11, 67–69, 72, 73, 81–83, 85, 97, 99, 102, 103, 113, 116, 128, 129, 157, 158*, 158, 160, 166, 167, 177–181, 195, 210, 211*, 212, 219, 238
Turkish, 5, 12, 37*

Ungarinji, 28*

Walapai, 61, 64, 73, 190–193, 195, 200*, 217
Wappo, 10, 15, 16, 53, 58, 59, 63, 64, 73, 91, 92, 97, 112, 126–129, 139, 142, 143, 148–150, 166, 167, 189, 191–195, 207, 210–213, 217, 221, 223, 224, 226, 227, 238
Warao, 25*
Waskia, 108, 111, 122, 123, 125, 126, 129, 200*
Wolaytta, 18, 65–67, 73, 87, 88, 97, 182–186, 195, 210, 212

Yapese, 25*
Yavapai, 10, 61, 64, 73, 90–92, 97, 127–129, 146–150, 167, 190, 191, 193, 195, 210, 212, 217

Yawuru, 108, 123–125, 129, 200*

Zayse, 65, 67, 73, 88, 97, 182, 184, 186, 195, 210, 212

Subject index

Accessibility Hierarchy, 28
agreement, *see* verbal indexing
alignment, 3
    behavioral factors, 28–29
    ergative-absolutive, 3
    marked-absolutive, 6–8, 15, 20
    marked-nominative, 5–6
    nominative-accusative, 3
    splits, 31–33, 39–44, 155–156
    through case-marking, 3, 24
    through verbal indexing, 24–25
    through word order, 24–28
antipassive, *see* valency-decreasing construction, antipassive
argument
    definiteness of, 75, 77, 78, 86
    omission of, 46–47

case, 35
    comparative concepts, 4
        S-case, 13
        zero-case, 13
    default, 18, 21–23, 234–236
    individual forms
        absolute, 11–12
        absolutive, 3, 6, 7, 9, 13, 19, 20, 33, 42, 47, 96, 137, 165*, 188, 234–236
        accusative, 3, 5, 8, 10–12, 19, 23, 33, 36, 41, 58, 63, 65–69, 82, 83, 92, 102, 105, 113, 115, 116, 119, 141, 144, 146, 158, 160, 177, 178, 180–189, 192–194
        allative, 125, 126
        antigenitive, 171–172, 174–175, 184
        dative, 36, 142
        ergative, 3, 6, 7, 10, 13, 15, 16, 23, 33, 41*, 47, 48, 100, 107–109, 123, 124, 126, 137, 155, 188, 231*, 234–236
        genitive, 152, 171, 172, 178, 179, 182, 185–189, 191, 193, 194
        nominative, 3, 9–12, 20, 41, 69, 82–91, 93, 94, 109, 110, 112–116, 122, 126, 127, 140–142, 145–148, 152, 154–158, 160–163, 172, 173, 175, 178, 189, 193, 194
        predicative, 66, 117
        vocative, 169, 172, 176, 177, 180, 181, 184, 185, 189, 192–194
    overt marking, 29
    terminology, 9–13
case-marking, 24
    absence of, 47
        morphophonologically conditioned, 43–44, 106–107, 121
    optional, 47–48, 48, 89, 100, 107–108, 145
    via adposition, 29, 93, 186
    via nominal mutation, 7*, 44

Subject index

via tone, 29, 67*, 114, 178, 181
caseterminology, 4
causative, *see* valency-increasing construction
citation form, 11, 20, 38, 169, 173–174, 176, 181–182, 185–186, 188–189, 193–194, 203, 205, 215, 226
clause-chaining, 133
clause-type, 132
    adverbial clause, 38, 131, 133–134, 139–140, 143, 145, 147–148, 152–153, 155–156, 161–162, 166
    complement clause, 38, 133–140, 143, 145–146, 157–158, 162–163, 166
    dependent, 38, 131–135, 139–142, 146, 150, 155, 161, 166–167
    relative clause, 28, 38, 131–134, 139–147, 150–154, 156–157, 161–163, 166
construction, 35
copula, 53
    absence versus presence, 53–54, 59–60, 62, 65*, 67–69, 72, 82, 104, 128
copula construction, *see* nominal predication
cross-referencing, *see* verbal indexing

Elsewhere Principle, 22
emphatic subject, 38, 99–100, 102–103, 107, 110–128, 200*, 205, 206, 208, 209, 215, 225
ergativity, *see* alignment
    optional, *see* case-marking, optional

existential predication, 38, 75, 205, 207–209, 217, 225
    positive versus negative, 76, 78–80, 82, 84–86, 91–97
    semantics of, 76–77
    syntax of, 77, 78

focus, 101, 106–108, 110, 111*, 111, 112, 114, 116, 118, 120, 121, 122*
    cleft-analysis, 104–106
    constituent, 102
    overt marker, 112, 120*, 126, 164
    sentence, 102
frequency, 44–46

grammatical relation
    object, 12
grammatical relations,
    subject, 14–15, 38

impersonal construction, *see* valency-decreasing construction

language change, *see* marked-S languages, historical explanations
language contact, *see* typology, areal
language-independent level, 34
language-specific level, 34
Lexical Decomposition Grammar, 22–23, 234–236
locational predication, 38, 75, 203, 205, 217
    semantics of, 75–77
    syntax of, 77

marked-S languages
    formal definition, 3–4, 8, 18
    functional definition, 8, 17–20, 31, 231–233

261

Subject index

strong versus weak hypothesis, 19, 203, 206
historical explanations, 14–17
markedness, 8–9
overt versus zero-coding, 3
micro-alignment approach, 33–36, 233–234
multidimensional scaling, 220–221
mutated form, *see* case-marking, via nominal mutation

NeighborNet, 199, 215
nominal mutation, *see* case-marking, via nominal mutation
nominal predication, 53, 75
    class-membership, 54
    class=membership, 57
    identity, 54, 57–58, 69
    predicate nominal, 38, 53–58, 60, 62–66, 68–72, 104–105, 128, 205, 209, 217, 226
    subject of, 53, 55, 60, 205, 208

Optimality Theory, 237–238

passive, *see* valency-decreasing construction, passive
phylogenetic networks, 199, 213–221
possession
    alienable versus inalienable, 171, 176, 186–191, 193
    attributive, 38, 170–172, 174–187, 189–191, 193–194, 203–209, 215, 226, 227
    predicative, 75–76
pro-drop, *see* argument, omission of

Silverstein Hierarchy, 29, 32–33, 40
subordinate clause, *see* clause-type, dependent

terms of address, 38, 169, 172, 174, 176–177, 180–182, 184–188, 192–194, 205, 207, 209, 226
topic, 38*, 46, 101, 106, 110, 113, 115, 118, 120, 121, 166
    afterthought, 101–102, 122, 127
    contrastive, 101
typology
    areal, 30, 200, 221–225
        Ethiopian language area, 222
    sampling
        genealogical grouping, 30, 201–202
    tertium comparationis, 34

unmutated form, *see* case-marking, via nominal mutation

valency-decreasing construction, 38, 131–132, 136–139, 141–142, 148–149, 153–154, 158–160, 163–165, 167, 205, 207, 209, 217
    antipassive, 131, 136–138, 141, 158, 160
    detransitivizing, 138, 154
    impersonal construction, 132, 136, 138, 141, 153, 159, 160, 165
    middle, 136, 138, 141–142, 160
    passive, 131, 132, 136–137, 141, 148–151, 153–154, 158–160, 163–165, 165, 167
valency-increasing construction, 131
verb class, 19
    'have', 75, 83
    positional verb, 79, 80, 83, 89, 92
    splits base on, 42–43
verbal indexing, 6, 24–25, 115, 139, 155

word order, 25–28, 77, 78, 126, 128, 139, 155

basic, 111, 113, 120, 128
in emphatic contexts, 111, 118, 128